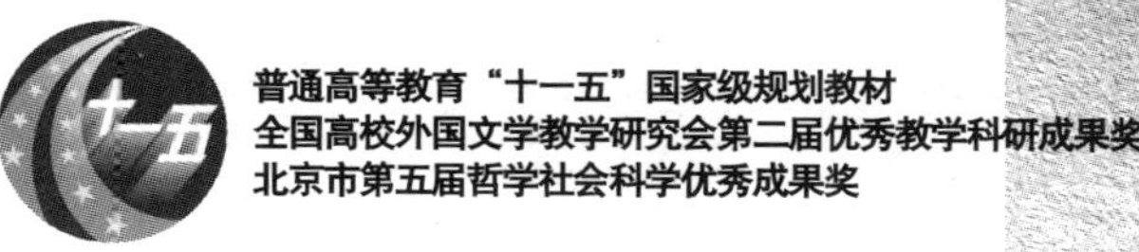

普通高等教育“十一五”国家级规划教材
全国高校外国文学教学研究会第二届优秀教学科研成果奖
北京市第五届哲学社会科学优秀成果奖

21世纪英语专业系列教材

新编 英国文学选读（下）

（第四版）

罗经国 阮炜 编注

A New Anthology of English Literature

Volume II Fourth Edition

北京大学出版社
PEKING UNIVERSITY PRESS

图书在版编目 (CIP) 数据

新编英国文学选读·下 / 罗经国，阮炜编注 .–4 版 .—北京：北京大学出版社，2016.3

（21 世纪英语专业系列教材）

ISBN 978-7-301-26823-0

Ⅰ. ①新… Ⅱ. ①罗… ②阮… Ⅲ. ①英语—阅读教学—高等学校—教材 ②英国文学—作品—介绍 Ⅳ. ①H319.4:I

中国版本图书馆 CIP 数据核字 (2016) 第 025176 号

书　　名　新编英国文学选读（下）（第四版）
XINBIAN YINGGUO WENXUE XUANDU（XIA）（DI–SI BAN）

著作责任者　罗经国　阮　炜　编注

责 任 编 辑　李　娜

标 准 书 号　ISBN 978-7-301-26823-0

出 版 发 行　北京大学出版社

地　　址　北京市海淀区成府路 205 号　100871

网　　址　http://www.pup.cn　　新浪微博：@ 北京大学出版社

电 子 信 箱　zpup@ pup.cn

电　　话　邮购部 62752015　发行部 62750672　编辑部 62759634

印 刷 者　三河市博文印刷有限公司

经 销 者　新华书店

650 毫米 ×980 毫米　16 开本　21 印张　420 千字

1996 年 5 月第 1 版　2005 年 7 月第 2 版　2011 年 6 月第 3 版

2016 年 3 月第 4 版　2024 年 7 月第 9 次印刷（总第 41 次印刷）

定　　价　45.00 元

FOREWORD TO THE FOURTH EDITION

As this nationally well-accepted textbook compiled by the late Professor Luo Jing-guo is still in great demand on book market, revisions become necessary to keep it up with the progressing time. Therefore, its publisher, Peking University Press, asked us, who had been invited by Professor Luo to compose certain parts of the first edition, to produce the fourth edition. When we received this revision proposal, we immediately consulted Professor Luo's wife Professor Li Shu about it. And it was with her permission and support that the two of us then agreed to take up the work.

The current 4th edition is, therefore, revised by Liu Yiqing and Ruan Wei, in which Liu Yiqing is responsible for Book One, and Ruan Wei for Book Two. And we'd like to mention here that in fulfilling the revision task, we tried to keep all the good points of the previous editions and replaced a few excerpts or writers with those we believe to be more suitable or important. We hope the result of our effort will meet the users' approval.

Liu Yiqing
Professor of English, Peking University
Ruan Wei
Professor of English, Shenzhen University

ABOUT THE THIRD EDITION

There is some reorganization of texts in this edition.

In the first volume "Sir Gawain and the Green Knight", and Robert Herrick's "To the Virgins, To Make Much of Time" are deleted, and thanks to Dr Su Yong, an excerpt from Tobias Smollet's "The Expedition of Humphry Clinker" is added.

Luo Jingguo
Peking University
January, 2011

FOREWORD TO THE FIRST EDITION

This textbook, composed of two volumes, is intended for the teaching of English literature to both English and non-English majors in higher educational institutions as well as for those who learn English in their spare time and whose English has reached such a level that guidance for further study seems necessary. The main aim of this textbook is to cultivate in the reader an interest in English literature and a sense of the development of English literature.

In editing this textbook, I paid particular attention to the following points:

1. All materials chosen are excerpts or full texts of well known literary works written by the best English authors, and they have stood the test of the time, as many of them are time and again collected in selected readings or anthologies both at home and abroad. They are not only the quintessence of English literature, but also the best of English writings, which will be beneficial to students in their learning of the English Language.

2. As literature takes its root in social life and is inseparable from the economic, political, religious, and intellectual factors of a given historical period, a brief summary of the period is given at the beginning of each chapter. Thus, the questions of why Shakespeare's great tragedies were all written during the first decade of the 17th century, why romanticism became prevalent in the beginning of the 19th century, and why there appeared a galaxy of novelists in the Victorian age, etc. are offered in brief introduction from a historical perspective in each chapter.

3. Special effort has been made to guide students to appreciate the aesthetic value of the selected pieces. The Notes serve not only to interpret the meanings of difficult words or passages, but also to call students' attention to the stylistic characteristics and rhetorical devices of the excerpts. Suggestive questions concerning the artistic techniques of the selected pieces are asked to arouse students' interest.

4. As the emphasis of the book is on the interpretation and appreciation of the selected readings, the biographies of most writers are reduced to the

minimum. It is meaningless and boring to give students the detailed biographies of writers, a long list of their works, and the synopses of their representative works, without offering them first-hand materials. Regrettably, such a style of teaching foreign literature is still practised in some institutions. Students who want the above information can easily find them in any history of English literature or in an encyclopaedia.

5. Literature in the twentieth century is very complex. Various trends and schools come and go. Few writers are generally accepted as representative writers of the modern age. No consensus has been reached as to which novels, poems, or prose selections represent the characteristic features of a particular writer. Attempts are made in this textbook to introduce students to T. S. Eliot, James Joyce, John Osborne, Samuel Beckett, William Golding, Iris Murdoch, V. S. Naipaul, Martin Amis and Seamus Heaney as major writers, representing the different trends of twentieth century English literature.

6. As the total teaching hours for English literature course vary widely in different higher-education institutions, this textbook provides sufficient materials for a year course of 4 hours per week. Teachers in various institutions can choose texts from the book at their own will according to the teaching hours of their institutions.

I have to express my thanks to all my colleagues and friends who encouraged me in my writing, especially to my wife, Professor Li Shu (李淑), who has been supporting and helping me throughout my forty years' teaching career. Special thanks should also be given to Professor Liu Yi-qing (刘意青), who, being an expert in 18th century English literature, generously helped me in formulating my discussion of four writers: Edmund Spenser, Daniel Defoe, Alexander Pope, and Henry Fielding. I also owe my gratitude to Professor Ruan Wei (阮炜) for his selections of Golding, Murdoch, Naipaul, and Amis, and to Professor Xu Wenbo (徐文博) for his selection of Heaney. Finally I have to thank my Canadian friend Sean MacDonald, who read over the manuscripts of the first five chapters of Volume I, my American friend Joshua Goldstein, who read over the manuscripts of the rest of Volume I, and my American colleague Professor Iris Maurer, who read over the manuscripts of Volume II. They offered many valuable suggestions.

Luo Jingguo
Peking University
March, 2005

ACKNOWLEDGMENTS

Acknowledgments must be made to the following reference books and dictionaries. The list is not arranged in alphabetical order, but according to their importance to me in my editing work:

The Norton Anthology of English Literature

Wang Zuoliang, et al. : *An Anthology of English Literature* Annotated in Chinese

Chen Jia: *A History of English Literature*

Chen Jia: *Selected Readings in English Literature*

William Long: *English Literature*

Paul Harvey: *The Oxford Companion to English Literature*

Christopher Gillie: *Longman Companion to English Literature*

Albert C. Baugh: *A Literary History of England*

Cleanth Brooks, Jr. and Robert Penn Warren: *Understanding Poetry*

The Complete Works of William Shakespeare, edited by Alfred Harbrace

Sixteen Plays of Shakespeare, edited by George Lyman Kittredge

Encyclopaedia and dictionaries:

The Everyman Encyclopaedia

Oxford American Dictionary

The Scribner-Bantam English Dictionary

Chambers Twentieth Century Dictionary

Longman Dictionary of Contemporary English

The Shorter Oxford Dictionary

Webster's Third New International Dictionary

CONTENTS

目　录

Chapter Eight

The Age of Romanticism(1798—1832)

From the publication of *Lyrical Ballads* by Wordsworth and Coleridge in 1798 to the death of Sir Walter Scott in 1832, a new movement appeared on the literary arena. The essence of this new movement is the glorification of instinct and emotion, a deep veneration of nature, and a flaming zeal to remake the world.

1. Historical background

The political and social factors that gave rise to the romantic movement were the three revolutions. Under the influence of the American and French revolutions, national liberation movements and democratic movements swept across many European countries. England was no exception. Though the government allied hand in glove with the reactionary forces on the Continent, political reforms and mass demonstrations violently shook the very foundation of aristocratic rule in England. No less important were the consequences of the industrial revolution. It brought great wealth to the rich and worsened working and living conditions of the poor. With the invention of new machines, many skilled workers were replaced by women and children and working hours for young children lasted fourteen to sixteen hours a day. Ignorant of the real causes that brought them such disaster, workers in various places attributed their miseries and growing poverty to the introduction of the new machines. Hence there broke out a machine-breaking movement, called the Luddite movement, named after Ned Ludd, who in a fit of temper, destroyed some stocking frames in 1779. Workers organized themselves and gave voice to their distress by breaking machines. The riots lasted from 1811 to 1818. The government took repressive measures against it.

2. Intellectual background

The shift in literature from emphasis on reason to instinct and emotion was intellectually prepared for by a number of thinkers in the later half of the 18th century.

Rousseau (1712—1778), the French philosopher, is generally regarded as the father of romanticism. He rejects the worship of reason. Reason, he maintains, has its use, but it is not the whole answer. In the really vital problems of life it is much safer to rely on feelings, to follow our instincts and emotions. He contrasts the freedom and innocence of primitive men with the tyranny and wickedness of civilized society, and even insists that the progress of learning is destructive to human happiness. He preaches that civilized men should "return to nature", to a primitive state of life. He praises the natural man as "the noble savage" and attacks the civilized man as "the depraved animal". *The New Heloise* (1761) and *Emile* (1762) sowed the seeds of romanticism.

Another thinker who contributed to this shift of emphasis from reason to instinct and emotion was Edmund Burke (1729—1797). As a political philosopher he is known for his *Reflection on the Revolution in France* (1790), in which he repudiates the revolution, claiming that no one has the right to destroy the institutions and traditions that have been passed down to him through generations and to destroy them is to destroy civilization itself. However, Burke's early work *A Philosophical Enquiry into the Origin of Our Ideas of the Sublime and the Beautiful* (1756) is an important piece that deals with aesthetics, i.e., the theory of beauty. He distinguishes between two kinds of beauty—the sublime and the beautiful. The idea of sublimity is first found in *The Poetics* by Aristotle (382 B.C. — 322 B.C.) and *On the Sublime* by Longinus (213? —273?). According to Longinus, sublimity is a kind of masculine beauty, more powerful and loftier than the beautiful. Burke further associates this kind of beauty with the feeling of danger and power whereas the beautiful is associated with smallness, elegance, and smoothness. He links the sublime and the beautiful to human emotions and physical senses as well as imagination, thus elevating the function of instincts and emotions.

Still another thinker who exerted much influence on this change was Thomas Paine (1737—1809). He published *The Rights of Man* in 1791, an answer to Burke's *Reflection* published in the previous year. *The Rights of Man* asserts that "man has no property in man" and justifies the radical actions of the French people in the revolution, claiming that it is the right of the people to overthrow a government that opposes humanity. This assertion of individual rights is in direct opposition to Neo-classicist's thinking of binding oneself to traditions and conventions.

3. Characteristic features of the romantic movement

(1) Subjectivism: Instead of regarding poetry as "a mirror to nature", the source of which is in the outer world, romantic poets describe poetry as "the spontaneous overflow of powerful feelings" which expresses the poet's mind. The interest of the romantic poets is not in the objective world or in the action of men, but in the feelings, thoughts, and experiences of the poets themselves. Even the description of natural and human objects is modified by the poets' feelings. In short, romanticism is related to subjectivism, whereas neo-classicism is related to objectivism. The poetry of the Romantic Age in England is distinctive for its high degree of imagination.

(2) Spontaneity: Wordsworth defines poetry as "the *spontaneous* overflow of feelings". This emphasis on spontaneity is opposed to the "rules" and "regulations" imposed on the poets by neo-classic writers. Romanticism is an assertion of independence, a departure from the neo-classis rules. A work of art must be original. The role of instinct, intuition, and the feelings of "the heart" is stressed instead of neo-classicists' emphasis on "the head", on regularity, uniformity, decorum, and imitation of the classical writers.

(3) Singularity: Romantic poets have a strong love for the remote,

the unusual, the strange, the supernatural, the mysterious, the splendid, the picturesque, and the illogical. All these qualities are those that the neo-classic writers tried to avoid.

(4) Worship of nature: The romantic poets are worshippers of nature, especially the sublime aspect of a natural scene. Romantic poets read in nature some mysterious force. Some treat nature as a living entity that shares the poet's feelings. Some even regard nature as the revelation of God.

(5) Simplicity: Romantic poets take to using everyday language spoken by the rustic people as opposed to the poetic diction used by neo-classic writers. Under the influence of the American and French revolutions, there was a growth of democratic feelings, and an increasing belief that every human being is worth being praised. Hence there was a revival of folk literature, a real awakening of interest in the life of the common people, a sense of universal brotherhood, and a growing sympathy for the suffering of the people. The romantic movement is characterized by a humanitarian idealism. Many poets had a vision of the brotherhood of mankind, universal sharing, and the ultimate freedom of human spirits.

(6) There is a dominating note of melancholy in the poems of the romantic poets. The theme of exile, isolation, and a longing for the infinite, for an indefinable and inaccessible goal is commonly found in their works.

(7) It was an age of poetry by which the poets outpoured their feelings and emotions. Romantic poets loved to use a freer verse form, not the standard form of "heroic couplets" preferred by neo-classic writers.

Romanticism is a term that denotes most of the writings that were written between 1798 and 1832. However, it cannot be applied to all writings. Nor is it applicable to all writings of a particular writer. Many different qualities contradicting each other are seen in the works of different writers or in the work of a single writer, so there might be elements that are not romantic.

It should be known that the term "romanticism" was not known to the poets themselves in their lifetime. It was a term applied to them half a century later by literary historians. Contemporary critics treated them as independent individuals or grouped them into separate schools.

William Wordsworth (1770—1850)

Wordsworth was born and grew up near the Lake district, a beautiful scenic spot in northwestern England. From his very early years, he had a profound love for nature, which characterizes all his works. His parents died when he was very young, and he was put under the care of his relatives. He went to study at Cambridge from 1787 to 1791. In 1791 he went to France to learn French in preparation for the career of a tutor. There he was greatly impressed by the revolutionary zeal, and he would have joined in the revolution if there had not been pressures from his relatives across the channel to call him back to England. He was also involved in a love affair with a French girl and would have married her if the war had not broken out between England and France. His revolutionary enthusiasm died down as he was shocked at the massacre during the Reign of Terror under the rule of Robespierre. From 1799 to his death he was politically very conservative and lived in retirement at Grasmere in the Lake district in the company of his sister Dorothy Wordsworth and his friend Coleridge. In 1843 after the death of Southey he was made poet laureate.

The life and thinking of Wordsworth are illustrated in the long poem *The Recluse* which remains unfinished. *The Prelude* (1850) is also a long poem which tells the growth of his mind. In 1798 he published *Lyrical Ballads* in collaboration with Coleridge. The preface to this collection of poems is an important piece of literary criticism in English literature. It can be read as a declaration of romanticism, in which Wordsworth openly expresses his theory of poetry, which is contrary to the theory of neo-classicism.

Wordsworth is most celebrated for his poetry of nature. His love for nature is boundless. To him nature means more than rivers, trees, rocks, mountains, lakes, and so on. Nature has a moral value and has its philosophical significance. Nature is for him the embodiment of the Divine Spirit. He believes that God and universe are identical, that God is everything and everything is God. To Wordsworth nature is the greatest of all teachers, and those who are uncorrupted by urban society, especially those simple rustic people, can communicate directly with nature which gives them power, peace, and happiness.

Grasmere Lake Wordsworth lived from 1799

Preface to *Lyrical Ballads*

In the preface Wordsworth makes clear the points below.

(1) He will write about the life of common people, especially the humble life of rustic people.

(2) He will try to transform the incidents and situations of the common people by his imagination and present them in such a way that they will seem novel and wonderful.

(3) He will try to trace through these humble incidents the essence of humanity—the primary laws of humanity.

(4) He will try to compose the poems in the kind of language that comes naturally to people in normal conversation. For people in the countryside live in close contact with nature and lead a simple life.

(5) There is a moral purpose in every poem he writes. The moral of a poem should not be arbitrarily added to it. A poem is the outcome of the strong emotions of a poet. The poet should train and regulate his feelings by deep and long thinking, to such a degree that these feelings will be connected with important subjects.

... The principal object, then, which I proposed[1] to myself in these poems was to choose incidents[2] and situations[3] from common life, and to relate or describe them, throughout, as far as was possible, in a selection of language really used by men; and, at the same time, to throw over them a certain colouring of imagination,[4] whereby ordinary things should be presented to the mind in an unusual way; and, further, and above all, to make these incidents and situations interesting by tracing[5] in them, truly though not ostentatiously,[6] the primary laws of our nature: chiefly, as far as regards the manner in which we associate ideas in a state of excitement. Low and rustic life was generally chosen, because in that condition, the essential passions of the heart find a better soil in which they can attain their maturity,[7] are less under restraint, and speak a plainer and more emphatic[8] language; because in that condition of life our elementary feelings co-exist in a state of greater simplicity, and, consequently, may be more accurately contemplated,[9] and more forcibly communicated; because the manners of rural life germinate[10] from those elementary feelings; and, from the necessary character of rural occupations, are more easily comprehended; and are more durable; and lastly, because in that condition the passions of men are incorporated with[11] the beautiful and permanent forms of nature. The language, too, of these men is adopted[12] (purified indeed from what appear to be its real defects, from all lasting and rational causes of dislike or disgust) because such men hourly communicate with the best objects from which the best part of language is originally derived;[13] and because, from their rank in society and the sameness and narrow circle of their intercourse, being less under the influence of social vanity they convey their feelings and notions in simple and unelaborated expressions.[14] Accordingly, such a language, arising out of repeated experience and regular feelings, is a more permanent, and a far more philosophical language, than that which is frequently substituted for it by poets, who think that they are conferring[15] honour upon themselves and their art, in proportion as they separate themselves from the sympathies[16] of men, and indulge in[17] arbitrary and capricious[18] habits of expression, in order to furnish food for fickle[19] tastes, and fickle appetites, of their own creation.

I cannot, however, be insensible of the present outcry against the triviality and meanness both of thought and language, which some of my contemporaries have occasionally introduced into their metrical compositions; and I acknowledge, that this defect, where it exists, is more dishonorable to the writer's own character than false refinement or arbitrary innovation,[20] though I should contend at the same time that it is far less pernicious in the sum of its consequences. From such verses the poems in these volumes will be found distinguished at least by one mark of difference, that each of them has a worthy *purpose*. Not that I mean to say, that I always began to write with a distinct purpose formally conceived; but I believe that my habits of meditation have so formed my feelings, as that my descriptions of such objects as strongly excite those feelings, will be found to carry along with them a *purpose*. If in this opinion I am mistaken, I can have little right to the name of a poet. For all good poetry is the spontaneous[21] overflow of powerful feelings: but though this be true, poems to which any value can be attached, were never produced on any variety of subjects but by a man who, being possessed of more than usual organic sensibility, had also thought long and deeply. For our continued influxes[22] of feeling are modified and directed by our thoughts, which are indeed the representatives of all our past feelings;[23] and, as by contemplating the relation of these general representatives to each other we discover what is really important to men, so, by the repetition and continuance of this act, our feelings will be connected with important subjects, till at length, if we be originally possessed of much sensibility, such habits of mind will be produced, that, by obeying blindly and mechanically the impulses of those habits, we shall describe objects, and utter sentiments, of such a nature and in such connection with each other, that the understanding of the being to whom we address ourselves, if he be in a healthful state of association, must necessarily be in some degree enlightened, and his affections ameliorated.[24]

... For a multitude of causes, unknown to former times, are now acting with a combined force to blunt[25] the discriminating powers[26] of the mind, and, unfitting it for all voluntary exertion, to reduce it to a state of almost savage torpor.[27] The most effective of these causes are the great national events[28] which are daily taking place, and the increasing accumulation of men in cities, where the uniformity[29] of their occupations produces a craving for extraordinary incident, which the rapid communication of intelligence hourly gratifies. To this tendency of life and manners the literature and theatrical exhibitions[30] of the country have conformed themselves.[31] The invaluable works of our elder writers, I had almost said the works of Shakespeare and Milton, are driven into neglect by frantic novels,[32] sickly and stupid German tragedies,[33] and deluges[34] of idle and extravagant[35] stories in verse....

Taking up the subject, then, upon general grounds, I ask what is meant by the word "poet" ? What is a poet? To whom does he address himself? And what language is to be expected from him? He is a man speaking to men: a man, it is true, endued with more lively sensibility, more enthusiasm and tenderness, who has a greater knowledge of human nature, and a more comprehensive soul, than are supposed to be common among mankind; a man pleased with his own passions and volitions,[36] and who rejoices more than other men in the spirit of life that is in him; delighting to contemplate similar volitions and passions as manifested in the going-on of the universe, and habitually impelled to create them where he does not find them. To these qualities he has added a disposition to be affected more than other men by absent things as if they were present; an ability of conjuring up in himself passions, which are indeed far from being the same as those produced by real events, yet(especially in those parts of the general sympathy which are pleasing and delightful) do more nearly resemble the passions produced by real events, than any thing which, from the motions of their own minds merely, other men are accustomed to feel in themselves; whence, and from practice, he has acquired a greater readiness and power in expressing what he thinks and feels, and especially those thoughts and feelings which, by his own choice, or from the structure of his own mind, arise in him without immediate[37] external excitement.

1. **proposed**: put forward for consideration.
2. **incident**: an event, especially a minor one.
3. **situation**: state of affairs.
4. **to throw over them a certain colouring of imagination**: a metaphor of painting, i. e. , to add to the beauty of the picture by putting on some colour. Here it means that the poet would add his own imagination to the incidents and situations of the common people.
5. **tracing**: discovering.
6. **ostentatiously**: showily.
7. **maturity**: "Maturity" means "ripeness, full development". Here it means that in the rustic people the essential passions are fully developed.
8. **emphatic**: more clearly spoken.

9. **contemplated**: considered or looked at attentively.
10. **germinate**: begin to grow.
11. **incorporated with**: joined with.
12. **adopted**: used. Here it means that Wordsworth will use the language of the rustic people.
13. **derived**: obtained.
14. **unelaborated expressions**: "Elaborated" means "worked out in detail"; "unelaborated expressions" means "simple and plain expressions".
15. **conferring**: granting.
16. **sympathy**: the ability to share another person's feelings or sensations.
17. **indulge in**: gratify one's desire freely.
18. **arbitrary and capricious**: "Arbitrary" means "based on personal opinion or choice rather than on reason"; "capricious" means "often changing".
19. **fickle**: often changing.
20. **false refinement or arbitrary innovation**: They may refer to the ostentatious expressions or conceits invented by neo-classic poets.
21. **spontaneous**: produced from natural feelings or causes without outside force.
22. **influx**: inflow.
23. **thoughts... representatives of all our past feelings**: Here we can see Wordsworth's emphasis on the importance of feelings. According to him, our thoughts come from our feelings.
24. **ameliorated**: made better.
25. **blunt**: become dull.
26. **discriminating power**: the power to distinguish difference.
27. **torpor**: condition of lazy inactivity.
28. **the great national events**: referring to the wars against France, the industrial urbanization, and the rapid popularization of daily newspapers.
29. **uniformity**: monotony.
30. **theatrical exhibitions**: performance in theatres.
31. **have conformed themselves (to)**: are in agreement with.
32. **frantic novels**: here referring to the Gothic novels.
33. **German tragedies**: here referring to the melodramas written by German playwrights.
34. **deluge**: an overwhelming flow.
35. **extravagant**: going beyond what is reasonable.
36. **volition**: one's power to control, decide, or choose.
37. **immediate**: direct.

Composed upon Westerminster Bridge[1]

The sonnet was written in the early morning on September 3, 1802. London in the early hours of the day was as serene and peaceful as nature itself, and to Wordsworth, even more beautiful than nature. Wordsworth's mystic thinking is clear in the last two lines.

Earth has not anything to show more fair[2]:
Dull would he be of soul who could pass by
A sight so touching in its majesty:
This City now doth, like a garment, wear
The beauty of the morning; silent, bare[3],
Ships, towers, domes, theaters, and temples lie
Open unto the fields, and to the sky;
All bright and glittering in the smokeless air.
Never did sun more beautifully steep[4]
In his first splendour valley, rock, or hill;
Ne'er saw I, never felt, a calm so deep!
The river glideth at his own sweet will;[5]
Dear God! the very houses seem asleep;
And all that mighty heart is lying still![6]

1. The sonnet is written in the Petrarchan form, with the rhyme scheme abba, abba in the octave and cdcdcd in the sestet.
2. **fair**: beautiful.
3. **bare**: empty, here referring to the fogless and smokeless air in London.
4. **steep**: soak.
5. **The river glideth at his own sweet will**: Wordsworth adds beauty to nature by treating it as a living thing.
6. **all that mighty heart is lying still**: What "mighty heart" refers to is ambiguous; here it might refer to earth and heaven (nature) around him in the early morning.

The Solitary Reaper[1]

The poem was suggested by a passage in Thomas Wilkinson's *Tour of Scotland* (1824) in which Wilkinson wrote: "Passed by a female who was reaping alone, she sung in Erse as she bended over her sickle, the sweetest human voice I ever heard. Her strains were tenderly melancholy, and felt delicious long after they were heard no more." The beauty of the song is presented to the reader through two well contrived comparisons in the second stanza.

Behold her, single in the field,
Yon solitary Highland[2] Lass[3]!
Reaping and singing by herself;
Stop here, or gently pass!
Alone she cuts and binds the grain,
And sings a melancholy strain[4];
O listen! for the Vale profound
Is overflowing with the sound.

No Nightingale did ever chaunt[5]
More welcome notes to weary bands
Of travellers in some shady haunt,
Among Arabian sands[6]:
A voice so thrilling ne'er was heard,
In spring time from the Cuckoo bird,
Breaking the silence of the seas
Among the farthest Hebrides[7,8].

Will no one tell me what she sings?[9]—
Perhaps the plaintive numbers[10] flow
For old, unhappy, far-off things,
And battles long ago:
Or is it some more humble lay[11],
Familiar matter of today?
Some natural sorrow, loss, or pain,
That has been, and may be again?

Whate'er the theme, the Maiden sang

As if her song could have no ending;
I saw her singing at her work,
And o'er the sickle bending;—
I listened, motionless and still;
And, as I mounted up the hill,
The music in my heart I bore,
Long after it was heard no more.

1. The poem is written in iambic tetrameter. The rhyme scheme of each stanza is ababccdd.
2. **Highland**: the mountainous area of Scotland.
3. **Lass**: (*Scottish*) a young girl.
4. **strain**: a tune, notes of music.
5. **chaunt**: old form of "chant".
6. **Arabian sands**: Arabian desert.
7. **Hebrides**: islands off the western coast of Scotland.
8. Notice the two comparison. Is it possible to hear the song of the nightingale in the Arabian deserts or the cry of the cuckoo-bird in the Hebrides? If not, why did Wordsworth use these comparisons?
9. **Will no one tell me what she sings?**: Wordsworth did not understand the language of the Erse.
10. **plaintive numbers**: a mournful song.
11. **lay**: a poem meant to be sung.

I Wandered Lonely as a Cloud[1]

In this poem Wordsworth sings of the harmony between things in nature and the harmony between nature and the poet himself.

I wandered lonely as a cloud
That floats on high o'er vales and hills,
When all at once I saw a crowd,
A host of[2] golden daffodils;
Beside the lake, beneath the trees,

Fluttering and dancing in the breeze.

Continuous[3] as the stars that shine
And twinkle on the Milky Way,
They stretched in never-ending line
Along the margin[4] of a bay:
Ten thousand saw I at a glance,
Tossing their heads in sprightly[5] dance[6].

The waves beside them danced; but they
Outdid the sparkling waves in glee:
A poet could not but be gay,
In such a jocund company:
I gazed—and gazed—but little thought
What wealth the show to me had brought:

For oft, when on my couch I lie
In vacant or in pensive mood,[7]
They flash upon that inward eye
Which is the bliss of solitude;[8]
And then my heart with pleasure fills,
And dances with the daffodils.

1. The poem is written in iambic tetrameter. The rhyme scheme of each stanza is ababcc.
2. **a host of**: a large number of.
3. **continous**: extending without break.
4. **margin**: edge or border.
5. **sprightly**: lively, full of energy.
6. **dance**: Notice the repetition of "dance" in the poem.
7. **in vacant or in pensive mood**: in a mood in which the mind is devoid of any thought or in a deeply thoughtful mood.
8. **They flash upon the inward eye/Which is the bliss of solitude**: When alone, Wordsworth recalls the beautiful scene, which gives him great happiness.

Lines Composed a Few Miles Above Tintern Abbey[1]

Wordsworth first made a tour of the Wye valley and the ruins of Tintern Abbey in August of 1793 when he was 23 years old. Five years later he revisited the place with his sister Dorothy Wordsworth. From the beautiful natural scene he meditates on the effect of nature on the growth of his mind.

Five years have past; five summers, with the length
Of five long winters[2]! and again I hear
These waters, rolling from their mountain-springs
With a soft inland murmur[3]. —Once again
Do I behold these steep and lofty cliffs,
That on a wild secluded scene[4] impress
Thoughts of more deep seclusion; and connect
The landscape with the quiet of the sky.
The day is come when I again repose
Here, under this dark sycamore, and view
These plots of cottage-ground, these orchard-tufts[5],
Which at this season, with their unripe fruits,
Are clad[6] in one green hue, and lose themselves[7]
'Mid groves and copses. Once again I see
These hedge-rows, hardly hedge-rows, little lines
Of sportive wood[8] run wild: these pastoral farms,
Green to the very door; and wreaths of smoke
Sent up, in silence, from among the trees!
With some uncertain notice[9], as might seem
Of vagrant dwellers[10] in the houseless woods,
Or of some hermit's cave, where by his fire
The hermit sits alone.
These beauteous forms,
Through a long absence, have not been to me
As is a landscape to a blind man's eye:
But oft, in lonely rooms, and 'mid the din
Of towns and cities, I have owed to them
In hours of weariness, sensations sweet,
Felt in the blood, and felt along the heart;

And passing even into my purer mind[11],
With tranquil restoration:[12]—feelings too
Of unremembered pleasure[13]: such, perhaps,
As have no slight or trivial influence
On that best portion of a good man's life,
His little, nameless, unremembered acts
Of kindness and of love[14]. Nor less, I trust,
To them I may have owed another gift,
Of aspect more sublime[15]; that blessed mood,
In which the burthen[16] of the mystery,
In which the heavy and the weary weight
Of all this unintelligible world,
Is lightened:—that serene and blessed mood
In which the affections gently lead us on,—
Until, the breath of this corporeal frame[17]
And even the motion of our human blood
Almost suspended, we are laid asleep
In body, and become a living soul:
While with an eye made quiet by the power
Of harmony, and the deep power of joy,
We see into the life of things[18].
If this
Be but a vain belief, yet, oh! how oft—
In darkness and amid the many shapes[19]
Of joyless daylight; when the fretful stir
Unprofitable,[20] and the fever of the world,[21]
Have hung upon the beatings of my heart—
How oft, in spirit, have I turned to thee,
O sylvan[22] Wye! thou wanderer thro' the woods,
How often has my spirit turned to thee!
And now, with gleams of half-extinguished thought,[23]
With many recognitions dim and faint,
And somewhat of a sad perplexity[24],
The picture of the mind revives again:
While here I stand, not only with the sense
Of present pleasure, but with pleasing thoughts
That in this moment there is life and food
For future years. And so I dare to hope,
Though changed, no doubt, from what I was when first

I came among these hills; when like a roe
I bounded o'er the mountains, by the sides
Of the deep rivers, and the lonely streams,
Wherever nature led: more like a man
Flying from something that he dreads, than one
Who sought the thing he loved. For nature then
(The coarser pleasures[25] of my boyish days[26],
And their glad animal movements all gone by)
To me was all in all. —I cannot paint
What then I was.[27] The sounding cataract
Haunted me like a passion; the tall rock,
The mountain, and the deep and gloomy wood,
Their colours and their forms, were then to me
An appetite,[28] a feeling and a love,
That had no need of a remoter charm,
By thought supplied, nor any interest
Unborrowed from the eye. —That time is past,
And all its aching joys[29] are now no more[30],
And all its dizzy raptures. Not for this
Faint[31] I, nor mourn, nor murmur; other gifts
Have followed; for such loss, I would believe,
Abundant recompense. For I have learned
To look on nature, not as in the hour
Of thoughtless youth; but hearing oftentimes
The still, sad music of humanity,
Nor harsh nor grating, though of ample power
To chasten and subdue.[32]

Notes

1. This poem is written in blank verse.
2. **Five years have past; five summers, with the length of five long winters**: Notice the repetition of the word "five" and the variation of the nouns it nodifies.
3. **soft inland murmur**: Here suggests the quietude of the place, as contrasted with the roaring waves in the sea.
4. **wild secluded scene**: a deserted place undisturbed by the outside world. Notice the harmony between the secluded scene and the more secluded mind of the poet.
5. **orchard-tufts**: "Tuft" is "toft", a hillock. The little hill was overgrown with fruit trees.

6. **clad**: clothed.
7. **lose themselves**: As the fruits are still green, it is impossible to distinguish them from the green leaves.
8. **sportive wood**: playful twigs and branches of trees in the wood.
9. **uncertain notice**: information the source of which is uncertain.
10. **vagrant dwellers**: wanderers who take rest somewhere in the wood.
11. **my purer mind**: In Wordsworth's philosophy, mind (heart) is contrasted with objective reality; "my purer mind" means mind in its "purer form".
12. **with tranquil restoration**: tranquility is restored in the mind.
13. **unremembered pleasure**: pleasure the source of which is forgotten.
14. **His little, nameless, unremembered acts of kindness and love**: Here Wordsworth is modest about his acts of kindness and love. He describes his good acts as little, nameless, and unremembered.
15. **Of aspects more sublime**: Of a more sublime nature.
16. **burthen**: burden.
17. **this corporeal frame**: this human body.
18. **We see into the life of things**: This is Wordsworth's mystic philosophy.
19. **shapes**: the appearances.
20. **the fretful stir/Unprofitable**: human activity which is irritating and useless.
21. **the fever of the world**: eager desire of the people at large.
22. **sylvan**: of the woods.
23. **with gleams of half extinguished thought**: with the memory about this secluded place growing dim.
24. **a sad perplexity**: The poet becomes sad because the scene he sees now is different from what he visualized in his memory.
25. **coarser pleasures**: pleasures during his boyhood, which were rough and crude.
26. **my boyish days**: Wordsworth in these lines illustrates the growing up of his mind, his relation to nature in the three stages of his life. In the first stage (the boyish days) he was part of nature and his movements were like animals.
27. **To me was all in all. —I cannot paint/What then I was**: This was what he was like five years ago during his first visit. Nature then was the most beloved thing to him.
28. **An appetite**: A strong desire.
29. **aching joys**: intense joys. The putting together of two words of entirely different meanings is called oxymoron in rhetoric.
30. **now no more**: the present stage, the third stage, of the growth of his mind.
31. **Faint**: Lose courage of spirit.
32. **hearing oftentimes... /To chasten and subdue**: Here Wordsworth means that as he advances in age, he is aware of the sorrows and miseries of human life, but with the influence of nature on him, they appear to him like quiet, soothing music, which has the power to purify and refine his soul.

Samuel Taylor Coleridge (1772—1834)

The other two lake poets beside Wordsworth are Samuel Taylor Coleridge and Robert Southey (1774—1834).

Like his friend Wordsworth whom he met in 1795 and with whom he began a lifelong friendship, Coleridge was progressive in his early years. He had been studying in the Charity School of Christ's Hospital in London for seven or eight years, where he met Charles Lamb. At nineteen he entered Cambridge and was there for three years and left in 1793 without taking a degree. In the next year he met Robert Southey, and the two of them were excited at what was happening in France. Inspired by the idea of egalitarianism, the two planned to establish a new community, a utopian society in America and name it Pantisocracy. Twelve couples were chosen for this undertaking, and for this purpose Coleridge even married the sister of Southey's wife. But the idea turned out to be a failure. In his later years, he was also shocked by the Reign of Terror and became very conservative in politics.

In his youth Coleridge suffered acute pain in the head and to ease the pain, he took opium. For the rest of his life he became a slave to the drug and lived in poverty. He lived in the Lake district after 1800.

His representative work is *The Rime of the Ancient Mariner*. The long poem is written in ballad form. He deliberately uses this form to tell a simple story. But when reading it, we discover many subtle places, and the musical effect is wonderful. The albatross, a sea bird, is an omen of luck. A seaman for no reason at all kills the bird, and for this reason the whole ship is punished by God and the seaman is punished by his fellow seamen. The theme is about sin and its expiation. The language is irresistible. A guest is detained by the mariner to listen to his tale. The reader, like the reluctant guest, is enchanted by the tale. Coleridge is very good at making supernatural things appear real and true to life. He uses his own words by saying he has the ability to secure from the reader "that willing suspension of disbelief which constitutes poetic faith."

Besides *The Ancient Mariner*, another of his well known poems is *Kubla Khan*, which is also collected in *Lyrical Ballads*. It is an unfinished poem of 54 lines. He claimed that one day in his dream he composed a poem of 200—300 lines when he was taking a nap. On waking up he hurriedly found his pen and wanted to write them down but he was interrupted by an unexpected guest and he stopped at the 54th line.

In addition to his poems, Coleridge also wrote a very important work of literary criticism, *Biographia Literaria* (1817), in which he emphasizes the importance of the imagination and makes a distinction between imagination and fancy. A creative writer should be able to transform reality into something higher. He was likewise a good lecturer and his lectures on Shakespeare are still considered valuable Shakespearean critical materials. Besides poetry and criticism Coleridge also wrote plays. His only play that was on the stage was *Remorse*, and it was through Byron's efforts that it was received by the Drury Lane Theatre (1813).

Kubla Khan[1]

Or a vision in a dream. A fragment

In Xanadu[2] did Kubla Khan
A stately pleasure-dome[3] decree[4]:
Where Alph[5], the sacred river, ran
Through caverns measureless to man
Down to a sunless sea.
So twice five miles of fertile ground
With walls and towers were girdled[6] round:
And there were gardens bright with sinuous rills[7],
Where blossom'd many an incense-bearing tree;
And here were forests ancient as the hills,
Enfolding sunny spots of greenery.
But oh! that deep romantic chasm[8] which slanted

Down the green hill athwart a cedarn cover![9]
A savage[10] place! as holy and enchanted
As e'er beneath a waning moon was haunted
By woman wailing for her demon-lover![11]
And from this chasm, with ceaseless turmoil seething[12],
As if this earth in fast thick pants[13] were breathing,

A mighty fountain momently[14] was forced:[15]
Amid whose swift half-intermitted burst
Huge fragments[16] vaulted like rebounding hail,
Or chaffy grain beneath the thresher's flail:
And 'mid these dancing rocks at once and ever
It flung up momently the sacred river.
Five miles meandering with a mazy motion[17]
Through wood and dale the sacred river ran,
Then reached the caverns measureless to man,
And sank in tumult to a lifeless ocean:
And 'mid this tumult Kubla heard from far
Ancestral voices prophesying war!

The shadow[18] of the dome of pleasure
Floated midway on the waves;
Where was heard the mingled measure
From the fountain and the caves.
It was a miracle of rare device,
A sunny pleasure-dome with caves of ice!

A damsel[19] with a dulcimer[20]
In a vision once I saw:
It was an Abyssinian[21] maid,
And on her dulcimer she played,
Singing of Mount Abora[22].
Could I revive[23] within me
Her symphony and song,
To such a deep delight 'twould win me,
That with music loud and long,
I would build that dome in air,
That sunny dome! those caves of ice!
And all who heard should see them there,
And all should cry, Beware! Beware!
His flashing eyes, his floating hair[24]!
Weave a circle round him thrice,[25]
And close your eyes with holy dread,
For he on honey-dew hath fed,

And drunk the milk of Paradise.

Notes

1. The poem is written in lines of irregular meters and rhyme scheme. Kubla Khan (忽必烈汗)(1216—1294) was the grandson of Genghis Khan(成吉思汗) and was the founder of the Mongol dynasty in China. Coleridge might have read about him in Marco Polo's *Travels*. "Khan" was the supreme ruler of Turkish, Tartar, and Mongol tribes, and emperors of China in the Mongol dynasty.
2. **Xanadu**: It might be Shangdu(上都), a place in Inner Mongolia, where Kubla Khan built his court when he came to power in 1260 and four years later made it the capital. Later the capital was moved to Beijing.
3. **pleasure-dome**: a great palace for entertainment with a round top.
4. **decree**: order.
5. **Alph**: a fictitious river.
6. **girdled**: surrounded.
7. **sinuous rills**: winding small streams.
8. **chasm**: a deep opening in rock.
9. **athwart a cedarn cover**: across a place covered by cedars.
10. **savage**: wild and fierce.
11. **As e'er beneath a waning moon was haunted / By woman wailing for her demon-lover**: The place was frequented by a woman who used to cry under the waning moon for the return of her lover from the underground. The scene adds to the savage place a romantic atmosphere.
12. **seething**: boiling; the water was tumbling as if boiling.
13. **thick pants**: short breaths in quick succession.
14. **momently**: every moment.
15. **was forced**: was spurted out.
16. **Huge fragments**: huge spouts of water.
17. **Five miles meandering with a mazy motion**: a celebrated example of the effect of alliteration; the "m" sound suggests the twisting movement of the lengthy river.
18. **shadow**: reflection.
19. **damsel**: (*archaic*) girl.
20. **dulcimer**: a musical instrument with strings struck by two hammers.
21. **Abyssinian**: Of Abyssinia, the old name for Ethiopia.
22. **Mount Abora**: a fictitious mount.
23. **Could I revive**: If I could sing the song that the girl sang.
24. **His flashing eyes, his floating hair**: The poet, stimulated by inspiration, is like one under magic charm, with his eyes shining and his hair flowing in the air.
25. **Weave a circle round him thrice**: It was believed in old times that anyone who was

bewitched by evil spirits or witches should be separated from other people by drawing a circle around him three times.

The Rime of the Ancient Mariner[1,2]

A paragraph from Coleridge's *Biographia Literaria* will help us to understand the creation of the long poem: "... In this idea originated the plan of the *Lyrical Ballads*; in which it was agreed that my endeavours should be directed to persons and characters supernatural, or at least romantic; yet so as to transform from our inward nature a human interest and semblance of truth sufficient to procure for these shadows of imagination that willing suspension of disbelief for the moment, which constitutes poetic faith. Mr. Wordsworth, on the other hand, was to propose to himself as his object to give charm of novelty of things of everyday, and to excite a feeling analogous to the supernatural... "

Argument[3]

How a Ship, having first sailed to the Equator, was driven by storms to the cold Country towards the South Pole; how the Ancient Mariner cruelly and in contempt of the laws of hospitality killed a Seabird and how he was followed by many and strange Judgments; and in what manner he came back to his own Country.

Part 1

An ancient Mariner meeteth three Gallants bidden to a wedding feast, and detaineth one.

It is an ancient Mariner
And he[4] stoppeth[5] one of three.[6]
—"By thy long gray beard and glittering eye,
Now wherefore[7] stopp'st thou me?

The Bridegroom's doors are opened wide,
And I am next of kin[8];
The guests are met, the feast is set.
May'st[9] hear the merry din.[10]"
He holds him with his skinny hand,
"There was a ship," quoth[11] he.
"Hold off![12] unhand me,[13] graybeard loon[14]!"
Eftsoons[15] his hand dropped he.

The Wedding-Guest is spellbound by the eye of the old sea faring man, and constrained to hear his tale.

He holds him with his glittering eye—[16]
The Wedding-Guest stood still,
And listens like a three years' child:
The Mariner hath his will.

The Wedding-Guest sat on a stone:
He cannot choose but hear;[17]
And thus spake on that ancient man,
The bright-eyed Mariner.

"The ship was cheered,[18] the harbor cleared,
Merrily did we drop
Below the kirk,[19] below the hill,
Below the lighthouse top.[20]

The Mariner tells how the ship sailed southward with a good wind and fair weather, till it reached the Line.

The Sun came up upon the left,[21]
Out of the sea came he!
And he shone bright, and on the right
Went down into the sea.

Higher and higher every day,
Till over the mast at noon[22]—"
The Wedding-Guest here beat his breast,
For he heard the loud bassoon[23].

The bride hath paced into the hall,
Red as a rose is she; [24]
Nodding their heads before her goes
The merry minstrelsy.
The Wedding-Guest he beat his breast,
Yet he cannot choose but hear;
And thus spake on that ancient man,
The bright-eyed Mariner.

The ship driven by a storm toward the South Pole.

"And now the STORM-BLAST came, and he[25]"
Was tyrannous[26] and strong;
He struck with his o'ertaking wings,
And chased us south along[27].

With sloping masts and dipping prow,[28]
As who pursued with yell and blow
Still treads the shadow of his foe,[29]
And forward bends his head,
The ship drove fast, loud roared the blast,
And southward aye[30] we fled.

And now there came both mist and snow,
And it grew wondrous cold[31]:
And ice, mast-high, came floating by,
As green as emerald.

The land of ice, and of fearful sounds where no living thing was to be seen.

And through the drifts[32] the snowy clifts[33]
Did send a dismal sheen[34]:
Nor shapes of men nor beasts we ken[35]—
The ice was all between.

Till a great sea bird, called the Albatross, came through the snowfog, and was received with great joy and hospitality.

The ice was here, the ice was there,
The ice was all around:[36]
It cracked and growled, and roared and howled,
Like noises in a swound![37]
At length did cross an Albatross[38],
Thorough[39] the fog it came;
As if it had been a Christian soul[40],
We hailed it in God's name.

It ate the food it ne'er had eat,
And round and round it flew.
The ice did split with a thunder-fit[41];
The helmsman steered us through!

And lo! the Albatross proveth a bird of good omen, and followeth the ship as it returned northward through fog and floating ice.

And a good south wind sprung[42] up behind;
The Albatross did follow,
And every day, for food or play,
Came to the mariner's hollo!

In mist or cloud, on mast or shroud[43],
It perched for vespers nine[44];
Whiles[45] all the night, through fog-smoke white,
Glimmered the white Moon-shine."

The ancient Mariner inhospitably killeth the pious bird of good omen.

"God save thee, ancient Mariner!
From the fiends, that plague thee thus! —
Why look'st thou so?"—With my crossbow
I shot the ALBATROSS.[46,47]

1. The poem is written in ballad form, i. e. , quatrains with the first and third lines containing four stresses and the second and fourth lines three stresses, and with rhymes in the even-numbered lines. The general movement of the verse is iambic, though many lines are anapaestic. There are many lines with internal rhymes. Notice the mechanisms of poetry; its meter, rhyme, and melody are in their perfect form in this poem.
2. **ancient**: The word has a double meaning. It means both "old age" and "old times". The atmosphere of "bygone days" permeates the whole poem.
3. **argument**: Here the word means "the summary of the story".
4. **he**: The abrupt beginning is typical of ballad form.
5. **stoppeth**: (*archaic*) The use of archaic words helps to create the atmosphere of "bygone days".
6. **one of the three**: The numbers 3,5,7,9 has a mystic and supernatural significance in western countries, as the three witches in Shakespeare's *Macbeth* and the Seven Deadly Sins in the *Bible*.
7. **wherefore**: (*archaic*) why.
8. **kin**: mear relative.
9. **May'st**: You may.
10. **din**: a loud resonant noise.
11. **quoth**: (*archaic*) says. Notice the joy of the feast is in sharp contrast with the strange mystery of the ancient mariner's tale.
12. **Hold off**: Get away.
13. **unhand me**: take your hands off me.
14. **loon**: worthless fellow, rascal.
15. **Eftsoons**: Immediately.
16. **He holds him with his glittering eye**: The eye of the mariner is several times mentioned in the poem and it has the magic power to stop the wedding guest. Notice how the guest changes his attitude toward the mariner step by step.
17. The fascination is now complete. There is no need to stop the wedding guest with the hand.
18. **The ship was cleared**: The ancient mariner plunges directly into the story without any introduction, and the listener is led into the story at once. In the reader's imagination, he visualizes a little village harbour and a ship putting out on its voyage, amid the cheers of the onlookers assembled on the quay. Those who are gathered on the quay little dream of the mysterious journey awaiting the ship (cheered=the shoutings of the onlookers; cleared=the ship sailed off the quay).
19. **kirk**: church.

20. Notice the order the different objects disappear from the sights of those on the ship. At the end of the story when the ship comes back, these objects reappear in reversed order.
21. **The Sun came up upon the left**: The ship was sailing southward, so the sun rose up on the left side of the ship.
22. **Till over the mast at noon**: The sun was just over the ship as it had reached the Equator.
23. **bassoon**: a woodwind musical instrument of deep base note.
24. **Red as a rose is she**: The redness of the bride and the revelry of the feast is in sharp contrast with the tragic story of the mariner.
25. **he**: the storm blast.
26. **tyrannous**: severe and cold.
27. **along**: The word suggests the length of the journey.
28. **sloping masts and dipping prow**: the masts turning downward and the forepart of the ship touching the water, a vivid description of the speedy movement of the ship.
29. **Still treads the shadow of his foe**: can get no further ahead than the shadow of his enemy whom he is pursuing(Still=always).
30. **aye**: ever, always.
31. **wondrous cold**: extremely cold.
32. **drifts**: currents of mist and snow.
33. **clifts**: cliffs, here means snow-capped icebergs.
34. **dismal sheen**: dismal=gloomy, sorrowful; sheen=radiance, brightness.
35. **ken**: see.
36. **The ice was here... /The ice was all around**: The repetition of the simple, monosyllabic word adds to the intensity of the ice scene. Some scholars think the description of the sea in the poem has no equal in English literature.
37. **It cracked and growled... /in a swound**: The onomatopoeia (拟声词) helps to create a scene of heterogeneous echoing sounds at the South Pole. Notice the different shades of meanings of the verbs(cracked=made a sharp snapping sound; growled=made a deep rough sound, as made by dogs; roared=gave forth a loud, deep, rumbling sound, as that of thunder; howled = uttered a loud, wailing sound, as made by wolves). swound=(*archaic*)swoon.
38. **Albatross**: a large, long-winged seabird of remarkable power of flight(信天翁).
39. **Thorough**: (*archaic*)Through.
40. **a Christian soul**: "Soul" means "human being". The albatross is believed to be a bird of good omen.
41. **a thunder-fit**: a sudden burst of thunder.
42. **sprung**: sprang.
43. **shroud**: ropes supporting the mast.
44. **vespers nine**: nine evenings.
45. **Whiles**: (*archaic*)While.
46. **God save thee... /I shot the ALBATROSS**: Notice the terseness of the speech

between the wedding guest and the ancient mariner. The guest is now wholly attracted by the mariner and has totally forgot the wedding ceremony. He has noticed the look of horror that has gradually deepened on the mariner's face.

47. **ALBATROSS**: Notice the first five parts of the poem end with the albatross. It suggests the irresistible mysterious power that the albatross had on the mariner.

George Gordon Byron (1788—1824)

Byron was born of noble blood both on the paternal and maternal lines. On his father's side, he was descended from an aristocratic family which came to England with William the Conqueror. He inherited the title of baron when he was ten years old upon the death of his great-uncle, and he came back to England from Scotland where he had been living with his mother, a Scottish heiress, to inherit the estate of Newstead. He was sent to study at Harrow and later at Cambridge. In 1807 while a student at Cambridge, he showed talent in verse writing by publishing a collection of lyrical verse *Hours of Idleness*, which incurred the harsh criticism from *The Edinburgh Review*, a conservative magazine. He was provoked to write in reply his first important poem *English Bards and Scotch Reviewers*, in which he, in the style of Pope, satirically attacked Wordsworth, Coleridge, and Southey, and the Edinburgh critics. After he attained his M. A. degree, he stayed for some time on his estate and led a dissipated life. From 1809 to 1811, he made a grand tour of the Continent. He visited Portugal, Spain, Albania, and Greece, countries which were under foreign domination. After his return, he took his seat in the House of Lords and made a famous speech on Feb. 27, 1812 opposing the government's cruel measures against the Luddites (the machine breakers). In the same year he published the first two cantos of *Childe Harold's Pilgrimage*. The book made him famous overnight, as he himself said, "(I) awoke one morning and found myself famous". In the next four years appeared his *Oriental Tales*, a series of romantic narrative verses, the stories of which took place in the Near-Eastern countries, with heroes rebellious in character, defying conventional morality and even fate, but moody and sometimes misanthropic. In 1815 he married an heiress but was soon separated from her. There arose a scandal, and Byron was to leave England forever. He first went to Switzerland, where he met Shelley. The two poets formed a close friendship, and under the influence of Shelley, he wrote *Prometheus*, *Sonnet on Chillon*, and *The Prisoner of Chillon*. Then he went to Italy and published the third and fourth cantos of *Childe Harold's Pilgrimage* (1816, 1818). They were followed by many other works, among which was *Don Juan* (1818—1820). In Italy he met Shelley for the second time. In 1824 he equipped a troop of soldiers with his own money to support the Greeks in their struggle against the Turks. He died of fever in 1824 in Greece. His body was brought home from Greece and buried near his family seat.

Childe Harold's Pilgrimage[1]

Childe Harold, a young man waiting to be knighted, disillusioned with and disgusted at a life of pleasure and revelry, sets out for the European Continent for diversion. In Europe he visited many countries dominated by foreign powers. The long poem records what Harold sees and feels on his journey, but it actually expresses Byron's feelings and his views on the political situations in these countries. In the fourth canto Byron gives up the imaginary Harold and speaks in the first person.

Below are three excerpts from the long poem. In the first excerpt we witness the pride and the misanthropic view of the Byronic hero and the influence of Wordsworth on Byron. The second excerpt is the description of the famous ball on the eve of the Battle of Quatre Bras. The third excerpt is a description of a stormy night on Lake Leman. In the tempest and thunder, the night, the lake, and the mountains became living things and they give voice to Byron's revolutionary spirit.

Excerpt I

Canto III

12

But soon he knew himself the most unfit
Of men to herd with Man, with whom he held
Little in common; untaught to submit
His thoughts to others, though his soul was quelled[2]
In youth by his own thoughts; still uncompelled[3].
He would not yield dominion of his mind
To spirits against whom his own rebelled,

Proud though in desolation; which could find
A life within itself, to breathe without mankind.

13

Where rose the mountains, there to him were friends;
Where rolled the ocean, thereon was his home;
Where a blue sky, and glowing clime[4], extends,
He had the passion and the power to roam;
The desert, forest, cavern, breaker's foam,
Were unto him companionship; they spake
A mutual language, clearer than the tome[5]
Of his land's tongue, which he would oft forsake
For Nature's pages glassed[6] by sunbeams on the lake.

Excerpt II

21

There was a sound of revelry by night,
And Belgium's capital had gather'd then
Her Beauty and her Chivalry, and bright
The lamps shone o'er fair women and brave men;
A thousand hearts beat happily; and when
Music arose with its voluptuous swell[7]
Soft eyes look'd love to eyes which spake again,
And all went merry as a marriage bell;
But hush! hark! a deep sound strikes like a rising knell[8]!

22

Did ye not hear it? —No; 'twas but the wind,
Or the car rattling o'er the stony street;
On with the dance! let joy be unconfined;
No sleep till morn, when Youth and pleasure meet
To chase the glowing Hours with flying feet—

But hark! —that heavy sound breaks in once more,
As if the clouds its echo would repeat;
And nearer, clearer, deadlier[9] than before!
Arm! arm! it is—it is—the cannon's opening roar!

23

Within a window'd niche[10] of that high hall
Sate[11] Brunswick's fated chieftain[12]; he did hear
That sound, the first amidst the festival,
And caught its tone with Death's prophetic ear;
And when they smiled because he deem'd it near,
His heart more truly knew that peal too well
Which stretch'd his father on a bloody bier[13];
And roused the vengeance blood alone could quell;
He rush'd into the field, and, foremost fighting, fell.

24

Ah! then and there was hurrying to and fro,
And gathering tears, and tremblings of distress[14],
And cheeks all pale, which but an hour ago
Blush'd at the praise of their own loveliness;
And there were sudden partings, such as press
The life from out young hearts, and choking sighs
Which ne'er might be repeated; who could guess
If ever more should meet those mutual eyes,
Since upon night so sweet such awful morn could rise!

25

And there was mounting in hot haste: the steed,
The mustering[15] squadron, and the clattering car,
Went pouring forward with impetuous speed,
And swiftly forming in the ranks of war;
And the deep thunder peal on peal afar;
And near, the beat of the alarming drum

Roused up the soldier ere the morning star;
While throng'd[16] the citizens with terror dumb,
Or whispering, with white lips— "The foe! they come! they come!"

Excerpt III

92

The sky is changed! —and such a change ! Oh night,
And storm, and darkness, ye are wondrous strong,
Yet lovely in your strength, as is the light
Of a dark eye in woman! Far along,
From peak to peak, the rattling crags among,[17]
Leaps the live thunder! Not from one lone cloud,
But every mountain now hath found a tongue,
And Jura answers, through her misty shroud,
Back to the joyous Alps, who call to her aloud!

93

And this is in the night—Most glorious night!
Thou wert not sent for slumber! let me be
A sharer in thy fierce and far delight—
A portion of the tempest and of thee!
How the lit lake shines, a phosphoric sea,
And the big rain comes dancing to the earth!
And now again'tis black—and now, the glee
Of the loud hills shakes with its mountain mirth,
As if they did rejoice o'er a young earthquake's birth.

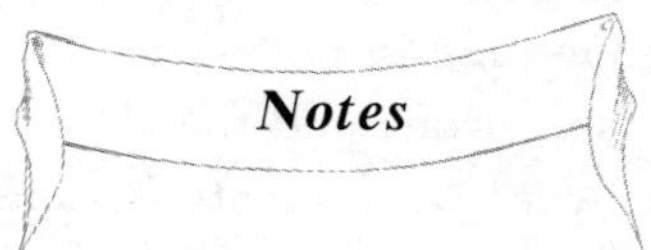

1. The poem is written in the Spenserian stanza, i. e. , a stanza consisting of 8 lines of iambic pentameter plus an Alexandrine (six-stress iambic meter), with the rhyme scheme ababbcbcc.

2. **quelled**: suppressed, reduced to submission.
3. **uncompelled**: unyielding.
4. **glowing clime**: warm climate; here means warm region.
5. **tome**: a book, especially a large and heavy one.
6. **glassed**: made glassy.
7. **voluptuous swell**: the sound of music growing louder and louder and gratifying sensual pleasure.
8. Notice "bell" rhymes with "knell" but with entirely different meanings.
9. **And nearer, clearer, deadlier**: Notice how these words build up to a climax.
10. **niche**: a hollow place in the wall.
11. **Sate**: (*archaic*) Sat.
12. **Brunswick's fated chieftain**: The Duke of Brunswick, nephew of George Ⅲ, was killed in the Battle of Quatre Bras(the ball described in the poem was held on the eve of the Battle of Quatre Bras, two days before the Battle of Waterloo), just as his father had been killed at Jena in 1806.
13. **bier**: a frame to carry the dead body to the grave.
14. **distress**: great sufferings.
15. **mustering**: collecting.
16. **throng'd**: gathered.
17. **From peak to peak, the rattling crags among**: Notice how the words "peak", "rattling", and "crags" resemble the sound of thunder.

Don Juan

Don Juan, a satirical epic, is Byron's masterpiece. It consists of 16 cantos and remains unfinished. It is about the romantic adventures of a legendary Spanish youth who has many love affairs with various woman. At first he has an illicit love with a married woman. Being discovered by the women's husband, he is sent aboard at the age of 16 by his mother. He is shipwrecked and is cast up on a Greek island where he is cared for by Haidee, the daughter of a pirate who is away from the island and is believed to be dead. There Don Juan marries Haidee and a wedding ceremony is held. Haidee's father returns unexpectedly and is enraged when he finds that his daughter has been married to a stranger. Don Juan is put on a slave ship and Haidee goes mad and dies. Juan is sold in Constantinople as a slave to a sultana who falls in love with him. He manages to escape from the harem and joins the Russian troops which are besieging Ismail. He distinguishes himself in the fighting and is sent to St. Petersburg, where he wins the favour of the Russian Empress, Catherine the Great, who dispatches him on a political mission to England. Although the poem is about the adventures of a Spanish libertine, the real significance of the poem lies in the vivid descriptions of the lives and manners of many lands, Byron's fiery passions for the liberation of the Greek people, and his bitter satire on the sham and hypocrisy in love, religion, and the social relations of his time.

The following excerpt is *The Isles of Greece*, a song sung by a singer at the wedding ceremony between Don Juan and Haidee, in which the singer (Byron) contrasts the past glory of the Greek people with their present state of enslavement by the Turks.

Canto III

The Isles of Greece[1]

1

The isles of Greece, the isles of Greece!
    Where burning[2] Sappho[3] loved and sung,
Where grew the arts of war and peace,[4]
    Where Delos[5] rose, and Phoebus[6] sprung[7]!
Eternal summer gilds them yet,
But all, except their sun, is set.

2

The Scian[8] and the Teian[9] muse[10],
    The hero's harp,[11] the lover's lute,[12]
Have found the fame your shores refuse[13];
    Their place of birth alone is mute
To sounds which echo further west
Than your sires'[14] 'Islands of the Blest'[15].

3

The mountains look on Marathon[16]—
    And Marathon looks on the sea;
And musing there an hour alone,
    I dream'd that Greece might still be free;
For standing on the Persian's grave[17],
I could not deem myself a slave.

4

A king[18] sate on the rocky brow
　　Which looks o'er sea-born Salamis;
And ships, by thousands, lay below,
　　And men in nations[19],—all were his!
He counted them at break of day—
And when the sun set where were they?

5

And where are they? and where art thou,
　　My country?[20] On thy voiceless shore
The heroic lay[21] is tuneless now—
　　The heroic bosom beats no more!
And must thy lyre, so long divine,
Degenerate into hands like mine?

6

'T is something, in the dearth of fame[22],
　　Though link'd among a fetter'd race,
To feel at least a patriot's shame,
　　Even as I sing, suffuse[23] my face;
For what is left the poet here?
For Greeks a blush—for Greece a tear.[24]

7

Must we but weep o'er days more blest?
    Must we but blush? —Our fathers bled.[25]
Earth! render back from out thy breast
    A remnant of our Spartan dead[26]!
Of the three hundred grant but three,
To make a new Thermopylae!

8

What, silent still? and silent all?
    Ah! no; —the voices of the dead
Sound like a distant torrent's fall,
    And answer, "Let one living head[27],
But one arise,—we come, we come!"
'T is but the living who are dumb.

9

In vain—in vain: strike other chords[28];
    Fill high the cup with Samian wine[29]!
Leave battles to the Turkish hordes,
    And shed the blood of Scio's vine![30]
Hark! rising to the ignoble call[31]—
How answer each bold Bacchanal[32]!

1. The versification of the song is different from the rest of the long poem. The song is composed of 16 stanzas, each stanza consisting of 6 lines of iambic tetrameter, with a rhyme scheme ababcc.
2. **burning**: passionate.
3. **Sappho**: a famous poetess in ancient Greece(ca. 612 B. C.), well-known for her love poems.

4. **arts of war and peace**: skill in military affairs and in ruling over the country in peacetime.
5. **Delos**: an island in the Aegean Sea, supposed to be the place where Apollo, the sun god was born.
6. **Phoebus**: the Greek name for Apollo.
7. **sprung**: sprang.
8. **Scian**: of Scio, supposed to be the birthplace of Homer.
9. **Teian**: of Teos, supposed to be the birthplace of Anacreon(570 B. C. ? —480 B. C. ?), a poet in ancient Greece, who was noted for his lyric singing in praise of wine, women, and song.
10. **muse**: a goddess of poetry in Greek mythology, here referring to Homer and Anacreon.
11. **The hero's harp**: here refers to Homer whose *Iliad* and *Odyssey* are about the exploits of heroes.
12. **the lover's lute**: Here refers to Anacreon.
13. **the fame your shores refuse**: Greece does not give honour to Homer and Anacreon who are worshipped in other counties.
14. **sires**: (*archaic*)ancestors.
15. **Islands of the Blest**: islands in Greek mythology where the blessed people live after death. The line means that the fame of Homer and Anacreon go beyond the geographical limit of the earth known to people in Byron's time.
16. **Marathon**: a plain to the northwest of Athens, where the Greeks defeated the invading Persians(490 B. C.).
17. **Persians' grave**: Here refers to the Persian soldiers killed at the Battle of Marathon.
18. **A King**: Here refers to the Persian king Xerxes(529 B. C. ?—465 B. C. ?), who witnessed the defeat of his mighty navy force of about two thousand ships by the Greeks' fleet of three hundred and eighty ships after a day's sea battle near the island of Salamis on September 29,480 B. C. (sate=〈*archaic*〉sat; rocky brow= the edge of a cliff).
19. **men in nations**: In the Persian navy there were many soldiers conscripted in different nations.
20. **And where are they? and where art thou,/My country?** :Notice the past tense is changed to the present tense. The singer is calling the attention of the Greek people to their enslavement by the Turks.
21. **lay**: song.
22. **in the dearth of fame**: in this age of dishonour(dearth=in lack of).
23. **suffuse**: spread line.
24. **For Greeks a blush —for Greece a tear**: Notice the conciseness of the language in this line.
25. **Must we but blush? —Our fathers bled**: Notice the contrast in this line.
26. **Spartan dead**: Here refers to the three hundred Spartans killed in the Battle of

Thermopylae(a mountain pass in Greece) fought between the Spartans and the Persian invaders in 480 B. C.

27. **one living head**: one living person.
28. **strike other chords**: play other tunes.
29. **Samian wine**: Samos is an island in the Aegean sea, famous for its wine. Since the Greeks refuse to answer his call to rise up against the invaders, the singer tries to goad them into action.
30. **And shed the blood of Scio's vine!**: Notice the singer's satirical tone in the line. Scio, the birthplace of Homer, is also noted for its wine.
31. **the ignoble call**: the dishonourable call in the previous four lines.
32. **Bacchanal**: worshipper of Bacchus, Roman god of wine.

When We Two Parted[1]

This poem and the following one are two of the most well-known love lyrics by Byron. The poem expresses the sorrow of a lady who is betrayed by her lover, and she is reproaching him for his cold-heartedness.

When we two parted
   In silence and tears,
Half broken-hearted
   To sever[2] for years,
Pale grew thy cheek and cold,
   Colder thy kiss;
Truly that hour foretold
   Sorrow to this[3].

The dew of the morning
   Sunk chill on my brow—
It felt like the warning
   Of what I feel now.
Thy vows are all broken,
   And light[4] is thy fame;
I hear thy name spoken,
   And share in its shame.

They name thee before me,

A knell to mine ear;
A shudder comes o'er me—
Why wert[5] thou so dear?
They know not I knew thee,
Who knew thee too well—
Long, long shall I rue[6] thee,
Too deeply to tell.
In secret we met—
In silence I grieve,
That thy heart could forget,
Thy spirit deceive.
If I should meet thee
After long years,
How should I greet thee? —
With silence and tears.

1. The metrical movement of this poem is basically a combination of iambic and anapaestic feet, with a rhyme scheme ababcdcd.
2. **sever**: separate.
3. **this**: this moment.
4. **light**: of small account.
5. **wert**: were.
6. **rue**: to be sorry for.

She Walks in Beauty[1]

This poem is chosen from *Hebrew Melodies* (1815). On June 11, 1814, Byron attended a party where he for the first time met his young cousin, Lady Wilmot Horton, who was dressed in a black mourning gown. Byron was so struck by her beauty that, on returning home, he wrote this poem in a single night.

1

She walks in beauty, like the night

Of cloudless climes[2] and starry skies;
And all that's best of dark and bright
Meet in her aspect[3] and her eyes:
Thus mellowed[4] to that tender light
Which heaven to gaudy day[5] denies[6].

2

One shade[7] the more, one ray[8] the less,
Had half impaired[9] the nameless grace[10]
Which waves in every raven tress[11],
Or softly lightens o'er her face;
Where thoughts serenely sweet express
How pure, how dear their dwelling place[12].

3

And on that cheek, and o'er that brow,
So soft, so calm, yet eloquent,
The smiles that win,[13] the tints that glow,[14]
But tell of days in goodness spent[15],
A mind at peace with all below,[16]
A heart whose love is innocent!

1. The poem contains three stanzas of iambic tetrameter, with a rhyme scheme ababab.
2. **climes**: climates.
3. **aspect**: appearance.
4. **mellowed**: become rich and soft.
5. **gaudy day**: brilliantly fine day.
6. **denies**: refuses to give.
7. **shade**: darkness.
8. **ray**: brightness.
9. **Had... impaired**: would have damaged.
10. **nameless grace**: indescribable elegance.
11. **raven tress**: dark-coloured lock of hair.

12. **their dwelling place**: Here refers to the body.
13. **The smiles that win**: The smiles that capture people's attention.
14. **the tints that glow**: the radiant reddish colour that shines.
15. **tell of days in goodness spent**: show that she has been living a life of purity and moral excellence.
16. **A mind at peace with all below**: The implied meaning is that she is kind towards everything below the heaven.

Percy Bysshe Shelley (1792—1822)

Like Byron, Shelley was born of noble blood. His ancestors had been Sussex aristocrats since early in the 17th century. At eighteen he entered Oxford University after he had graduated from Eton. But he was expelled from the university for the publication of a pamphlet *On the Necessity of Atheism* (1811). His father forbade him to return home. He eloped with a young girl, Harriet Westbrook. In 1813 he published his first important poem *Queen Mab*, an allegorical poem in which through the mouth of Queen Mab, the fairy queen, he attacks "kings, priests, and statesmen", and human institutions such as marriage, commerce, and religion. The fairy queen finally predicts the future state of a regenerated world when "all things are recreated, and the flame of consentaneous love inspires all life." For the atheist idea in the poem, he was indebted to William Godwin (1765—1836), a radical who published *The Inquiry Concerning Political Justice* (1793). In 1814 Shelley met Godwin and fell in love with his daughter Mary Godwin. Her mother was Mary Wollstonecraft (1759—1797), a champion for women's rights and the authoress of *A Vindication of the Rights of Woman* (1792). Although Godwin was an atheist and believed in free love, he did not allow his daughter to be Shelley's lover and the two eloped. In 1816 Harriet committed suicide and this caused a scandal. Shelley's enemies launched attacks on him and Shelley had to leave England for good in 1818, and spent the rest of his life in Italy with his wife Mary Shelley. In Italy Shelley met Byron again, and the two poets became close friends. On July 8, 1822, Shelley was drowned in a tempest while sailing in a boat along the coast of Italy. His ashes were buried in Rome.

Besides *Queen Mab* Shelley wrote a number of other allegorical poems. They are *Alastor* (1816), *The Revolt of Islam* (1818), *The Mask of Anarchy* (1819). He also wrote some lyrical dramas among which are *Prometheus Unbound* (1820), *Hellas* (1822), and *The Cenci* (1819), a tragedy in verse form. On the death of Keats he wrote an elegiac poem *Adonais* (1821). His lyrics are best known among the English poets. The most well-known is *Ode to the West Wind* (1819). Besides poetry Shelley also wrote prose. *The Defence of Poetry* was written in 1821 and published in 1840 after the poet's death.

Shelley's funeral

Song to the Men of England[1]

On August 16, 1819, when about 60,000 people were holding a rally in St. Peter's Field near Manchester, demanding universal suffrage, parliamentary reform, and the repeal of the Corn Law, a troop of cavalry opened fire on them, killed more than a dozen, and wounded several hundreds. The killing was ironically referred to as "Peterloo Massacre", a combination of "Waterloo" and "St. Peter's". Upon hearing the news of the massacre, Shelley, being exiled in Italy, wrote several political lyrics in protest against the government's barbarous action and calling the working people to rise up to overthrow the rule of the idle class.

I

Men of England, wherefore[2] plough
For the lords who lay ye low[3]?
Wherefore weave with toil and care
The rich robes your tyrants wear?

II

Wherefore feed, and clothe, and save,
From the cradle to the grave,
Those ungrateful drones[4] who would
Drain your sweat—nay[5], drink your blood?

III

Wherefore, Bees of England[6], forge
Many a weapon, chain and scourge[7],
That these stingless drones[8] may spoil[9]
The forced produce of your toil?[10]

IV

Have ye leisure, comfort, calm,
Shelter, food, love's gentle balm?
Or what is it ye buy so dear
With your pain and with your fear?

V

The seed ye sow, another reaps;
The wealth ye find, another keeps;
The robes ye weave, another wears;
The arms ye forge, another bears.

VI

Sow seed,—but let no tyrant reap;
Find wealth,—let no impostor heap;
Weave robes,—let not the idle wear;
Forge arms,—in your defence to bear.

VII

Shrink to your cellars, holes, and cells;
In halls ye deck[11] another dwells.
Why shake the chains ye wrought?[12] Ye see
The steel ye tempered glance on ye.[13]

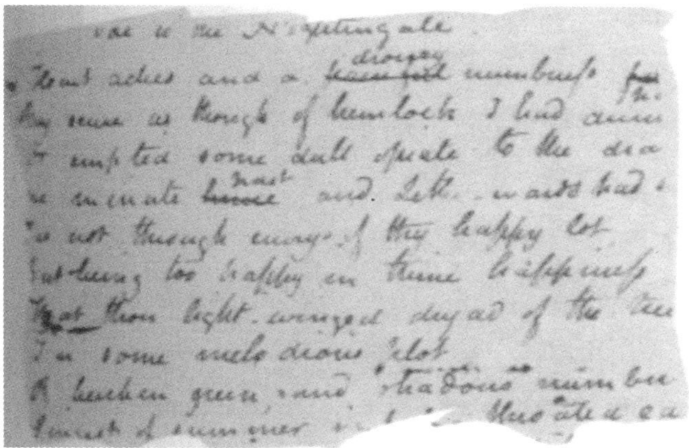

Shelley's manuscript

VIII

With plough and spade, and hoe and loom,
Trace your grave, and build your tomb,
And weave your winding-sheet[14], till fair[15]
England be your sepulchre.[16,17]

1. The song consists of eight quatrains, the metrical pattern of each line being iambic tetrameter and the rhyme scheme of each quatrain being aabb.
2. **wherefore**: (*archaic*) why.
3. **lay ye low**: reduce you to an economically and socially humble situation.
4. **drones**: male honeybees, here referring to the people of the exploiting class who do not work and live on the labours of the working class.
5. **nay**: not only so, but.
6. **Bees of England**: Here refers to the working class of England.
7. **scourge**: a whip used formerly for punishment.
8. **these stingless drones**: Here refers to the people of the exploiting class.
9. **spoil**: plunder.
10. **The forced produce of your toil**: the products you have produced with great effort.
11. **deck**: decorate.
12. **Why shake the chains you wrought**: Why should you shake off the chains that bind you which you have made yourself?

13. **The steel ye tempered glance on ye**: The sword you have forged is flashing on you.
14. **winding-sheet**: shroud, i. e., a piece of cloth that wraps up a corpse.
15. **fair**: beautiful.
16. **sepulchre**: a burial place, tomb.
17. In the last two stanzas the poet is reprimanding the workers who do not answer his call to fight for their freedom.

Ode to the West Wind[1]

In the turbulent year of 1819, Shelley wrote many political lyrics. This poem is most representative of Shelley's feelings and thoughts at the time. It is a mixture of death and rebirth. Shelley is concerned with the regeneration of himself spiritually and poetically and of Europe politically. He is appealing to the west wind to effect this regeneration. In the first three stanzas, the dynamic force of the west wind is manifested in its power on the land, in the air, and in the sea in different seasons. It is the destroyer and preserver. It will destroy the old world and herald in a new one. In the fourth stanza Shelley wishes that he were a leaf, a cloud, and a wave, so that he could feel the power of the west wind; but he is aware of his age and his sufferings in life which have bent him down. Finally, he appeals to the wind, the wind of aspiration and change, to reinvigorate him and to give force and persuasiveness to his poetry.

Shelley in his note says, "This poem was conceived and chiefly written in a wood that skirts the Arno, near Florence, and on a day when that temptuous wind, whose temperature is at once mild and animating, was collecting the vapours which pour down the autumnal rains. They began, as I foresaw, at sunset with a violent tempest of hail and rain, attended by that magnificent thunder and lightning peculiar to the Cisalpine region(阿尔卑斯山南侧的意大利地区)".

I

O wild West Wind,[2] thou breath of Autumn's being,[3]
Thou, from whose unseen presence[4] the leaves dead
Are driven like ghosts from an enchanter fleeing,

Yellow, and black, and pale, and hectic red,[5]
Pestilence-stricken multitudes:[6] O thou,
Who chariotest[7] to their dark wintry bed[8]

The winged seeds,[9] where they lie cold and low[10],
Each like a corpse within its grave, until
Thine azure sister[11] of the Spring shall blow

Her clarion[12] o'er the dreaming earth, and fill
(Driving sweet buds like flocks to feed in air)[13]
With living hues[14] and odours plain and hill:

Wild Spirit, which art moving everywhere[15];
Destroyer and Preserver; hear, oh, hear!

II

Thou on whose stream[16], 'mid the steep sky's commotion,[17]
Loose clouds like earth's decaying leaves are shed,
Shook from the tangled boughs of Heaven and Ocean,[18]

Angels of rain and lightning:[19] there are spread
On the blue surface of thine aery surge[20],
Like the bright hair uplifted from the head

Of some fierce Maenad[21], even from the dim verge[22]
Of the horizon to the zenith's[23] height,
The locks[24] of the approaching storm. Thou dirge[25]

Of the dying year, to which this closing night[26]
Will be the dome of a vast sepulchre[27],
Vaulted[28] with all thy congregated might

Of vapours,[29] from whose solid atmosphere[30]
Black rain, and fire, and hail will burst: oh hear!

III

Thou who didst waken from his summer dreams
The blue Mediterranean, where he[31] lay,
Lulled by the coil of his crystalline streams,[32]

Beside a Pumice Isle[33] in Baiae's bay[34],
And saw in sleep old palaces and towers
Quivering within the wave's intenser day,[35]

All overgrown with azure moss and flowers
So sweet, the sense faints picturing them![36] Thou
For whose path the Atlantic's level powers[37]

Cleave[38] themselves into chasms[39], while far below
The sea-blooms and the oozy woods which wear
The sapless foliage of the ocean, know

Thy voice, and suddenly grow gray with fear;
And tremble and despoil themselves:[40] oh, hear!

IV

If I were a dead leaf thou mightest bear;
If I were a swift cloud to fly with thee;
A wave to pant[41] beneath thy power, and share

The impulse of thy strength, only less free
Than thou, O uncontrollable![42] If even
I were as in my boyhood, and could be

The comrade of thy wanderings over Heaven,
As then, when to outstrip thy skiey speed
Scarce seemed a vision; I would ne'er have striven

As thus with thee in prayer in my sore need[43].
Oh, lift me as a wave, a leaf, a cloud!
I fall upon the thorns of life! I bleed!

A heavy weight of hours has chained and bowed
One too like thee:[44] tameless, and swift, and proud.[45]

V

Make me thy lyre, even as the forest is:[46]
What if my leaves are falling[47] like its own[48]!
The tumult of thy mighty harmonies

Will take from both[49] a deep, autumnal tone,
Sweet though in sadness. Be thou, Spirit fierce,
My spirit! Be thou me, impetuous one!

Drive my dead thoughts over the universe
Like withered leaves to quicken a new birth!
And, by the incantation of this verse,

Scatter, as from an unextinguished hearth
Ashes and sparks, my words among mankind!
Be through my lips to unawakened earth

The trumpet of a prophecy![50] O, Wind,
If Winter comes, can Spring be far behind?

1. An ode(颂诗),in ancient literature, is an elaborate lyrical poem composed for a chorus to chant and to dance to; in modern use, it is a rhymed lyric expressing noble feelings, often addressed to a person or celebrating an event. This ode consists of five stanzas, each a sonnet formed of four units of terza rima completed by a couplet. Terza rima(三行诗节)was used by Dante(1265—1321)in *The Divine Comedy*. The first and third lines rhyme second line is in rhyme with the fourth and sixth lines, the rhyme scheme being aba, bcb, cdc, ded, ee. This linked chain gives a feeling of onward motion; the verse has a breathless quality which is in keeping with the onward motion of the wind's movement. The metrical pattern of each line is basically iambic pentameter.
2. **O wild West Wind**: Notice the grammatical structure of the whole stanza. It is an invocation to the west wind. Notice the sound effect of the alliterated "w".
3. **thou breath of Autumn's being**: Here Autumn is personified, and the west wind is

compared to the air breathed out of Autumn, a living being. Throughout the poem the west wind appears like a deity, or at least a living thing.

4. **unseen presence**: invisible existence; the word "presence" further intensifies the idea of the west wind as a living thing.
5. **Yellow, and black, and pale, and hectic red**: the varied colours of the decaying leaves (hectic: affected with hectic fever, the kind of fever occuring in connection with certain wasting diseases). It has been suggested that these are the colours of the different races of human beings.
6. **Pestilence-stricken multitudes**: The leaves are like human beings hit by epidemic disease.
7. **chariotest**: The ending "est" is added to the verb in Middle English in the second person singular (chariot is a car used in ancient warfare or racing; here "chariot" is a verb, meaning "to carry").
8. **their dark wintry bed**: In winter time, the seeds of plants are buried in the earth. Here "the dark bed" means "the grave". The theme of death and rebirth recurs throughout the poem.
9. **The winged seeds**: Many plants, including trees, perpetrate themselves by seeds borne on the wind.
10. **lie cold and low**: The seeds are compared to the dead bodies in the grave.
11. **Thine azure sister**: The west wind that will blow in the spring (azure: sky blue).
12. **clarion**: a kind of trumpet whose note is clear and shrill.
13. **Driving sweet buds like flocks to feed in air**: as if the new seeds are being shepherded to pastures after winter.
14. **living hues**: vivid colours.
15. **art moving everywhere**: The west wind is sweeping through the universe.
16. **stream**: flow of the wind.
17. **'mid the steep sky's commotion**: in the midst of the great turbulence high up in the sky.
18. **Loose clouds... boughs of Heaven and Ocean**: Loose clouds are torn by the wind like decaying leaves from the confused mass of clouds which are like boughs, formed by the air and the vapour that the sun draws from the ocean's water.
19. **Angels of rain and lightning**: Angels refer to the loose clouds in the previous line, which are compared to heralds of rain and lightning.
20. **aery surge**: airy wave.
21. **Maenad**['miːnæd]: a frenzied female follower of Bacchus, the god of wine in Greek mythology. In comparing the loose clouds in the wind to the hair of Maenad, Shelley is suggesting the demonic power of the approaching storm.
22. **dim verge**: The sky at the horizon is dark with clouds.
23. **zenith**: the highest point in the sky.
24. **locks**: the hair of the head, here referring to the loose clouds.

25. **dirge**: a song of mourning for the dead, here referring to the west wind.
26. **this closing night**: The clouds are thickening, and the darkness is deepening as the night falls.
27. **dome of a vast sepulchre**: the round top of a huge tomb.
28. **Vaulted**: Covered with an arched roof.
29. **congregated might/Of vapours**: The clouds (vapours) are so condensed that they carry a great force.
30. **solid atmosphere**: The clouds are so dense that the sky appears solid.
31. **he**: referring to the Mediterranean. Here the Mediterranean is personified.
32. **Lulled by the coil of his crystalline streams**: soothed, or almost hypnotized by the soft sound of the clear currents in the water.
33. **Pumice Isle**: the name of an isle near Naples (pumice: porous rock formed by volcanic lava〈浮石〉).
34. **Baiae's bay**: Baiae, a famous resort near Naples where ancient Roman emperors built luxurious palaces.
35. **Quivering within the wave's intenser day**: The reflections of palaces and towers trembling in the intenser daylight in the water. Palaces and towers are symbols of the aristocratic rule.
36. **the sense faints picturing them**: The sense loses its consciousness while describing them.
37. **the Atlantic's level powers**: the powerful tides of the Atlantic Ocean, which move ahead horizontally.
38. **cleave**: cut, split.
39. **chasm**: a very deep crack.
40. **And tremble and despoil themselves**: Shelley's note, "The phenomenon alluded to at the conclusion of the third stanza is well-known to naturalists. The vegetation at the bottom of the sea, of rivers, and of lakes, sympathizes with that of the land in the change of seasons, and is consequently influenced by the winds which announce it." "Despoil" means "to take away by force".
41. **pant**: breathe quickly.
42. **O uncontrollable**: the west wind.
43. **in my sore need**: in my painful need.
44. **One too like thee**: Here refers to Shelley himself.
45. **tameless, and swift, and proud**: In his boyhood Shelley was wild, swift, and proud as the west wind.
46. **Make me thy lyre, even as the forest is**: The aeolian harp(风弦琴) gives musical sounds as the wind blows through it. Here the forest is compared to the aeolian harp(lyre), and the poet prays that he also may be the aeolian harp so that he could feel the power of the west wind.
47. **What if my leaves are falling**: What does it matter if I am depressed?

48. **its own**: the leaves of the forest. Here "it" refers to the forest.
49. **take from both**: "Both" refers to Shelley and the forest.
50. **The trumpet of a prophecy**: The prophecy is the last line of the poem, here Shelley refers to his ideal world which he describes in many of his poems.

John Keats (1795—1821)

Unlike Byron and Shelley, Keats was born in London, of lowly origin. His father was a hostler and stable keeper and then married his employer's daughter. When he was eight, his father died, and his mother died of tuberculosis when he was fourteen. His guardian forced him to leave school at fifteen and apprenticed him to a surgeon. For five years he served his apprenticeship and then worked as the surgeon's helper for two more years. In 1817 he abandoned his profession and published his first collection of poems. In 1818 he published his long allegorical poem *Endymion*, which was about the love between a Greek shepherd and the moon goddess. Both collections were severely attacked by conservative critics. It is said that the attacks were the cause of his illness that took away his life. He went on writing, however, and most of his best poems were written in the short three years from 1817 to the time of his death.

On First Looking into Chapman's Homer[1]

It was said that Keat's former school teacher Charles Cowden Clarke introduced him to Homer's *The Iliad*, translated by George Chapman (ca. 1557—1634), an Elizabethan poet and dramatist. The two read through the epic until dawn, and Keats walked home. The sonnet reached Clarke by the ten o'clock mail on that day.

Much have I travell'd in the realms of gold,[2]
  And many goodly states and kingdoms[3] seen;
  Round many western islands[4] have I been
Which bards in fealty to Apollo hold.[5]
Oft of one wide expanse[6] had I been told
  That deep-browed[7] Homer rules as his demesne[8];
  Yet did I never breathe its pure serene[9]
Till I heard Chapman speak out loud and bold[10];

Then felt I like some watcher of the skies[11]
　　When a new planet swims into his ken[12];
Or like stout Cortez[13] when with eagle eyes
　　He star'd at the Pacific—and all his men
Look'd at each other with a wild surmise[14]—
　　Silent, upon a peak in Darien.

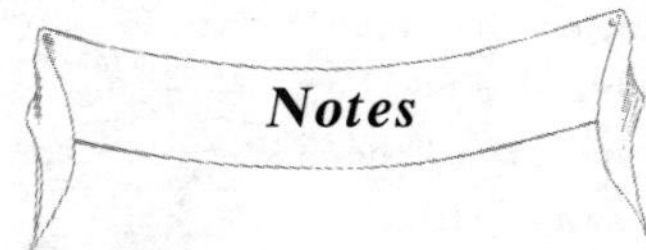

1. This sonnet is written in the Petrarchan form; each line is in iambic pentameter, and the rhyme scheme of the sonnet is abba, abba, cdcdcd.
2. **Much have I travell'd in the realms of gold**: Keats in the sonnet is comparing himself to a traveller and great ancient literary works to kingdoms of gold.
3. **goodly states and kingdoms**: The word "goodly" means "beautiful"; "states and kingdoms" continues the idea of "realms of gold" in the previous line.
4. **western islands**: also referring to ancient classic works.
5. **Which bards in fealty to Apollo hold**: The ancient poets(bards) of the isles of Greece (western islands) vowed loyalty to the god of poetry (Apollo is the Greek sun god, patron of poetry and music, medicine, archery, etc.).
6. **wide expanse**: vast territory, as different from "western islands".
7. **deep-browed**: "Brow" is regarded as seat of expression or intellectual quality; "deep-browed" refers to Homer's profound thinking and knowledge.
8. **demesne**[dɪˈmeɪn]: realm, feudal possession.
9. **pure serene**: clear air.
10. **bold**: daring.
11. **watcher of the skies**: astrologer.
12. **ken**: the range of sight or knowledge.
13. **Cortez**: A Spanish colonist(1485—1547)who conquered Mexico in 1519. In fact it was Vasco Nunex de Balboa(1475—1517), a Portuguese colonist, who first saw the Pacific Ocean at the top of a mountain in Dairen, a place in Panama.
14. **surmise**: a guess.

Ode to a Nightingale[1]

Charles Brown wrote about the situation in which Keats wrote this beautiful poem: "In the spring of 1819 a nightingale had built her nest near my house. Keats felt a tranquil and continual joy in her song; and one morning he took his chair from the breakfast table to the grass plot under a plum tree, where he sat for two or three hours. When he came into the house, I perceived he had some scraps of paper in his hand, and these he was quietly thrusting behind the books. On inquiry, I found those scraps, four or five in number, contained his poetic feeling on the song of our nightingale."

In the poem Keats identifies the nightingale with his Ideal Beauty and hopes that the song of the nightingale will help him to escape from the world of actuality, where "to think is to be full of sorrow", into the world of Ideal Beauty, a place of eternal happiness.

I

My heart aches[2], and a drowsy numbness[3] pains
  My sense, as though of hemlock[4] I had drunk,
Or emptied some dull opiate[5] to the drains[6]
  One minute past, and Lethe-wards[7] had sunk;
'Tis not through envy of thy happy lot,
  But being too happy in thine happiness,—
    That thou, light winged Dryad[8] of the trees,
      In some melodious plot[9]
Of beechen green[10], and shadows numberless[11]
  Singest of summer in full-throated[12] ease.

II

O, for a draught of vintage![13] that hath been
  Cool'd a long age in the deep-delved earth[14],
Tasting of Flora[15] and the country green[16],
  Dance, and Provençal song[17], and sun-burnt mirth[18]!
O, for a beaker full of the warm South[19],
  Full of the true, the blushful[20] Hippocrene[21],
    With beaded bubbles[22] winking[23] at the brim,
      And purple stained mouth[24];
That I might drink, and leave the world unseen,
  And with thee fade away into the forest dim:

III

Fade[25] far away, dissolve[26], and quite forget

What thou among the leaves hast never known,
The weariness, the fever, and the fret[27]
Here, where men sit and hear each other groan;
Where palsy shakes a few, sad, last gray hairs,[28]
Where youth grows pale, and spectre-thin, and dies;[29]
Where but to think is to be full of sorrow
And leaden-eyed despairs[30],
Where Beauty cannot keep her lustrous eyes,
Or new Love[31] pine at them[32] beyond to-morrow.

IV

Away! away! for I will fly to thee,
Not charioted by Bacchus and his pards[33],
But on the viewless[34] wings of Poesy,
Though the dull brain perplexes and retards:[35]
Already with thee![36] tender is the night,[37]
And haply[38] the Queen-Moon is on her throne,
Cluster'd around by all her starry Fays[39];
But here[40] there is no light,
Save[41] what from heaven is with the breezes blown
Through verdurous glooms[42] and winding mossy ways.

V

I cannot see what flowers are at my feet,[43]
Nor what soft incense[44] hangs upon the boughs,
But, in embalmed darkness[45], guess each sweet[46]
Wherewith[47] the seasonable month[48] endows
The grass, the thicket and the fruit-tree wild;
White hawthorn, and the pastoral eglantine;
Fast fading violets cover'd up in leaves;
And mid-May's eldest child,
The coming musk-rose,[49] full of dewy wine,
The murmurous haunt of flies on summer eves.[50]

VI

Darkling[51] I listen; and, for many a time
I have been half in love with easeful Death,
Call'd him soft names in many a mused rime,
To take into the air my quiet breath;
Now more than ever seems it rich to die,
To cease upon the midnight with no pain,
While thou art pouring forth thy soul abroad[52]
In such an ecstasy!
Still[53] wouldst thou sing, and I have ears in vain[54]—
To thy high requiem[55] become a sod[56].

VII

Thou wast not born for death, immortal Bird!
No hungry generations[57] tread thee down;
The voice I hear this passing night was heard
In ancient days by emperor and clown[58]:
Perhaps the self-same song that found a path
Through the sad heart of Ruth[59], when, sick for home,
She stood in tears amid the alien corn;
The same that oft-times hath
Charm'd magic casement, opening on the foam
Of perilous seas, in faery lands forlorn.[60]

VIII

Forlorn![61] the very word is like a bell
To toll me back from thee to my sole self![62]
Adieu! the fancy[63] cannot cheat so well
As she is fam'd to do, deceiving elf.[64]
Adieu! adieu! thy plaintive anthem[65] fades
Past the near meadows, over the still stream,
Up the hill-side; and now 'tis buried deep
In the next valley-glades:

Was it a vision, or a waking dream?
  Fled is that music:—Do I wake or sleep?[66]

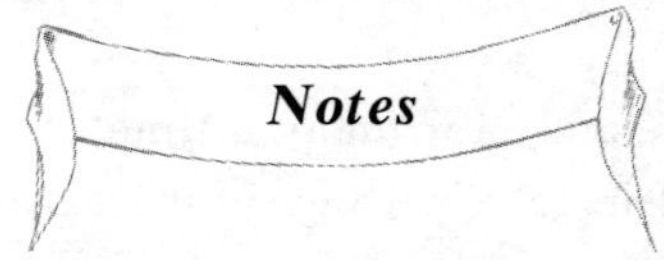

1. The poem contains eight stanzas, each consisting of ten lines, with nine lines in five-stress iambic meter and the eighth line in three-stress iambic meter. The poem is remarkable for its imagery and its music. They appeal to readers' senses—tactile(触觉), gustatory(味觉), olfactory(嗅觉), as well as visual and auditory.
2. **My heart aches**: People sometimes feel acute pain when in extreme happiness.
3. **drowsy numbness**: in a half-sleeping state in which one is deprived of the power to feel or move.
4. **hemlock**: a poisonous plant which first benumbs the person who takes it and then deprives him of his life.
5. **dull opiate**: a sedative drug containing opium, which makes people benumbed.
6. **drains**: dregs.
7. **Lethe-wards**: towards the Lethe, a river in Hades, which causes the dead souls to forget things on the earth.
8. **Dryad**: a spirit who lived in a tree in ancient Greek stories, here "the winged Dryad"referring to the nightingale.
9. **melodious plot**: the place where the nightingale is singing.
10. **beechen green**: the green leaves of the beechen(山毛榉树)trees.
11. **shadows numberless**: Here refers to the thick leaves which cast numberless shadows.
12. **full-throated**: singing with the whole power of the voice.
13. **O, for a draught of vintage**: In the second stanza, the poet wishes that with the help of the wine (vintage), he could go into the forest with the nightingale.
14. **deep-delved earth**: Good wine should be kept cool in the underground cell(delved: dug).
15. **Flora**: Roman goddess of flowers; here referring to flowers.
16. **country green**: green country, referring to the place where flowers blossom.
17. **Provençal song**: Provence, in southern France, was famous for its troubadours, singers of love songs in the Middle Ages.
18. **sun-burnt mirth**: the joyous life of the people who live in warm climate where the sun shines.
19. **the warm South**: the wine brewed in the south.
20. **blushful**: The word"blush"means"to become red in the face"; here the word is used to modify the colour of the wine which is as red as the blushes on people's faces.

21. **Hippocrene**: a fountain on the northern slopes of Mount Helicon, sacred to the Muses and Apollo and was supposed to be a source of poetic inspiration. Here "Hippocrene" means "the vintage" in the previous lines.
22. **beaded bubbles**: the bubbles of the wine at the edge(brim) of the cup are like beads.
23. **winking**: sparkling.
24. **purple stained mouth**: The wine leaves its purple colour on the drinker's mouth.
25. **Fade**: Disappear. The word "fade" echoes "fade" in the last line of the previous stanza. In the third stanza the poet wants to escape from the world of actuality.
26. **dissolve**: to melt away. See Hamlet's soliloquy in *Hamlet* Ⅱ. ii. :"O that this too too solid flesh would melt,/Thaw, and resolve itself into a dew." Here Keats is expressing his death wish.
27. **fret**: worry.
28. **Where palsy shakes a few, sad, last gray hairs**: The poet is using a visual image to describe the miserable old people who are paralysed.
29. **Where youth grows pale, and spectre-thin, and dies**: Here perhaps refers to Keat's brother, Tom Keats, who died of tuberculosis in the previous winter (spectre-thin:as thin as a ghost).
30. **leaden-eyed despairs**: the dull eyes of the people who are in despair (here "despairs" is personified).
31. **new Love**: lovers newly fallen in love.
32. **them**: Here refers to the lustrous eyes.
33. **Bacchus and his pards**: Bacchus is the god of wine in Greek mythology, and his chariot is drawn by leopards(pards). In the third stanza, the poet, finding that wine cannot bring him to the dream world(the world of the nightingale), is appealing to fancy (Poetry) to bring him there.
34. **viewless**: invisible.
35. **Though the dull brain perplexes and retards**: The word "perplexes" means "confuses"; "retards" means "makes dull". The line echoes his state of mind in the first stanza.
36. **Already with thee**: It shows that the poet is successful in getting at the dream world with the help of Poetry.
37. **tender is the night**: a very beautiful sentence. Francis Scott Fitzgerald(1896—1940)used it as the title of one of his novels.
38. **haply**: by chance.
39. **Fays**: Fairies. The moon is like a fairy queen surrounded by fairy-like stars.
40. **here**: in the wood in which the nightingale is singing.
41. **Save**: Except.
42. **verdurous glooms**: The word "verdurous" means "fresh green of growing leaves and grass"; "glooms" means "a deeply shaded or darkened place". This is a very beautiful description of the darkness of the place. Can darkness be green?
43. **I cannot see what flowers are at my feet**: Notice how the poet appeals to the sense

of smell in this stanza.

44. **soft incense**: tender fragrance, here refers to the flowers around him.
45. **embalmed darkness**: The word "embalmed" means "fragrant and soothing". It is another example of the beautiful description of darkness.
46. **each sweet**: each fragrant odour.
47. **Wherewith**: With which.
48. **the seasonable month**: The word "seasonable" means "occuring in good or proper time". June is the proper time for the blooming of flowers.
49. **The coming musk-rose**: The season of the musk-rose is coming.
50. **The murmurous haunt of flies on summer eves**: The alliterated "m" sound suggests the sound made by the flies that make people drowsy and intoxicated.
51. **Darkling**: In the dark. In the dream world, Keats is again thinking of death.
52. **abroad**: in the open air.
53. **Still**: (*archaic*) Always.
54. **I have ears in vain**: Though I am dead and can no longer hear you, you will continue to sing.
55. **requiem** [ˈrekwɪəm]: music for the Roman Catholic religious ceremony for a dead person, at which people pray that his soul shall rest quietly.
56. **sod**: earth with grass and roots growing in it.
57. **hungry generations**: suffering generations. In this stanza the poet, by means of allusions, is describing eternal beauty as represented by the song of the nightingale.
58. **clown**: a rustic or country fellow.
59. **Ruth**: a woman in "The Book of Ruth" in The Old Testament(《圣经·旧约》"路得记"), who, after the death of her husband, went to live in her husband's native country with her mother-in-law. There she married Boaz, a relative of her late husband, and through this marriage she became the great-grandmother of King David, king of the Israelites(11th century B. C. —962 B. C.). Keats, out of his poetic imagination, described Ruth's sadness in living in a foreign country.
60. **The same that oft-times hath/... /Of perilous seas, in faery lands forlorn**: These three lines are typical of romantic characteristics. In the romances in the Middle Ages, there were stories about a princess who was kept by some magician in a castle near the sea and who was waiting for a prince or knight who would come to break the charm imposed upon her. The song of the nightingale attracted (charm'd) the princess to the window(casement) of the castle which was under magic power.
61. **Forlorn**: Left alone and unhappy. The word in the last stanza is used to describe the remote castle in which the princess was kept. Here the poet in his trance picks up the word and applies it to himself and with it he again returns to the world of actuality.
62. **to my sole self**: A minute ago I was in the company of the nightingale.
63. **fancy**: his poetic imagination, i. e. , the "viewless wings of Poesy" in the fourth

stanza.

64. **elf**: a type of small fairy which is said to play tricks on people.
65. **plaintive anthem**: An "anthem" is a short musical composition to be sung in religious services or on solemn ceremonies. The word "plaintive" means "mournful"; it is because the poet has returned to the world of actuality.
66. **Do I wake or sleep**: The question brings the reader back to the very beginning of the poem.

To Autumn[1]

On September 22, 1819 Keats wrote to his friend J. H. Reynolds: "I never liked stubble fields so much as now—Aye, better than the chilly green of the spring. Somehow a stubble plain looks warm—in the same way that some pictures look warm—this struck me so much in my Sunday's walk that I compose upon it." Enclosed in the letter was this poem.

Like *Ode to a Nightingale*, this poem is also representative of Keats's poetic creation. Through a series of images he presents to the reader a picture of golden autumn, which, according to Keats, is no less beautiful than spring. Special attention should be paid to how the poem appeals to our visual, tactile, and aural senses.

I[2]

Season of mists and mellow[3] fruitfulness,
Close bosom-friend of the maturing sun[4],
Conspiring[5] with him how to load and bless
With fruit the vines[6] that round the thatch-eves[7] run;
To bend with apples the mossed cottage-trees,
And fill all fruit with ripeness to the core;
To swell the gourd, and plump the hazel shells
With a sweet kernel; to set budding more,
And still more, later flowers for the bees,
Until they think warm days will never cease,
For Summer has o'er-brimmed their clammy cells[8].

II

Who hath not seen thee[9] oft amid thy store[10]?
Sometimes whoever seeks abroad[11] may find

Thee sitting careless on a granary[12] floor,
　Thy hair soft-lifted by the winnowing[13] wind;
Or on a half-reaped furrow[14] sound asleep,
　Drowsed[15] with the fume of poppies, while thy hook[16]
　　Spares the next swath[17] and all its twined flowers:
And sometimes like a gleaner thou dost keep
　Steady thy laden head across a brook;
　Or by a cider-press, with patient look,
　　Thou watchest the last oozings[18] hours by hours.

III

Where are the songs of Spring? Ay, where are they?
　Think not of them, thou hast thy music[19] too,—
While barred clouds[20] bloom[21] the soft-dying day,
　And touch the stubble-plains with rosy hue;
Then in a wailful choir the small gnats mourn
　Among the river sallows[22], borne aloft
　　Or sinking as the light wind lives or dies;
And full-grown lambs loud bleat from hilly bourn[23];
　Hedge-crickets sing; and now with treble soft
　The red-breast whistles from a garden-croft[24];
　　And gathering swallows twitter in the skies.

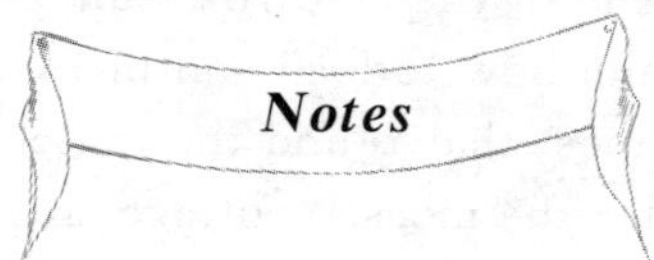

1. The poem contains three stanzas, each stanza consisting of eleven lines in iambic pentameter with a rhyme scheme ababcdecdde.
2. Notice the grammatical structure of the first stanza.
3. **mellow**: soft and rich, indicating the full ripeness of the fruit.
4. **the maturing sun**: the sun that causes fruit to ripen(maturing).
5. **Conspiring**: Both autumn and the sun are personified. "Conspiring" means "planning something together secretly"; the word further brings out the idea that autumn and the sun are close bosom friends.
6. **bless/With fruit the vines**: Here "bless with" has the same meaning as in the sentence "The marriage is blessed with a child."
7. **eves**: eaves, the projecting edge of the roof.
8. **clammy cells**: Overspilled honey makes the beehive sticky (clammy).

9. **thee**: Here autumn is identified with the farm labourer.
10. **store**: what is harvested.
11. **seeks abroad**: goes out of one's house.
12. **granary**: a storehouse for grain.
13. **winnowing**: separating the chaff from the grain by fanning.
14. **furrow**: a long cut in the ground made by a plow.
15. **Drowsed**: Fallen in half asleep.
16. **hook**: scythe.
17. **swath**: the space that a scythe cuts in one sweep.
18. **oozings**: the slowly flowing down fluid that is squeezed from fruit.
19. **thy music**: Here autumn is identified with the varied sounds heard in autumn.
20. **barred clouds**: clouds in the shape of bars.
21. **bloom**: make glowing and radiant.
22. **sallows**: willows.
23. **bourn**: domains, limits, boundary.
24. **croft**: a small piece of arable land, especially adjoining a dwelling.

Charles Lamb (1775—1834)

The name of Charles Lamb is familiar to Chinese readers, for his *Tales from Shakespeare* is widely read either in translation or in original by Chinese youth.

Side by side with the Lake poets, there were a number of essayists, who, like the Lake poets, were not interested in the national events, did not care about national democratic movements and national liberation movements in England and on the Continent, nor the miserable conditions of the people. Like the Lake poets, they were indulged in contemplation and imagination, looking backward to the past and took literature as an expression of their own subjective world that has nothing to do with the real one. In short, to them, literature is a means to escape from the turbulence and revolutions of the real world, a shelter where they can find their spiritual consolation.

Charles Lamb was important in English literature for his contribution to the Familiar Essay, a type of essay which dates back to those of the French essayist Montaigne (1533—1592) and was later developed by Addison and Steele.

There are similarities between Wordsworth and Lamb. Both of them emphasized the function of imagination. Lamb's essays are expressions of his own feelings, taking as their subject matter insignificant things and daily events, especially the recollections of the good old days, the remembrance of childhood. Like Wordsworth, Lamb contrasted the present with the past, eulogizing the carefreeness (innocence) of the bygone days and consoling himself by the fact that age had brought him as recompense a contemplative mind, which somehow made up for the loss of innocence. We can compare this idea with what Wordsworth wrote in *The Tintern Abbey* in which he describes the growth of his mind.

Another similarity between the two writers is that Lamb also took great delight in awakening within himself passions recollected in tranquility. What he described in his essays is usually experiences half a lifetime away, but these experiences were always fresh in his mind when he recollected them in tranquility. Recollection and nostalgia play an important part in his essays.

A striking difference between the two is that while Wordsworth took great delight in natural scenes, Lamb had nothing of Wordsworth's feeling for nature, his main interest being the city of London.

Lamb was born and grew up in London. He was the son of a poor clerk. At seven he was sent to the Charity School of Christ's Hospital where he made the acquaintance of Coleridge and where they began to make a lifelong friendship. It was through Coleridge that Lamb came to know Wordsworth. Lamb was very poor in his early years. After leaving school, he worked for some time in the South Sea House as a small clerk, and in 1792 he entered the East India House where he worked steadily for thirty-three years. As there was a strain of madness in the family, Lamb himself was mad for six weeks in the winter of 1795 — 1796, and his sister Mary Lamb (1764—1847), a talented girl, was also mad and killed her mother in 1796. Lamb took upon himself to take care of her, or she would have been put in the asylum.

Lamb's most well-known literary work is *Tales from Shakespeare*, which he wrote with his sister (1807). They were stories retold from the plays of Shakespeare. The other work is a collection of essays he contributed to the London magazine. The essays were written under the pen name of an Italian clerk named Ilia, who was supposed to be working in the South Sea House. The first collection *Essays of Ilia* was published in 1823, and the second collection *Last Essays of Ilia* was published in 1833. These essays began from 1832 and deal with subject matters such as roasted pig, a chimney sweeper, old china, and a dream child.

Charles Lamb never married. His house in London was frequented by many literary figures, among whom were Wordsworth, Coleridge, Hazlitt, and Leigh Hunt. Lamb devoted his life to the care of his sister, who appears in his essays as Cousin Bridget.

The style of his essays echoes that of 17th century essayists, such as Robert Burton and Thomas Browne. His essays are full of long and curious words and are interrupted by frequent exclamations and parentheses.

Old China

I have an almost feminine[1] partiality for old china. When I go to see any great house[2], I inquire for the china closet[3], and next for the picture gallery. I cannot defend[4] the order of preference, but by saying that we have all some taste or other, of too ancient a date to admit of our remembering distinctly that it was an acquired one[5]. I can call to mind the first play, and the first exhibition, that I was taken to; but I am not conscious of a time when china jars and saucers were introduced into my imagination.

I had no repugnance then—why should I now have? —to those little, lawless[6], azure-tinctured grotesques[7], that under the notion of men and women float about, uncircumscribed[8] by any element, in that world before perspective[9]—a china teacup.

I like to see my old friends—whom distance cannot diminish[10]—

figuring up in the air (so they appear to our optics[11]), yet on terra firma[12] still—for so we must in courtesy interpret that speck of deeper blue, which the decorous[13] artist, to prevent absurdity[14], had made to spring up beneath their sandals.

I love the men with women's faces, and the women, if possible, with still more womanish expressions.

Here is a young and courtly mandarin[15], handing tea to a lady from a salver[16]—two miles off. See how distance seems to set off[17] respect! And here the same lady, or another—for likeness is identity[18] on teacups—is stepping into a little fairy boat, moored on the hither side[19] of this calm garden river, with a dainty mincing foot, which in a right angle of incidence[20] (as angles go[21] in our world) must infallibly land her in the midst of a flowery mead[22]—a furlong[23] off on the other side of the same strange stream!

Farther on—if far or near can be predicated of their world—see horses, trees, pagodas, dancing the hays[24].

Here—a cow and rabbit couchant[25], and coextensive[26]—so objects show, seen through the lucid atmosphere of fine Cathay[27].

I was pointing out to my cousin last evening, over our Hyson[28] (which we are old-fashioned enough to drink unmixed still of an afternoon), some of these *speciosa miracula*[29] upon a set of extraordinary old blue china (a recent purchase) which we were now for the first time using; and could not help remarking how favorable circumstances had been to us of late years that we could afford to please the eye sometimes with trifles of this sort—when a passing sentiment seemed to overshade the brows of my companion. I am quick at detecting these summer clouds in Bridget.

"I wish the good old times would come again," she said, "when we were not quite so rich. I do not mean that I want to be poor; but there was a middle state"—so she was pleased to ramble on[30]—"in which I am sure we were a great deal happier. A purchase is but a purchase, now that you have money enough and to spare[31]. Formerly it used to be a triumph. When we coveted[32] a cheap luxury[33] (and, O! how much ado I had to get you to consent in those times!)—we were used to have a debate two or three days before, and to weigh the *for* and *against*, and think what we might spare it out of, and what saving we could hit upon, that should be an equivalent. A thing was worth buying then, when we felt the money that we paid for it.

"Do you remember the brown suit, which you made to hang upon you, till all your friends cried shame upon you, it grew so threadbare—and all because of that folio Beaumont and Fletcher[34], which you dragged home late at night from Barker's in Covent Garden[35]? Do you remember how we eyed it for weeks before we could make up our minds to the purchase, and had not come to a determination till it was near ten o'clock of the Saturday night, when you set off from Islington[36], fearing you should be too late—and when the old bookseller with some grumbling opened his shop, and by the twinkling taper (for he was setting bedwards) lighted out the relic from his dusty treasures—and when you lugged[37] it home, wishing it were twice as cumbersome—and when you presented it to me—and when we were exploring the perfectness of it (*collating*[38], you called it)—and while I was repairing some of these loose leaves with paste, which your impatience would not suffer to be left till daybreak—was there no pleasure in being a poor man? or can those neat black clothes which you wear now, and are so careful to keep brushed, since we have become rich and finical[39], give you half the honest vanity[40] with which you flaunted[41] it about in that overworn suit—your old corbeau[42]—for four or five weeks longer than you should have done, to pacify your conscience for the mighty sum of fifteen—or sixteen shillings was it? —a great affair we thought it then—which you had lavished on the old folio. Now you can afford to buy any book that pleases you, but I do not see that you ever bring me home any nice old purchases now.

"You are too proud to see a play anywhere now but in the pit[43]. Do you remember where it was we used to sit, when we saw the *Battle of Hexham*, and the *Surrender of Calais*[44], and Bannister and Mrs. Bland in the *Children in the Wood*[45]—when we squeezed out our shillings apiece to sit three or four times in a season[46] in the one-shilling gallery[47]—where you felt all the time that you ought not to have brought me—and more strongly I felt obligation to you for having brought me—and the pleasure was the better for a little shame—and when the curtain drew up, what cared we for our place in the house, or what mattered it where we were sitting, when our thoughts were with Rosalind in Arden, or with Viola[48] at the Court of Ilyria. You used to say that the gallery was the best place of all for enjoying a play socially—that the relish[49] of such exhibitions[50] must be in proportion to the infrequency of going—that the company we met there, not being in general readers of plays, were obliged to attend the more, and did attend, to what was going on, on the stage—because a word lost would have been a chasm[51], which it was impossible for them to fill up. With such reflections we consoled our pride then—and I appeal to you whether, as a woman, I met generally with less attention and accommodation[52] than I have done since in more expensive situations in the house? The getting in indeed, and the crowding up those inconvenient staircases, was bad enough—but there was still a law of civility to woman recognized[53] to quite as great an extent as we ever found in the other passages—and how a little difficulty overcome heightened the snug seat and the play, afterwards! Now we can only pay our money and walk in. You cannot see, you say, in the galleries now. I am sure we saw, and heard too, well enough then—but sight, and all, I think, is gone with our poverty.

Bridget is so sparing of her speech on most occasions that when she gets into a rhetorical vein, I am careful how I interrupt it. I could not help. however, smiling at the phantom[54] of wealth which her dear imagination had conjured up out of a clear income of poor—hundred pounds a year. It is true we were happier when we were poorer, but we were also younger, my cousin. I am afraid we must put up with the excess[55], for if we were to shake the superflux[56] into the sea, we should not much mend ourselves. That we had much to struggle with, as we grew up together, we have reason to be most thankful. It strengthened and knit our compact closer. We could never have been what we have been to each other, if we had always had the sufficiency which you now complain of. The resisting power—those natural dilations[57] of the youthful spirit, which circumstances cannot straiten—with us are long since passed away. Competence[58] to age is supplementary youth, a sorry supplement indeed, but I fear the best that is to be had. We must ride where we formerly walked: live better and lie softer—and shall be wise to do so—than we had means to do in those good old days you speak of. Yet could those days return—could you and I once more walk our thirty miles a day—could Bannister and Mrs. Bland again be young, and you and I be young to see them—could the good old one-shilling gallery days return—they are dreams, my cousin, now—but could you and I at this moment, instead of this quiet argument, by our well-carpeted fireside, sitting on this luxurious sofa—be once more struggling up those inconvenient staircases, pushed about, and squeezed, and elbowed by the poorest rabble of poor gallery scramblers—could I once more hear those anxious shrieks of yours—and the delicious *Thank God, we are safe*, which always followed when the topmost stair, conquered, let in the first light of the whole cheerful theater down beneath us—I know not the fathom line[59] that ever touched a descent[60] so deep as I would be willing to bury more wealth in than Croesus[61] had, or the great Jew R—[62] is supposed to have, to purchase it. And now do just look at that merry little Chinese waiter holding an umbrella, big enough for a bedtester[63], over the head of that pretty insipid half Madonnaish[64] chit[65] of a lady in that very blue summer-house.

1. **feminine**: a delicate feeling or preference for old china that almost resembles a woman's.
2. **great house**: In England the great houses of the aristocrats sometimes are open to the public.
3. **china closet**: a cupboard in which pieces of china are kept.
4. **defend**: offer a justified reason.
5. **acquired one**: a liking gained through experience.
6. **lawless**: Here in the text "lawless" means "disregarding the law of perspective(透视画法)".
7. **grotesques**: comically distorted figures.
8. **uncircumscribed**: unrestricted.
9. **perspective**: technique of representing objects on a flat surface to show depth and relative distance.
10. **diminish**: make smaller.
11. **optics**: (*archaic*) eyes.
12. **terra firma**: (*Latin*) solid ground.
13. **decorous**: characterized by decorum and propriety.
14. **absurdity**: the state of being against reason or common sense.
15. **mandarin**: a high ranking influential officer in old China.
16. **salver**: a tray.
17. **to set off**: to make(something)more noticeable.
18. **likeness is identity**: Similar appearance may mean the same person on a tea cup.
19. **hither side**: on this side.

20. **incidence**: the falling of a ray on a surface(入射).
21. **as angles go**: as angles are accepted.
22. **mead**: (*poetical*) meadow.
23. **furlong**: one eighth of a mile.
24. **dancing the hays**: An English country dance with a serpentine movement (蛇行状,螺旋形前进). This is how Lamb explains the dances on the china tea cup.
25. **couchant**: lying down with the head up(抬头蹲伏的动物).
26. **coextensive**: extending over the same length.
27. **Cathy**: the old European name for China.
28. **Hyson**: a Chinese green tea.
29. **speciosa miracula**: (*Latin*) shining wonders.
30. **ramble on**: talk in a disordered and wandering way.
31. **enough and to spare**: more than enough.
32. **coveted**: desired eagerly.
33. **cheap luxury**: a luxurious thing, the price of which is cheap. This is an example of an oxymoron(逆喻), a figure of speech combining seemingly contradictory expressions, such as "cruel kindness", and "falsely true".
34. **Beaumont and Fletcher**: Francis Beaumont(1584—1616) and John Fletcher(1579—1625) were English dramatists. They wrote many plays in collaboration. That folio Beaumount and Fletcher: that book by Beaumount and Fletcher made of sheets of paper each folded once.
35. **Covent Garden**: a market place in London.
36. **Islington**: a place in the north of London where the Lambs lived.
37. **lugged**: dragged or carried with great effort.
38. **collating**: examining and comparing (copies of books, notes, etc.) carefully in order to find the differences between them(核对).
39. **finical**: too delicate and fussy about details.
40. **honest vanity**: Lamb had the vanity to show himself in the outworn suit, a vanity which he honestly acknowledged.
41. **flaunted**: showed something for public admiration.
42. **corbeau**: a dark green cloth, almost black("corbeau" is the French word for "raven").
43. **pit**: the ground floor of a theatre behind the stalls.
44. ***Battle of Hexham* and the *Surrender of Calais***: comedies by George Colman (1762—1836).
45. ***Children in the Wood***: a play by Thomas Morton (1764—1838).
46. **season**: a period of time in a year in which plays are performed.
47. **gallery**: the highest upper floor in a theatre.
48. **Rosalind... Viola**: Rosalind in *As You Like It*; Viola in *Twelfth Night*.
49. **relish**: great enjoyment.
50. **exhibitions**: performances.
51. **a chasm**: a gap.

52. **accommodation**: convenience.
53. **recognized**: acknowledged.
54. **phantom**: not real, something that exists in one's imagination.
55. **excess**: superfluity.
56. **superflux**: a greater amount than is needed.
57. **natural dilations**: the natural ability to cope with any circumstance.
58. **Competence**: Sufficiency, enough to live on with comfort.
59. **fathom line**: a line for measuring the depth of water or something else (fathom: a measure of six feet).
60. **descent**: depth.
61. **Croesus**: King of Lydia (560 B. C. —546 B. C.), a very rich king.
62. **R—**: Nathan Meyer Rothschild (1777—1836) founded the English branch of the great European banking house.
63. **bedtester**: a canopy over the bed.
64. **Madonnaish**: like the Virgin Mary.
65. **chit**: a small young woman.

Thomas de Quincey (1785—1859)

The romantic elements in De Quincey's essays are more striking than those in Charles Lamb's. The former was more imaginative, or more subjective, and his essays are more rambling than those of Lamb. Lamb's essays are characterized by love and a profound nostalgia for the past and the dream world, whereas De Quincey's essays are marked by an exploration of the subconscious.

De Quincey had received good education. He studied in Oxford, where he began to take opium because he was suffering from a sharp pain in the head. Then he became a lifelong opium addict. For many years he lived in Grasmere in the company of Wordsworth and Coleridge. He tried to decrease the use of opium, and it was the experiences he had during this decreasing the dosage that he wrote a series of essays which were first published in *London Magazine* and later collected in a collection *The Confessions of an English Opium-Eater*, which was published in 1821 and which made him famous. In it he described the pains and agonies he had, as well as the terrible reveries and day dreams.

In addition, De Quincey was very much interested in literary criticism, which was flourishing as a literary genre. Among the best of his critical essays is "On the Knocking at the Gate in Macbeth" (1823). It had much to do with the rise of aestheticism in the beginning of the 19th century and with the German idealistic philosophy, which emphasized the importance of the imagination. His criticism by no means rested on social analysis. Instead, it relied on his personal impression. He stretched his imagination in his criticism. He studied the psychological reaction of the audience of a play. He was one of the founders of the psychological analysis, which has become very popular in the twentieth century, especially in the twenties. The knocking at the gate after King Duncan was killed is a highlight in the murder, and De Quincey interprets the significance of the scene in his own light. He states that (1) Shakespeare wants the audience to sympathize temporarily with Macbeth rather than with Duncan (the use of the word "sympathy" is different from the common meaning we use: it is, to share the passions, feelings, and motives of others); (2) the knocking heightens the dramatic effect and reflects back upon the murder a peculiar awfulness; (3) he is absolutely opposed to the use of understanding (reason, comprehension) in literary criticism. In short, De Quincey insists on the dependence of literary criticism on psychology.

On the Knocking at the Gate in Macbeth[1]

From my boyish days I had always felt a great perplexity on one point in *Macbeth*. It was this: The knocking at the gate which succeeds to the murder of Duncan produced to my feelings an effect for which I never could account. The effect was that it reflected back upon the murderer a peculiar awfulness[2] and a depth of solemnity[3]; yet, however obstinately I endeavored with my understanding[4] to comprehend this, for many years I never could see *why* it should produce such an effect.

Here I pause for one moment, to exhort the reader never to pay any attention to his understanding when it stands in opposition to any other faculty of his mind. The mere understanding, however useful and indispensable, is the meanest faculty in the human mind, and the most to be distrusted; and yet the great majority of people trust to nothing else—which may do for ordinary life, but not for philosophical purposes...

But to return from this digression. My understanding could furnish no reason why the knocking at the gate in *Macbeth* should produce any effect, direct or reflected. In fact, my understanding said positively that it could not produce and effect. But I knew better; I felt that it did; and I waited and clung to the problem until further knowledge should enable me to solve it. At length, in 1812, Mr. Williams made his debut[5] on the stage of Ratcliffe Highway[6], and executed those unparalleled murders which have procured for him such a brilliant and undying reputation. On which murders, by the way, I must observe[7] that in one respect they have had an ill effect, by making the connoisseur in murder[8] very fastidious[9] in his taste, and dissatisfied by anything that has been since done in that line[10]. All other murders look pale by the deep crimson of his; and, as an amateur once said to me in a querulous tone, "There has been absolutely nothing *doing* since his time, or nothing that's worth speaking of." But this is wrong; for it is unreasonable to expect all men to be great artists, and born with the genius of Mr. Williams. Now, it will be remembered that in the first of these murders (that of the Marrs) the same incident (of a knocking at the door[11] soon after the work of extermination was complete) did actually occur which the genius of Shakespeare has invented; and all good judges, and the most eminent dilettanti[12], acknowledged the felicity[13] of Shakespeare's suggestion as soon as it was actually realized. Here, then, was a fresh proof that I was right in relying on my own feeling, in opposition to my understanding; and I again set myself to study the problem. At length I solved it to my own satisfaction; and my solution is this: Murder, in ordinary cases, where the sympathy[14] is wholly directed to the case of the murdered person, is an incident of coarse and vulgar horror; and for this reason—that it flings the interest exclusively upon the natural but ignoble instinct by which we cleave to[15] life: an instinct which, as being indispensable to the primal law of self-preservation, is the same in kind[16] (though different in degree) amongst all living creatures. This instinct, therefore, because it annihilates all distinctions, and degrades[17] the greatest of men to the level of "the poor beetle that we tread on,"[18] exhibits human nature in its most abject and humiliating attitude. Such an attitude would little suit the purposes of the poet. What then must he do? He must throw the interest on the murderer. Our sympathy must be with *him* (of course I mean a sympathy of comprehension, a sympathy by which we enter into his feelings, and are made to understand them—not a sympathy of pity or approbation). In the murdered person, all strife of thought, all flux and reflux[19] of passion and of purpose, are crushed by one overwhelming panic; the fear of instant death smites him "with its petrific mace."[20] But in the murderer, such a murderer as a poet will condescend to, there must be raging some great storm of passion—jealousy, ambition, vengeance, hatred—which will create a hell within him; and into this hell we are to look.

In *Macbeth*, for the sake of gratifying his own enormous and teeming[21] faculty of creation, Shakespeare has introduced two murderers: and, as usual in his hands, they are remarkably discriminated[22]; but—though in Macbeth the strife of mind is greater than in his wife, the tiger spirit not so awake, and his feelings caught[23] chiefly by contagion from her—yet, as both were finally involved in the guilt of murder, the murderous mind of necessity[24] is finally to be presumed in both. This was to be expressed; and, on its own account, as well as to make it a more proportionable antagonist to the unoffending nature of their victim, "the gracious Duncan",[25] and adequately to expound "the deep damnation of his taking off",[26] this was to be expressed with peculiar energy. We were to be made to feel that the human nature—i. e. , the divine nature of love and mercy, spread through the hearts of all creatures, and seldom utterly withdrawn from man—was gone, vanished, extinct, and that the fiendish nature had taken its place. And, as this effect is marvelously accomplished in the *dialogues* and *soliloquies* themselves, so it is finally consummated[27] by the expedient[28] under consideration; and it is to this that I now solicit the reader's attention. If the reader has ever witnessed a wife, daughter, or sister in a fainting fit, he may chance to have observed that the most affecting moment in such a spectacle is *that* in which a sigh and a stirring announce the recommencement of suspended life. Or, if the reader has ever been present in a vast metropolis on the day when some great national idol was carried in funeral pomp to his grave, and, chancing to walk near the course through which it passed, has felt powerfully, in the silence and desertion of the streets, and in the stagnation of ordinary business, the deep interest which at that moment was possessing the heart of man—if all at once he should hear the deathlike stillness broken up by the sound of wheels rattling away from the scene, and making known that the transitory vision was dissolved, he will be aware that at no moment was his sense of the complete suspension and pause in ordinary human concerns so full and affecting as at that moment when the suspension ceases, and the goings-on of human life are suddenly resumed. All action in any direction is best expounded, measured, and made apprehensible[29], by reaction. Now, apply this to the case in *Macbeth*. Here, as I have said, the retiring of the human heart and the entrance of the fiendish heart was to be expressed and made sensible. Another world has stepped in; and the murderers are taken out of the region of human things, human purposes, human desires. They are transfigured:[30] Lady Macbeth is "unsexed"[31]; Macbeth has forgot that he was born of woman; both are conformed to[32] the image of devils; and the world of devils is suddenly revealed. But how shall this be conveyed and made palpable[33]? In order that a new world may step in, this world must for a time disappear. The murderers and the murder must be insulated—cut off by an immeasurable gulf from the ordinary tide and succession of human affairs—locked up and sequestered in some deep recess; we must be made sensible that the world of ordinary life is suddenly arrested[34], laid asleep, tranced[35], racked into a dread armistice[36]; time must be annihilated, relation to things without[37] abolished; and all must pass self-withdrawn into a deep syncope[38] and suspension of earthly passion. Hence it is that, when the deed is done, when the work of darkness is perfect, then the world of darkness passes away like a pageantry[39] in the clouds: the knocking at the gate is heard, and it makes known audibly that the reaction has commenced; the human has made its reflux upon the fiendish; the pulses of life are beginning to beat again; and the reestablishment of the goings-on of the world in which we live first makes us profoundly sensible of the awful parenthesis[40] that had suspended them.

O mighty poet[41]! Thy works are not as those of other men, simply are merely great works of art, but are also like the phenomena of nature like the sun and the sea, the stars and the flowers, like frost and snow, rain and dew, hailstorm and thunder, which are to be studied with entire submission of our own faculties, and in the perfect faith that in there there can be no too much or too little, nothing useless or inert, but that the farther we press in our discoveries, the more we shall see proofs of design and self-supporting arrangement where the careless eye had see nothing but accident!

1. Together with *Hamlet*, *Othello*, and *King Lear*, *Macbeth* was regarded as one of the four best known Shakespearean tragedies. It was probably finished in 1606.

   The story took place in ancient times, Duncan, King of Scotland, was crushing the rebellious forces of the thane of Cawdor, one of his noblemen, with the help of his two generals, Macbeth and Banquo. Macbeth was victorious in battle and won the king's favour.

   When Macbeth was returning from the battlefield, he met three witches who were waiting for him. They welcomed him by giving three mysterious prophecies: "All hail, Macbeth! hail to thee, thane of Glamis!" "All hail, Macbeth! hail to thee, thane of Cawdor!" "All hail, Macbeth! that thou shalt be king hereafter!"

   As Macbeth was already the thane of Glamis, he was not surprised at the first prophecy, but he was shocked when he was hailed the thane of Cawdor and King of Scotland. The witches also told Banquo that he could beget kings. Then they vanished.

As Macbeth did not believe that he would be the thane of Cawdor, a messenger came to announce that the king had conferred that title upon him. For a moment Macbeth was overpowered by an evil imagination of the way he could fulfill the prophecy and become the king of Scotland, but he refused this idea and thought to himself, "If chance will have me king, why, chance may crown me."

When Macbeth reached the palace, the king treated him with great courtesy and announced he would pay a visit to Macbeth's castle, and again Macbeth was shaken by the temptation.

A messenger was sent by Macbeth to his wife, carrying a letter in which he told her about the witches' prophecies and about the king's coming visit. Lady Macbeth called on all the evil forces to help her to be cruel. When her husband came back, she began to hint at the king's death.

When the king arrived, the two of them falsely gave him a cheerful welcome. But Macbeth hesitated to take action. He would have a guilty conscience, for the king was his kinsman and his guest, and moreover, a good man. His wife saw his hesitation and told him that he was a coward and did not love her. She told him that she herself would take two sharpened daggers and kill the king, who was sleeping in the bedroom, if he did not have the courage to do it. Spurred on by his wife, Macbeth killed the king in the middle of the night. Then there was an intense silence in the castle, which, however, was broken by a knocking at the south gate of the castle(Ⅱ. ii-iii). It was two noblemen who came to visit the king. One of them went to see the king and found that he was dead.

2. **peculiar awfulness**: particular quality of inspiring reverential wonder or fear.
3. **solemnity**: the state of being serious, dignified, or awe-inspiring.
4. **understanding**: the power of comprehension, analyzing, distinguishing, and judging.
5. **debut**: a first appearance on the stage, in society, etc.
6. **Ratcliffe Highway**: John Williams, a sailor, had thrown London into a panic(the date was actually December, 1811) by murdering the Marr family and twelve days later, the Williamson family.
7. **observe**: make a remark.
8. **connoisseur in murder**: a well informed judge in the art of murdering.
9. **fastidious**: difficult to please.
10. **line**: profession.
11. **a knocking at the door**: made by a maidservant of the Marrs, returning from the purchase of oysters for supper.
12. **dilettanti** [ˌdɪlɪˈtæntɪ]: one who loves the fine arts but in a superficial way and without serious purpose. Notice De Quincey humourously treats the serious matter of murder as a work of fine art.
13. **felicity**: a happy faculty in art.
14. **sympathy**: power of entering into another's feelings or mind.

15. **cleave to**: stick or adhere to.
16. **kind**: fundamental qualities.
17. **degrades**: reduces to a lower rank or status.
18. **"the poor beetle that we tread on"**: from Shakespeare's *Measure for Measure* Ⅲ. i. 79.
19. **flux and reflux**: flowing and reflowing.
20. **"with its petrific mace"**: from Milton's *Paradise Lost* X. 294. "Petrific" means "turning into stone"; a "mace" is "a ceremonial staff as the symbol of a public official's authority".
21. **teeming**: prolific or fertile.
22. **discriminated**: distinguished.
23. **caught**: became infected with.
24. **of necessity**: unavoidably.
25. **"the gracious Duncan"**: from *Macbeth* Ⅲ. i. 66.
26. **"the deep damnation of his taking off"**: from *Macbeth* I. vii. 20. "Taking off" means "killing".
27. **consummated**: made complete.
28. **expedient**: a means of achieving something, here, the knocking.
29. **apprehensible**: understandable.
30. **transfigured**: made a great change in outward appearance or form.
31. **"unsexed"**: from *Macbeth* I. v. 42.
32. **are conformed to**: are identical to.
33. **palpable**: able to be felt.
34. **arrested**: stopped.
35. **tranced**: brought into a deep sleep-like state.
36. **armistice**: a temporary suspension of hostilities.
37. **without**: outside.
38. **syncope**: a faint.
39. **pageantry**: a public show consisting of a procession of people in costume.
40. **parenthesis**: interlude.
41. **mighty poet**: Here refers to Shakespeare.

Walter Scott (1771—1832)

Although most of the romantic writers made their fame by poetry, Scott made his fame by his novels, which are not only characterized by romantic elements, but also are noted for their realistic description of historical events.

Scott was born into a lawyer's family in Edinburgh, Scotland. His father was a lawyer, and for a period of time Scott practiced law in Edinburgh. But he soon gave up the legal profession and engaged himself in writing as a professional writer. In his early years he took great interest in collecting the ballads of the old times written by the Scottish bards who lived on the border of England and Scotland. The result was a collection of ballads published in 1802—1803, entitled *Minstrelsey of the Scottish Border*. It was followed by a number of other collections and narrative poems, such as *The Lay of the Last Minstrel* (1805), *Marmion* (1808), and *The Lady of the Lake* (1810). These poems won him great fame as well as money, with which he bought an old castle. But after Byron published his *Childe Harold's Pilgrimage* in 1812, Scott was aware that in poetry he was no match for the young poet. So he gave up writing poetry and turned to novels. He published his first *Waverley* novel in 1812. and in the remaining eighteen years of his life, he wrote more than twenty novels. In 1820 he was made a baronet. In 1826, the publishing house he had set up with his friend went bankrupt, and though he had kept his partnership a secret, he assumed full responsibility to pay the debt of £130000. He worked harder than ever and succeeded in paying a considerable amount of the debt. He would have accomplished the task if he had lived a few years longer. His health was ruined, and a stroke of paralysis hit him in 1830, from which he never recovered. He died in 1832.

Scott's contribution to English literature, and even to world literature, is his historical novels. The stories of his novels are about incidents of historical significance, usually about the turning point of a nation's history. They are unfolded on a vast scale and cover a wide range of actions. Like most romantic poets, Scott has a deep interest in the role the masses play in the crucial moment of their country and has a profound pride in the nation's past glory. The fate of individual heroes in his novels is closely linked with the historical events. It should also be noticed that Scott is the first novelist who makes the scene an important factor in the action.

Ivanhoe

Published in 1819, *Ivanhoe* is the first of Scott's historical novels that deals with a purely English subject. The novels concerns the rivalry between King Richard I (1157—1199) and his wicked brother John who has taken over his authority during his absence, and between Saxons and the ruling Norman aristocrats. Wilfred of Ivanhoe, son of Cedric, of Saxon noble blood, loves his father's ward, Lady Rowena, a descendant of King Alfred. But Cedric intends to marry his ward to Athelstane of Coningsburgh, also of the Saxon blood royal, and banishes his son in anger. At the tournament at Ashby-de-la-Zouche, Ivanhoe, though victorious over his three opponents, is wounded seriously and is taken care of by a Jewish lady Rebecca. Richard, who has come back secretly from abroad, plays a very important role in the tournament to aid Ivanhoe, and later, with the help of Locksley (Robin Hood) and his men, to save the captured Saxons from the Norman nobles. The book ends with the union of Ivanhoe and Rowena and the compromise between the Saxons and the ruling Normans under King Richard I.

The the following excerpts is from chapter 20, in which Locksley and his followers, with the help of an unknown knight, are planning to attack Front-de-Boeuf's castle of Torquilstone, where are imprisoned Cedric and Rowena, with the wounded Ivanhoe, Athelstane, the Jew Isaac, and his beautiful and courageous daughter Rebecca.

Chapter Twentieth

When autumn nights were long and drear,
　And forest walks were dark and dim,
How sweetly on the pilgrim's ear
　Was wont[1] to steal the hermit's hymn!

Devotion borrows Music's tone,
　And Music took Devotion's wing;
And, like the bird that hails the sun,
They soar to heaven, and soaring sing.

THE HERMIT OF ST. CLEMENT'S WELL.

IT was after three hours' good walking that the servants of Cedric, with their mysterious guide, arrived at a small opening in the forest, in the centre of which grew an oaktree of enormous magnitude, throwing its twisted branches in every direction. Beneath this tree four or five yeomen[2] lay stretched on the ground, while another, as sentinel, walked to and fro in the moonlight shade.

Upon hearing the sound of feet approaching, the watch instantly gave the alarm, and the sleepers as suddenly started up and bent their bows. Six arrows placed on the string were pointed toward the quarter from which the travellers approached, when their guide, being recognized, was welcomed with every token of respect and attachment, and all signs and fears of a rough reception[3] at once subsided.

"Where is the Miller?" was his first question.

"On the road toward Rotherham."

"With how many?" demanded the leader, for such he seemed to be.

"With six men, and good hope of booty, if it please Saint Nicholas."

"Devoutly spoken," said Locksley; "and where is Allan-a-Dale?"

"Walked up toward the Watling Street, to watch for the Prior of Jorvaulx."

"That is well thought on also," replied the captain; "and where is the Friar?"

"In his cell."

"Thither will I go," said Locksley. "Disperse and seek your companions. Collect what force you can, for there's game afoot that must be hunted hard, and will turn to bay[4]. Meet me here by daybreak. And stay," he added "I have forgotten what is most necessary of the whole. Two of you take the road quickly toward Torquilstone, the Castle of Front-de-Bœuf[5]. A set of gallants[6], who have been masquerading in such guise as our own, are carrying a band of prisoners[7] thither. Watch them closely, for, even if they reach the castle before we collect our force, our honor is concerned to punish them, and we will find means to do so. Keep a close watch on them, therefore; and despatch one of your comrades, the lightest of foot, to bring the news of the yeomen thereabout."

They promised implicit obedience, and departed with alacrity on their different errands. In the meanwhile, their leader and his two companions, who now looked upon him with great respect, as well as some fear, pursued their way to the chapel of Copmanhurst.

When they had reached the little moonlight glade, having in front the reverend though ruinous chapel and the rude hermitage, so well suited to ascetic devotion, Wamba whispered to Gurth[8], "If this be the habitation of a thief, it makes good the old proverb, The nearer the church the farther from God. And, by my coxcomb[9]," he added, "I think it be even so. Hearken but to the black sanctus[10] which they are singing in the hermitage!"

In fact the anchorite and his guest were performing, at the full extent of their very powerful lungs, an old drinking song, of which this was the burden[11]:

Come, trowl[12] the brown bowl to me,
  Bully boy, bully boy,
Come, trowl the brown bowl to me:
  Ho! jolly Jenkin, I spy[13] a knave in drinking,
Come, trowl the brown bowl to me.

"Now, that is not ill sung," said Wamba, who had thrown in a few of his own flourishes to help out the chorus. "But who, in the saint's name, ever expected to have heard such a jolly chant come from out a hermit's cell at midnight?"

"Marry, that should I," said Gurth, "for the jolly Clerk[14] of Copmanhurst is a known man, and kills half the deer that are stolen in this walk. Men say that the keeper has complained to his official, and that he will be stripped of his cowl and cope[15] altogether if he keep not better order."

While they were thus speaking, Locksley's loud and repeated knocks had at length disturbed the anchorite and his guest. "By my beads," said the hermit, stopping short in a grand flourish, "here come more benighted guests. I would not for my cowl that they found us in this goodly exercise. All men have their enemies, good Sir Sluggard[16]; and there be those malignant enough to construe[17] the hospitable refreshment which I have been offering to you, a weary traveller, for the matter of three short hours, into sheer drunkenness and debauchery, vices alike alien to my profession and my disposition."

"Base calumniators!" replied the knight; "I would I had the chastising[18] of them. Nevertheless, Holy Clerk, it is true that all have their enemies; and there be those in this very land whom I would rather speak to through the bars of my helmet than barefaced."

"Get thine iron pot on thy head, then, friend Sluggard, as quickly as thy nature will permit," said the hermit, "while I remove these pewter flagons, whose late contents run strangely in mine own pate; and to drown the clatter—for, in faith, I feel somewhat unsteady—strike into the tune which thou hearest me sing; it is no matter for the words—I scarce know them myself."

So saying, he struck up a thundering *De profundis clamavi*[19], under cover of which he removed the apparatus of their banquet; while the knight, laughing heartily, and arming himself all the while, assisted his host with his voice from time to time as his mirth permitted.

"What devil's matins are you after at this hour?" said a voice from without.

"Heaven forgive you, Sir Traveller!" said the hermit, whose own noise, and perhaps his nocturnal potations[20], prevented from recognizing accents which were tolerably familiar to him. "Wend[21] on your way, in the name of God and Saint Dunstan, and disturb not the devotions of me and my holy brother."

"Mad priest," answered the voice from without, "open to Locksley!"

"All's safe—all's right," said the hermit to his companion.

"But who is he?" said the Black Knight; "it imports me much to know."

"Who is he?" answered the hermit; "I tell thee he is a friend."

"But what friend?" answered the knight; "for he may be friend to thee and none of mine."

"What friend?" replied the hermit; "that, now, is one of the questions that is more easily asked than answered. What friend? — why, he is, now that I bethink me a little, the very same honest keeper I told thee of a while since."

"Ay, as honest a keeper as thou art a pious hermit," replied the knight, "I doubt it not. But undo the door to him before he beat it from its hinges."

The dogs, in the meantime, which had made a dreadful baying at the commencement of the disturbance, seemed now to recognize the voice of him who stood without; for, totally changing their manner, they scratched and whined at the door, as if interceding for his admission. The hermit speedily unbolted his portal and admitted Locksley with his two companions.

"Why, hermit," was the yeoman's first question as soon as he beheld the knight, "what boon companion[22] hast thou here?"

"A brother of our order," replied the friar, shaking his head; "we have been at our orisons[23] all night."

"He is a monk of the church militant, I think," answered Locksley; "and there be more of them abroad. I tell thee, friar, thou must lay down the rosary and take up the quarter-staff; we shall need every one of our merry men, whether clerk or layman. But," he added, taking him a step aside, "art thou mad, to give admittance to a knight thou dost not know? Hast thou forgot our articles[24]?"

"Not know him!" replied the friar, boldly; "I know him as well as the beggar knows his dish."

"And what is his name, then?" demanded Locksley.

"His name," said the hermit, "his name is Sir Anthony of Scrablestone—as if I would drink with a man and did not know his name!"

"Thou hast been drinking more than enough, friar," said the woodsman, "and, I fear, prating more than enough too."

"Good yeoman," said the knight, coming forward, "be not wroth[25] with my merry host. He did but afford me the hospitality which I would have compelled from him if he had refused it."

"Thou compel!" said the friar; "wait but till I have changed this gray gown for a green cassock[26], and if I make not a quarterstaff ring twelve upon thy pate I am neither true clerk nor good woodsman."

While he spoke thus he stripped off his gown, and appeared in a close black buckram[27] doublet and drawers, over which he speedily did on a cassock of green, and hose of the same color. "I pray thee truss[28] my points," said he to Wamba, "and thou shalt have a cup of sack for thy labor."

"Gramercy for thy sack," said Wamba; "but think'st thou it is lawful for me to aid you to transmew[29] thyself from a holy hermit into a sinful forester?"

"Never fear," said the hermit; "I will but confess the sins of my green cloak to my gray friar's frock, and all shall be well again."

"Amen!" answered the Jester; "a broadcloth penitent should have a sackcloth confessor, and your frock may absolve[30] my motley doublet into the bargain."

So saying, he accommodated the friar with his assistance in tying the endless number of points, as the laces which attached the hose to the doublet were then termed.

While they were thus employed Locksley led the knight a little apart, and addressed him thus: "Deny it not, Sir Knight—you are he who decided the victory to the advantage of the English against the strangers on the second day of the tournament at Ashby."

"And what follows, if you guess truly, good yeoman?" replied the knight.

"I should in that case hold you," replied the yeoman, "a friend to the weaker party."

"Such is the duty of a true knight at least," replied the Black Champion; "and I would not willingly that there were reason to think otherwise of me."

"But for my purpose," said the yeoman, "thou shouldst be as well a good Englishman as a good knight; for that which I have to speak of concerns, indeed, the duty of every honest man, but is more especially that of a trueborn native of England."

"You can speak to no one," replied the knight, "to whom England, and the life of every Englishman, can be dearer than to me."

"I would willingly believe so," said the woodsman, "for never had this country such need to be supported by those who love her. Hear me, and I will tell thee of an enterprise in which, if thou be'st really that which thou seemest, thou mayest take an honorable part. A band of villains, in the disguise of better men than themselves, have made themselves master of the person of a noble Englishman, called Cedric the Saxon, together with his ward, and his friend, Athelstane of Coningsburgh, and have transported them to a castle in this forest, called Torquilstone. I ask of thee, as a good knight and a good Englishman, wilt thou aid in their rescue?"

"I am bound by my vow to do so," replied the knight; "but I would willingly know who you are, who request my assistance in their behalf?"

"I am," said the forester, "a nameless man; but I am the friend of my country, and of my country's friends. With this account of me you must for the present remain satisfied, the more especially since you yourself desire to continue unknown. Believe, however, that my word, when pledged, is as inviolate as if I wore golden spurs."

"I willingly believe it," said the knight; "I have been accustomed to study men's countenances, and I can read in thine honesty and resolution. I will, therefore, ask thee no farther questions, but aid thee in setting at freedom these oppressed captives; which done, I trust we shall part better acquainted, and well satisfied with each other."

"So," said Wamba to Gurth—for the friar being now fully equipped, the Jester, having approached to the other side of the hut, had heard the conclusion of the conversation—"So we have got a new ally? I trust the valor of the knight will be truer metal than the religion of the hermit or the honesty of the yeoman, for this Locksley looks like a born deer-stealer, and the priest like a lusty hypocrite."

"Hold thy peace, Wamba," said Gurth; "it may all be as thou dost guess; but were the horned devil to rise and proffer me his assistance to set at liberty Cedric and the Lady Rowena, I fear I should hardly have religion enough to refuse the foul fiend's offer, and bid him get behind me."

The friar was now completely accoutred as a yeoman, with sword and buckler, bow and quiver, and a strong partisan over his shoulder. He left his cell at the head of the party, and, having carefully locked the door, deposited the key under the threshold.

"Art thou in condition to do good service, friar?" said Locksley;

"or does the brown bowl still run in thy head?"

"Not more than a draught from Saint Dunstan's fountain will allay[31]," answered the priest; "something there is of a whizzing in my brain and instability in my legs, but you shall presently see both pass away."

So saying he stepped to the stone basin, in which the waters of the fountain as they fell formed bubbles which danced in the white moonlight, and took so long a draught as if he had meant to exhaust the spring.

"When didst thou drink as deep a draught of water before, Holy Clerk of Copmanhurst?" said the Black Knight.

"Never since my wine-butt leaked, and let out its liquor by an illegal vent," replied the friar, "and so left me nothing to drink but my patron's bounty here."

Then plunging his hands and head into the fountain, he washed from them all marks of the midnight revel.

Thus refreshed and sobered, the jolly priest twirled his heavy partisan round his head with three fingers, as if he had been balancing a reed, exclaiming at the same time, "Where be those false revishers who carry off wenches against their will? May the foul fiend fly off with me if I am not man enough for a dozen of them!"

"Swearest thou, Holy Clerk?" said the Black Knight.

"Clerk me no clerks," replied the transformed priest; "by Saint George and the Dragon, I am no longer a shaveling[32] than while my frock is on my back. When I am cased in my green cassock I will drink, swear, and woo a lass with any blithe forester in the West Riding."

"Come on, Jack Priest," said Locksley, "and be silent; thou art as noisy as a whole convent on a holy eve, when the Father Abbot has gone to bed. Come on you, too, my masters; tarry not to talk of it—I say come on, we must collect all our forces, and few enough we shall have, if we are to storm the castle of Reginald Front-de-Boeuf."

"What! is it Front-de-Boeuf," said the Black Knight, "who has stopped on the king's highway the king's liege subjects? Is he turned thief and oppressor?"

"Oppressor he ever was." said Locksley.

"And for thief," said the priest, "I doubt if ever he were even half so honest a man as many a thief of my acquaintance."

"Move on, priest, and be silent," said the yeoman; "it were better you led the way to the place of rendezvous than say what should be left unsaid, both in decency and prudence."

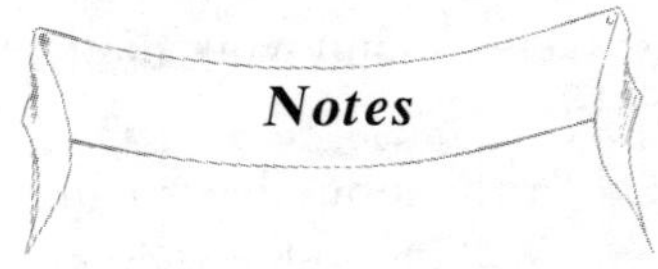

1. **wont**: accustomed.
2. **yeomen**: A yeoman is a freeholder under the rank of gentleman.
3. **rough reception**: not gentle or violent reception.
4. **bay**: a position of a person or animal forced to turn and face an enemy when no escape is possible.
5. **Front-de-Bœuf**: A Norman aristocrat with whom Ivanhoe fights at the tournament and in whose castle Cerdic and his followers are imprisoned.
6. **gallants**: a gallant is a man of fashion and pleasure. The gallants are, in fact, the Norman nobles in disguise.
7. **prisoners**: Here refers to Cedric and his followers, who are captured by the disguised Norman nobles in the previous chapter.
8. **Wamba... Gurth**: two of Cedric's servants who, fortunately, are not captured by the Normans.
9. **by my coxcomb**: an oath ("coxcomb" is a cap worn by a jester, like a cock's comb in shape and colour).
10. **black sanctus**: a burlesque hymn.
11. **burden**: refrain.
12. **trowl**: (*archaic*) troll, circulate.
13. **spy**: see.
14. **Clerk**: clergyman.
15. **cowl and cope**: hood and cloak.
16. **Sir Sluggard**: or called Black Knight, i. e., King Richard I in disguise.
17. **construe**: interpret, explain.
18. **chastising**: punishing severely by beating.
19. ***De profundis clamavi***: the name of a song.
20. **potations**: drinkings.
21. **Wend**: Go.
22. **boon companion**: pleasant, sociable companion.
23. **orisons**: (*archaic*) prayers.
24. **articles**: rules or conditions generally.
25. **wroth**: (*archaic*) wrathful, angry.
26. **cassock**: a long robe worn by a clergyman.
27. **buckram**: coarse cloth of hemp, stiffened with glue.
28. **truss**: tie.

29. **transmew**: transmute, transform.
30. **absolve**: *n.* absolution, a priest's formal declaration of the forgiveness of penitents' sins.
31. **allay**: abate.
32. **shaveling**: a cleric having his hair shaven off.

Chapter Nine

The Victorian Age (1832—1901)

1. Historical background

Though Queen Victoria lived from 1819 to 1901, she did not come to the throne until 1837. The English people were proud of the two queens in their history, i. e. , Queen Elizabeth (1533—1603) and Queen Victoria. There are similarities between the two queens. First, both queens were on the throne for a long period of time, Queen Elizabeth being on the throne for over forty years and Queen Victoria more than sixty years. Secondly, during their long reigns England developed rapidly both politically and economically. During the reign of Queen Elizabeth, capitalism first took its shape, and the small island country defeated the strong naval power Spain in 1588. During the long reign of Queen Victoria, England grew from an agricultural country into an industrialized one and became the workshop of the world as well as its financial and political center. Thirdly, during their reigns, literature flourished. In the age of Queen Elizabeth drama flourished and with it there was the greatest dramatist William Shakespeare whereas in the age of Queen Victoria, novel flourished and with it a galaxy of brilliant novelists appeared on the literary scene.

The Victorian age can be roughly divided into three periods: The early period 1832—1848, a time of social unrest; the middle period 1848—1870, a period of economic prosperity and religious controversy; the last period 1870—1901, a period of decay of Victorian values.

The first period: The passing of the first reform bill made it possible for the industrial capitalists to gain their power in Parliament. For up to 1832 the industrial capitalists, though they had been playing an increasingly important role in the economic life of the country, were barred from the political organ of the country, i. e. , Parliament. Prior to 1832, the system of voting and representation were controlled by the landed class and aristocrats, including the commercial capitalists. Out of a number of 650 seats in the House of Commons, no more than a third could be said to have been elected in any proper sense; the rest were appointed by local magnets or selected by petty groups of richest property holders. In some cases the positions were openly sold or offered for rent for a term of years. This situation remained unchanged although many new industrial towns emerged as the result of the development of industry. For example, many of the new cities, such as Birmingham and Manchester, with more than 100000 people each, were denied representation entirely. Yet there were represented a number of so called "rotten boroughs" where there were no people at all. For example, there was a village which had become a deserted hill (Old Sarum) and another village (Dunwich) which had slipped beneath the sea, but they were still sending delegates to the House of Commons.

The Reform Bill of 1832 extended the right to vote to all men owning property worth ten pounds or more. This bill extended the right to vote to the industrial capitalists and the lower middle class, but not the workers (they had to wait until 1867 when a second Reform Bill was passed). The second accomplishment of the Reform Bill was to eliminate the "rotten boroughs" and gave the vacant seats to the industrial cities. This Bill broke the monopoly in Parliament of the conservative landowners and ended the long reign of the Tory party which had been in power almost continuously from 1783 to 1830. The Whig party, which represented the interests of the industrial capitalists and businessmen, came into power.

With the introduction of the steam engine, it was possible for the capitalists to hire unskilled workers, such as women and children. It was not unusual that children of five years of age were dragging heavy loads of coal in the mine passages for 16 hours a day. Many skilled workers were unemployed, and what made the situations worse was the enforcement of the Corn Laws, which forbade importing any grain from foreign countries when the price of wheat dropped to a certain price; this measure kept wheat at a high price in the interests of the landed class. In 1845 serious crop failures in England and the potato blight in Ireland kept the price of bread still higher. Under the economic policy of Laissez faire (a policy based on the Utilitarian philosophy) which asserted that the function of the government was to preserve order and protect ownership of private property and not to interfere with the economic operation of the country, the capitalists did not feel they were responsible for the poverty of the working people. In order to demand their own rights, the working people launched large-scale demonstrations. They put forward their political demands in the form of a Charter and organized meetings to collect signatures. In the thirties and forties the country was threatened by social unrest. The Chartist Movement reached its peak in 1838, 1842, and 1848.

The most influential philosophy of the period was no doubt the philosophy of Utilitarianism(功利主义), which was founded by Jeremy Bentham(1772—1832) and continued by John Stuart Mill (1806—1873). According to them the value of any institution, government, and church depends on the question of whether it is useful as it is judged by human reason—that is, whether it contributes or not to the greatest happiness of the greatest number. This philosophy evidently was in the interests of the industrial capitalists. For they invariably argued that they were exploiting the working people for the great happiness of the greatest number.

Opposed to the Utilitarian philosophy were thinkers and writers such as Thomas Carlyle(1795—1881), Charles Dickens(1812—1870), Charles Kingsley (1819—1875), Elizabeth Gaskell (1810—1865), Elizabeth Barrett Browning(1806—1861), and Benjamin Disraeli(1804—1881). Disraeli, though he was himself the Prime Minister, wrote a novel entitled *Sybil*(1845) with the subtitle *Two Nations*, in which he made a distinction between two nations in England—the England of the rich and the England of the poor.

The mid-Victorian period: The mid-Victorian period was heyday of the Victorian age. Although there was war against Russia in Crimea (1854—1856), the country enjoyed two decades of peace and prosperity. In 1846 the Corn Laws were repealed and the price of labour lowered. By 1848 England had produced one half of the world's pig iron. The tremendous changes that took place in England in the forties were described in the novels of Charles Dickens. In the thirties Mr Pickwick in *The Posthumous Papers of the Pickwick Club* (1836) travelled from town to town in stage coaches, whereas in the forties Mr Dombey in *Dombey and Son*(1848) chased after his wife and Mr Carter by train. The railway had replaced the stage coach. By the early seventies England had become the workshop of the world and the world's banker. The factory had become the focal point of the nation's life. It was a period of complacency, stability, and optimism.

In the fifties and sixties even the conditions of the working people were improved, which Engels noticed in his preface to *The Condition of the English Working Class* (1845). In 1851 a gigantic greenhouse of glass and iron was built in Hyde Park. It was called the Crystal Palace where the Great Exhibition was held. It was a display of the nation's advanced technology and industry, as well as its prosperity. But the prosperity was on the surface, while beneath there were anxieties and worries, for in 1857 and following years, the economy was hit by crises from time to time.

In this period, the novelists Dickens, Mrs Gaskell, and George Eliot (1819—1880) realistically exposed the darker side of the seemingly prosperous society. Among the critics was John Ruskin (1819—1900), who, condemning the ugly modern capitalist civilization, glorified the dignity of labour and clamoured for a society in which an individual worker could fully express himself. The debate between the supporters of Utilitarianism and their opponents went on. On the side of the opponents there were two groups. One group was represented by Carlyle who did not like the Christian religion and believed that some spiritual belief was necessary. The other group belonged to the Oxford Movement headed by Cardinal Newman(1801—1890), a clergyman in Oxford University who held the opinion that only a powerful church could withstand Utilitarianism. But after Charles Darwin(1809—1882) published his *The Origin of Species* (1859), science came to the forefront in the debate against the church. Thomas Henry Huxley (1825—1895) succeeded Darwin in his endeavour. The influence of Darwin was great, as his discovery conflicted with the *Bible* and was applied in social science. Some thinkers defended the capitalist system by stating that life in society was also dominated by the principle of survival of the fittest.

The last period: England continued to grow in strength in this period. By 1890 the British Empire had comprised more than a quarter of all the territory on the surface of the earth and was called "the empire on which the sun never sets". To many Victorians this was a period of serenity and security, the age of house parties and long weekends in the country.

However, under the fierce competitions of the newly risen rivals, economic crisis continued to hit the country. Germany grew rapidly after she defeated France in the Franco-Prussian War in 1871. The United States, Japan, and Russia were her rivals too. Writers such as Matthew Arnold(1822—1888), Samuel Butler (1835—1902), Thomas Hardy, and Bernard Shaw exposed the cant and hypocrisy of the Victorian complacency. In the eighties there appeared the school of art for art's sake, which was represented by Walter Pater(1839—1894) and Oscar Wilde (1854—1900). In the nineties, melancholy became the spirit of the time and the intellectuals were tainted by a feeling of fin-de-siecle.

2. The Victorian novelists

1832 witnessed the end of poetry boom. In that year Scott died, and as most of the romantic poets had died, the romantic movement came to an end as a movement, although romantic elements continued to be found in the works of the writers and poets of the Victorian age. For example, Lord Alfred Tennyson was a follower of Keats; Matthew Arnold, a follower of Wordsworth; Robert Browning and Algernon Charles Swinburne(1837—1909) were followers of Shelley. The poetry of the Romantic age had given ways to novels. Many factors explain the rise of novels as a dominant literary genre during the Victorian age.

First, the growth of urban population resulted in the appearance of a new reading public. For example, in 1770 Manchester had only a population of 10,000, and by 1841 it had increased to 350,000. When Queen Victoria first came to the throne, London had a population of 2 million and by the time of her death it had increased to 6.5 million. The Education Acts, which came into effect in 1870, made a certain measure of education compulsory. Thus there was a fairly large reading public in the Victorian age.

Second, with the development of the method of printing and paper making, the price of books dropped, and besides regular books, there were serial publications. In addition, many libraries were set up by philanthropists so that books were now available to readers who could not afford to buy books.

Third, writing had become a profession, which made it possible for the writers to make a living by writing. Charles Dickens became a very wealthy person in his later years.

Fourth, with the ascendancy of the industrial capitalists, the majority of whom lived an idle life on interests, there was a large idle class who needed recreation and entertainment. Novels met with their desires.

Fifth, the conditions of the time and the dire poverty on the one hand and the enormous wealth on the other hand needed a secular form to explore human relations rather than sermons given in the church. The novel provided a marvelous mechanism for all sorts of things—exploring the conditions of the poor and the manners of society, satirizing individuals or institutions, advocating social reforms, and providing diversion for people at all levels.

Finally, the feminist movement had much to do with the growth of the novel. The struggle for women suffrage continued through the Victorian age and it was not until 1918 that women won their rights to vote. This struggle for women's rights was a recurring theme in the novels of the 19th century, and there were a number of woman writers who dealt with the issues of women. G. K. Chesterton (1874—1936), a critic and novelist, said, "When we come to the novelists, the women have, on the whole, equality; and certainly, in some points, superiority... The novel of the 19th century was female... Victorian women had a sort of unrest in their souls."

Although there is great divergence in style and subject matter, Victorian novels are characterized by the common features below:

(1) The plot is unfolded against a social background which is broader than what it had been in previous novels. The plot draws materials from society and relates them in such a way that the Victorian novels reflect the complexity of human relations in a capitalist society and reveal the writers' attitudes towards the society.

(2) The cause-effect sequence is much more striking than in previous novels. Generally speaking, a motive or a set of circumstances gives rise to an event which produces an effect on a character, and through the mechanics of internal causation, it gives rise to another event which in turns becomes another cause. And all this is centered around the central character. This kind of development of plot is called "linear causation", which makes the Victorian novels better constructed than previous ones.

(3) Most of the Victorian novels were first published in serial

form, that is, by installment, before they were fully published in a single book. They first appeared in pamphlets, periodicals, or newspapers. This was true of Charles Dickens' works and William Thackeray's *Vanity Fair*. The serial form may be detrimental to the plot, as Henry James (1843—1916) characterized the works of Dickens as "large loose baggy monsters". However, this was not necessary so. The later novels of Dickens were well constructed. Like an actor or a public speaker, the Victorian writers had a sense, during the process of their writing, of how their readers would respond to their works. They had to meet the challenge that was put to the writers to hold the interest of the readers in every issue and had to provide them delight and entertainment.

(4) The Victorian novels were tainted by the spirit of Puritanism of the Victorian age. The Victorian capitalists were notorious for their hypocrisy. Though cruelly exploiting the working class and living luxuriously themselves with little care for the miseries of the poor, they preached that the key to success was that they were sober, earnest, hard working, and that they abstained from worldly pleasures. Their Puritan standard of sexual behaviour was very strict. Women should be kept innocent, i. e. , ignorant. Their Puritan code had much bearings on the literature. For whenever sexual matter was touched, Victorian writers would try every means to keep away from it. It was especially so since novels were commonly read in family gatherings and it was necessary not to include the novel what might cause embarrassment to the ladies.

(5) The Victorian novels were characterized by their moral purpose. Many writers wrote novels with a purpose to edify readers and to bring about reforms. Of course, this was no new thing in English literature. But the Victorian writers, living in an age when there were striking differences between the rich and the poor and when the evils of the capitalist society were so conspicuous, invariably criticized certain aspects of the society and advocated their remedy. Some Chinese scholars called them critical realistic novelists, an epithet or label too vague to be applied to such a variety of writers.

Charles Dickens (1812—1870)

Dickens was born at Portsmouth in 1812, His father was a clerk in a Navy Pay Office. His grandparents were servants in an aristocrat's house. John Dickens, his father, though a kind-hearted man, did not know how to take care of his financial situation and always ran into pecuniary troubles. He was put into the debtors' prison when Dickens was only eleven years old, and while the family was living in the prison, Dickens was living by himself and working in the underground cell of a shoe blacking factory. Although he was there only for half a year, this experience of his childhood left such a deep impression on his mind that it became a recurring subject in his novels. When he all kinds of people, and his experience there provided him with an inexhaustible source for his creative work. While working there, he spent his spare time in learning shorthand and later became a parliamentary reporter, noting down in shorthand the speeches made by the members of Parliament and hurriedly sending his notes to the printing house to be published. These years as a reporter further enriched his knowledge of various classes in society. In 1836 he published his first book *Sketches by Boz* (1836). In the same year *The Posthumous Papers of the Pickwick Club* (1836—1837) began to appear in a fortnightly magazine in installments, which rapidly brought him fame and wealth. This book was followed by *Oliver Twist* (1837—1838), *Nicholas Nickleby* (1838—1839), *The Old Curiosity Shop* (1840—1841), and *Martin Chuzzlewit* (1843—1844). In the years 1843—1845 appeared his Christmas stories, which include *A Christmas Carol*, *The Chimes*, and *The Cricket on the Hearth*. In these stories Dickens showed his profound sympathy for the poor and described how the rich were converted after undergoing severe tests. These stories are permeated with the spirit of brotherhood and are regarded as representatives of the spirit of Christmas.

After 1844, Dickens, being a wealthy man, spent most of his time on the Continent of Europe. The revolutionary fervor of the forties both in England and on the Continent inspired him to write novels of bitter social criticism, such as *Dombey and Son* (1848), *Bleak House* (1853), *Hard Times* (1854), *Little Dorrit* (1857), and *Our Mutual Friend* (1865). In 1858 Dickens began to give public readings which continued until his death.

Dickens' artistic technique can be summarized as below:

(1) Dickens has a tendency to depict the grotesque (very odd or unusual, fantastically ugly or absurd) characters or events. This is true in his characterization and in his description of scenes. Most of Dickens's characters have a peculiar habit, manner, behaviour, dress, and catch phrase of his or her own. Evidently in this respect, Dickens was under the influence of Ben Jonson's comedies of humours, in which each character has his or her own peculiar humour.

(2) Dickens loves to instill life into inanimate things and to compare animate beings to inanimate things. For example, in *Hard Times* he compares the up and down movement of engines in a factory to the head of an elephant in a state of melancholy madness, and the smoke in the air above to snakes trailing themselves for ever and ever. *In Martin Chuzzlewit* he compares the hypocritical Pecksniff to a direction post, which always points out the direction for other people to go but it never moves an inch towards the direction it is pointing.

(3) Dickens is noted for his description of pathetic scenes that aim to arouse people's sympathy. Pathos is a distinctive quality in Dickens' writings. Though we may feel it affected, the readers of Dickens' time had great love of pathetic scenes as they were fond of melodramas which were very popular in their time and which are a kind of naively sensational entertainment with the main character either excessively virtuous or excessively evil. Dickens knew what his readers liked, and he loved to avail himself of every opportunity to appeal to the emotions of his readers.

Dombey and Son

Dombey and Son, published in serial form in 1847—1848, is one of the representative works of Dickens' mature period. Dombey, the owner of a shipping house, is a rich, proud, and heartless man, whose sole concern in life is the perpetuation of his name in connection with his firm. When the story begins, he has just been presented with a son and heir, Paul, and his wife dies in childbirth. He neglects his daughter and lays all his hopes on Paul, who would carry on his business. But Paul dies in childhood because of poor health and the strict discipline in the boarding school. Dombey remarries, but his wife, a cold and disillusioned lady who cannot stand Dombey's arrogant treatment, runs away with the villainous manager of Dombey's company. Having lost both his pride and wealth, Dombey lives in desolate solitude and finally is taken care of by his forgiving daughter. In the following excerpt, Dickens successfully describes the scene of the birth of Paul and the death of his mother.

Chapter I

Dombey sat in the corner of the darkened room in the great arm-chair by the bedside, and Son lay tucked up warm in a little basket bedstead, carefully disposed on a low settee immediately in front of the fire and close to it, as if his constitution were analogous to that of a muffin[1], and it was essential to toast him brown while he was very new.

Dombey was about eight-and-forty years of age. Son about eight-and-forty minutes. Dombey was rather bald, rather red, and though a handsome well-made man, too stern and pompous in appearance, to be prepossessing[2]. Son was very bald, and very red, and though (of course) an undeniably fine infant, somewhat crushed and spotty in his general effect, as yet. On the brow of Dombey, Time and his brother Care[3] had set some marks, as on a tree that was to come down in good time—remorseless twins they are for striding through their human forests[4] notching as they go-while the countenance of Son was crossed and recrossed with a thousand little creases, which the same deceitful Time would take delight in smoothing out and wearing away with the flat part of his scythe, as a preparation of the surface for his deeper operations[5].

Dombey, exulting in the long-looked-for event[6], jingled and jingled the heavy gold watch-chain[7] that depended[8] from below his trim blue coat, whereof the buttons sparkled phosphorescently in the feeble rays of the distant fire. Son, with his little fists curled up and clenched, seemed, in his feeble way, to be squaring at[9] existence for having come upon him so unexpectedly.

"The house will once again, Mrs. Dombey," said Mr. Dombey, "be not only in name but in fact Dombey and Son; Dombey and Son!"

The words had such a softening influence, that he appended[10] a term of endearment to Mrs. Dombey's name (though not without some hesitation, as being a man but little used to that form of address): and said, "Mrs. Dombey, my—my dear."

A transient flush of faint surprise overspread the sick lady's face as she raised her eyes towards him.

"He will be christened Paul, my—Mrs. Dombey—of course."

She feebly echoed, "Of course," or rather expressed it by the motion of her lips, and closed her eyes again.

"His father's name. Mrs. Dombey, and his grandfather's! I wish his grandfather were alive this day!" And again he said, "Dombey and Son," in exactly the same tone as before.

Those three words conveyed the one idea of Mr. Dombey's life. The earth was made for Dombey and Son to trade in, and the sun and moon were made to give them light. Rivers and seas were formed to float their ships; rainbows gave them promise of fair weather; winds blew for or against their enterprises; stars and planets circled in their orbits, to preserve inviolate a system of which they were the centre. Common abbreviations took new meanings in his eyes, and had sole reference to them: A. D. had no concern with anno Domini, but stood for anno Dombei— and Son[11].

He had risen, as his father had before him, in the course of life and death, from Son to Dombey[12], and for nearly twenty years had been the sole representative of the firm. Of those years he had been married, ten-married, as some said, to a lady with no heart to give him, whose happiness was in the past, and who was content to bind her broken spirit to the dutiful and meek endurance of the present. Such idle talk[13] was little likely to reach the ears of Mr. Dombey, whom it nearly concerned; and probably no one in the world would have received it with such utter incredulity as he, if it had reached him. Dombey and Son had often dealt in[14] hides, but never in hearts. They left that fancy ware to boys and girls, and boarding-schools and books. Mr. Dombey would have reasoned: That a matrimonial alliance with himself *must*, in the nature of things, be gratifying and honourable to any woman of common sense. That the hope of giving birth to a new partner in such a house, could not fail to awaken a glorious and stirring ambition in the breast of the least ambitious of her sex. That Mrs. Dombey had entered on that social contract of matrimony: almost necessarily part of a genteel and wealthy station, even without reference to the perpetuation of family firms: with her eyes fully open to these advantages. That Mrs. Dombey had had daily practical knowledge of his position in society. That Mrs. Dombey had always sat at the head of his table, and done the honours of his house in a remarkably lady-like and becoming manner. That Mrs. Dombey must have been happy. That she couldn't help it.

Or, at all events, with one drawback. Yes. That he would have allowed. With only one; but that one certainly involving much. They had been married ten years, and until this present day on which Mr. Dombey sat jingling and jingling his heavy gold watch-chain in the great arm-chair by the side of the bed, had had no issue[15].

—To speak of; none worth mentioning. There had been a girl some six years before, and the child, who had stolen into the chamber unobserved, was now crouching timidly, in a corner whence she could see her mother's face. But what was a girl to Dombey and Son! In the capital of the House's name and dignity, such a child was merely a piece of base coin[16] that couldn't be invested—a bad Boy—nothing more.

Mr. Dombey's cup of satisfaction was so full at this moment, however, that he felt he could afford a drop or two of its contents, even to sprinkle on the dust in the by-path of his little daughter.

So he said, "Florence, you may go and look at your pretty brother, if you like, I dare say. Don't touch him!"

The child glanced keenly at the blue coat and stiff white cravat, which, with a pair of creaking boots and a very loud ticking watch, embodied her idea of a father; but her eyes returned to her mother's face immediately, and she neither moved nor answered.

Next moment, the lady had opened her eyes and seen the child, and the child had run towards her; and, standing on tiptoe, the better to hide her face in her embrace, had clung about her with a desperate affection very much at variance with[17] her years.

"Oh Lord bless me!" said Mr. Dombey, rising testily. "A very ill-advised and feverish proceeding this, I am sure. I had better ask Doctor Peps if he'll have the goodness to step upstairs again perhaps. I'll go down. I'll go down. I needn't beg you," he added, pausing for a moment at the settee before the fire, "to take particular care of this young gentleman, Mrs. —"

"Blockitt, Sir?" suggested the nurse, a simpering[18] piece of faded gentility[19], who did not presume to state her name as a fact, but merely offered it as a mild suggestion.

"Of this young gentleman, Mrs. Blockitt."

"No, Sir, indeed. I remember when Miss Florence was born—"

"Ay, ay, ay," said Mr. Dombey, bending over the basket bedstead, and slightly bending his brows at the same time. "Miss Florence was all very well, but this is another matter. This young gentleman has to accomplish a destiny. A destiny, little fellow!" As he thus apostrophised[20] the infant he raised one of his hands to his lips, and kissed it; then, seeming to fear that the action involved some compromise[21] of his dignity, went, awkwardly enough, away.

Doctor Parker Peps, one of the Court Physicians, and a man of immense reputation for assisting at the increase of great families, was walking up and down the drawing-room with his hands behind him, to the unspeakable admiration of the family Surgeon, who had regularly puffed the case for the last six weeks, among all his patients, friends, and acquaintances, as one to which he was in hourly expectation day and night of being summoned, in conjunction with Doctor Parker Peps.

"Well, Sir," said Doctor Parker Peps, in a round, deep, sonorous voice, muffled for the occasion, like the knocker[22]; "do you fine that your dear lady is at all roused by your visit?"

"Stimulated as it were?" said the family practitioner faintly; bowing at the same time to the Doctor, as much as to say, "Excuse my putting in a word, but this is a valuable connexion[23]."

Mr. Dombey was quite discomfited by the question. He had thought so little of the patient, that he was not in a condition to answer it. He said that it would be a satisfaction to him, if Doctor Parker Peps would walk upstairs again.

"Good! We must not disguise from you, Sir," said Doctor Parker Peps, "that there is a want of power in Her Grace the Duchess—I beg your pardon; I confound names; I should say, in your amiable lady. That there is a certain degree of languor, and a general absence of elasticity, which we would rather—not—"

"See," interposed the family practitioner with another inclination of the head.

"Quite so," said Doctor Parker Peps, "which we would rather not see. It would appear that the system of Lady Cankaby—excuse me! I should say of Mrs. Dombey: I confuse the names of cases—"

"So very numerous," murmured the family practitioner—"can't be expected I'm sure—quite wonderful if otherwise—Doctor Parker Peps's West—End practice"—

"Thank you," said the Doctor, "quite so, it would appear, I was observing, that the system of our patient has sustained a shock, from which it can only hope to rally by a great and strong —"

"And vigorous," murmured the family practitioner.

"Quite so," assented the Doctor—"and vigorous effort, Mr. Pilkins here, who from his position of medical adviser in this family—no one better qualified to fill that position, I am sure."

"Oh!" murmured the family practitioner. "Praise from Sir Hubert Stanley[24]!"

"You are good enough," returned Doctor Parker Peps, "to say so. Mr. Pilkins who, from his position, is best acquainted with the patient's constitution in its normal state(an acquaintance very valuable to us in forming our opinions on these occasions), is of opinion, with me, that Nature must be called upon to make a vigorous effort in this instance; and that if our interesting friend the Countess of Dombey—I beg your pardon; Mrs. Dombey—should not be—"

"Able," said the family practitioner.

"To make that effort successfully," said Doctor Parker Peps, "then a crisis might arise, which we should both sincerely deplore."

With that, they stood for a few seconds looking at the ground. Then, on the motion—made in dumb show—of Doctor Parker Peps, they went upstairs; the family practitioner opening the room door for that distinguished professional, and following him out, with most obsequious politeness.

To record of Mr. Dombey that he was not in his way affected by this intelligence, would be to do him an injustice. He was not a man of whom it could properly be said that he was ever startled or shocked; but he certainly had a sense within him, that if his wife should sicken and decay, he would be very sorry, and that he would find a something gone from among his plate and furniture, and other household possessions, which was well worth the having, and could not be lost without sincere regret. Though it would be a cool, business-like, gentlemanly, self-possessed regret, no doubt.

His meditations on the subject were soon interrupted, first by the rustling of garments on the staircase, and then by the sudden whisking into the room of a lady rather past the middle age than otherwise, but dressed in a very juvenile manner, particularly as to the tightness of her bodice, who running up to him with a kind of screw in her face and carriage[25], expressive of suppressed emotion, flung her arms round his neck, and said in a choking voice.

"My dear Paul! He's quite a Dombey!"

"Well, Well!" returned her brother—for Mr. Dombey was her brother—"I think he is like the family. Don't agitate yourself, Louisa."

"It's very foolish of me," said Louisa, sitting down, and taking out her pocker-handkerchief, "but he's—he's such a perfect Dombey! I never saw anything like it in my life!"

"But what is this about Fanny, herself?" said Mr. Dombey. "How is Fanny?"

"My dear Paul," returned Louisa, "it's nothing whatever. Take my word, it's nothing whatever. There is exhaustion, certainly, but nothing like what I underwent myself, either with George or Frederick. An effort is necessary. That's all. If dear Fanny were a Dombey! —But I dare say she'll make it; I have no doubt she'll make it. Knowing it to be required of her, as a duty, of course she'll make it. My dear Paul, it's very weak and silly of me, I know, to be so trembly and shaky from head to foot; but I am so very queer[26] that I must ask you for a glass of wine and a morsel of that cake. I thought I should have fallen out of the staircase window, as I came down from seeing dear Fanny, and that tiddy ickle sing[27]." These last words originated in a sudden vivid reminiscence of the baby.

They were succeeded by a gentle tap at the door.

"Mrs. Chick," said a very bland female voice outside, "how are you now, my dear friend?"

"My dear Paul," said Louisa in a low voice, as she rose from her seat, "it's Miss Tox. The kindest creature! I never could have got here without her! Miss Tox, my brother, Mr. Dombey. Paul, my dear, my very particular friend Miss Tox."

The lady thus specially presented, was a long lean figure, wearing such a faded air that she seemed not to have been made in what linendrapers call "fast colours" originally and to have, by little and little, washed out. But for this she might have been described as the very pink of general propitiation and politeness[28]. From a long habit of listening admirably to everything that was said in her presence, and looking at the speakers as if she were mentally engaged in taking off impressions of their images upon her soul, never to part with the same but with life, her head had quite settled on one side. Her hands had contracted a spasmodic habit of raising themselves of their own accord as in involuntary admiration. Her eyes were liable to a similar affection. She had the softest voice that ever was heard; and her nose, stupendously aquiline, had a little knob in the very centre or key-stone of the bridge, whence it tended downwards her face, as in an invincible determination never to turn up at anything.

Miss Tox's dress, though perfectly genteel and good, had a certain character of angularity and scantiness. She was accustomed to wear odd weedy little flowers in her bonnets and caps. Strange grasses were sometimes perceived in her hair; and it was observed by the curious, of all her collars, frills, tuckers, wristbands, and other gossamer articles—indeed of everything she wore which had two ends to it intended to unite—that the two ends were never on good terms[29], and wouldn't quite meet without a struggle. She had furry articles for winter wear, as tippets, boas, and muffs, which stood up on end in a rampant manner, and were not at all sleek. She was much given to the carrying about of small bags with snaps to them that went off like little pistols when they were shut up; and when full-dressed, she wore round her neck the barrenest of lockets[30], representing a fishy old eye, with no approach to speculation in it[31]. These and other appearances of a similar nature, had served to propagate the opinion, that Miss Tox was a lady of what is called a limited independence, which she turned to the best account. Possibly her mincing gait encouraged the belief, and suggested that her clipping a step of ordinary compass[32] into two or three, originated in her habit of making the most of everything.

"I am sure," said Miss Tox. with a prodigious curtsey, "that to have the honour of being presented to Mr. Dombey is a distinction which I have long sought, but very little expected at the present moment. My dear Mrs. Chick—may I say Louisa!"

Mrs. Chick took Miss Tox's hand in hers, rested the foot of her wine-glass upon it, repressed a tear, and said in a low voice "Bless you!"

"My dear Louisa then," said Miss Tox, "my sweet friend, how are you now?"

"Better," Mrs. Chick returned, "take some wine. You have been almost as anxious as I have been, and must want it, I am sure."

Mr. Dombey of course officiated.

"Miss Tox, Paul," pursued Mrs. Chick, still retaining her hand, "knowing how much I have been interested in the anticipation of the event of today, has been working at a little gift for Fanny, which I promised to present. It is only a pin-cushion for the toilette table, Paul, but I do say, and will say, and must say, that Miss Tox has very prettily adapted the sentiment to the occasion. I call 'Welcome little Dombey 'Poetry myself!"

"Is that the device?" inquired her brother.

"That is the device," returned Louisa.

"But do me the justice to remember, my dear Louisa," said Miss Tox in a tone of low and earnest entreaty, "that nothing but the—I have some difficulty in expressing myself—the dubiousness of the result would have induced me to take so great a liberty: 'Welcome, Master Dombey,' would have been much more congenial to my feelings, as I am sure you know. But the uncertainty attendant on angelic strangers will, I hope, excuse what must otherwise appear an unwarrantable familiarity." Miss Tox made a graceful bend as she spoke, in favour of

Mr. Dombey, which that gentleman graciously acknowledged. Even the sort of recognition of Donbey and Son conveyed in the foregoing conversation, was so palatable to him, that his sister, Mrs. Chick—though he affected to consider her a weak good-natured person—had perhaps more influence over him than anybody else.

"Well!" said Mrs. Chick, with a sweet smile, "after this, I forgive Fanny everything!"

It was a declaration in a Christian spirit, and Mrs. Chick felt that it did her good. Not that she had anything particular to forgive in her sister-in-law, nor indeed anything at all, except her having married her brother—in itself a species of audacity—and her having, in the course of events, given birth to a girl instead of a boy: which, as Mrs. Chick had frequently observed, was not quite what she had expected of her, and was not a pleasant return for all the attention and distinction she had met with.

Mr. Dombey being hastily summoned out of the room at this moment, the two ladies were left alone together. Miss Tox immediately became spasmodic.

"I know you would admire my brother, I told you so before-hand, my dear," said Louisa.

Miss Tox's hands and eyes expressed how much.

"And as to his property, my dear!"

"Ah!" said Miss Tox, with deep feeling.

"Im—mense!"

"But his deportment, my dear Louisa!" said Miss Tox. "His presence. His dignity! No portrait that I have ever seen of any one has been half so replete with those qualities. Something so stately, you know, so uncompromising, so very wide across the chest, so upright! A pecuniary[33] Duke of York[34], my love, and nothing short of it!" said Miss Tox. "That's what I should designate him."

"Why, my dear Paul!" exclaimed his sister, as he returned, "you look quite pale! There's nothing the matter?"

"I am sorry to say, Louisa, that they tell me that Fanny—"

"Now, my dear Paul," returned his sister rising, "don't believe it. If you have any reliance on my experience, Paul, you may rest assured that there is nothing wanting but an effort on Fanny's part. And that effort," she continued, taking off—her bonnet, and adjusting her cap and gloves, in a business-like manner, "she must be encouraged, and really, if necessary, urged to make. Now, my dear Paul, come upstairs with me."

Mr. Dombey, who, besides being generally influenced by his sister for the reason already mentioned, had really faith in her as an experienced and bustling matron, acquiesced: and followed her, at once, to the sick chamber.

The lady lay upon her bed as he had left her, clasping her little daughter to her breast. The child clung close about her, with the same intensity as before, and never raised her head, or moved her soft cheek from her mother's face, or looked on those who stood around, or spoke, or moved, or shed a tear.

"Restless without the little girl," the Doctor whispered Mr. Dombey. "we found it best to have her in again."

There was such a solemn stillness round the bed; and the two medical attendants seemed to look on the impassive form with so much compassion and so little hope, that Mrs. Chick was for the moment diverted from her purpose. But presently summoning courage, and what she called presence of mind, she sat down by the bedside, and said in the low precise tone of one who endeavours to awaken a sleeper:

"Fanny! Fanny!"

There was no sound in answer but the loud ticking of Mr. Dombey's watch and Doctor Parker Peps's watch, which seemed in the silence to be running a race.

"Fanny, my dear," said Mrs. Chick, with assumed lightness, "here's Mr. Dombey come to see you. Won't you speak to him? They want to lay your little boy— the baby. Fanny, you know; you have hardly seen him yet, I think—in bed; but they can't till you rouse yourself a little. Don't you think it's time you roused yourself a little? Eh?"

She bent her ear to the bed, and listened: at the same time looking round at the bystanders, and holding up her finger.

"Eh?" she repeated, "what was it you said, Fanny? I didn't hear you."

No word or sound in answer. Mr. Dombey's watch and Dr. Parker Peps's watch seemed to be racing faster.

"Now, really, Fanny my dear," said the sister-in-law, altering her position, and speaking less confidently, and more earnestly, in spite of herself, "I shall have to be quite cross with you, if you don't rouse yourself. It's necessary for you to make an effort, and perhaps a very great and painful effort which you are not disposed to make; but this is a world of effort you know, Fanny, and we must never yield, when so much depends upon us. Come! Try! I must really scold you if you don't!"

The race in the ensuing pause was fierce and furious. The watches seemed to jostle, and to trip each other up.

"Fanny!" said Louisa, glancing round, with a gathering alarm. "Only look at me. Only open your eyes to show me that you hear and understand me; will you? Good Heaven, gentlemen, what is to be done!"

The two medical attendants exchanged a look across the bed; and the Physician, stooping down, whispered in the child's ear. Not having understood the purport of his whisper, the little creature turned her perfectly colourless face, and deep dark eyes towards him; but without loosening her hold in the least.

The whisper was repeated.

"Mama!" said the child.

The little voice, familiar and dearly loved, awakened some show of consciousness, ever at that ebb. For a moment, the closed eyelids trembled, and the nostril quivered, and the faintest shadow of a smile was seen.

"Mama!" cried the child sobbing aloud. "Oh dear Mama! Oh dear Mama!"

The Doctor gently brushed the scattered ringlets of the child, aside from the face and mouth of the mother. Alas how calm they lay there; how little breath there was to stir them!

Thus, clinging fast to that slight spar[35] within her arms, the mother drifted out upon the dark and unknown sea that rolls round all the world.

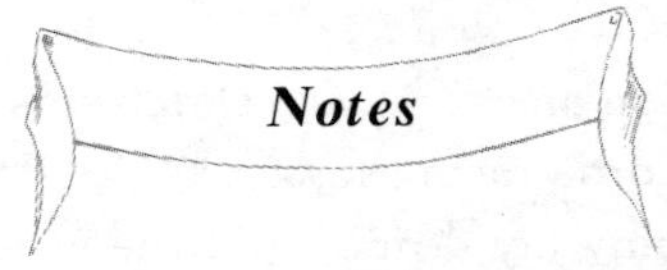

1. **as if his constitution were analogous to that of a muffin**: a very appropriate comparison, as the wrinkled face of a newborn baby is very much like a muffin (a soft, porous cake eaten hot with butter). Dombey handled the life of young Paul before he finally sent him to death.
2. **prepossessing**: attractive.
3. **Time and his brother Care**: Both Time and Care(worry) are personified. They are described as merciless twins ("remorseless twins") who leave marks (wrinkles) on the foreheads of people.
4. **human forests**: Human beings are compared to forests through which Time and Care stride.
5. **the same deceitful Time would take delight in smoothing out and wearing away with the flat part of his scythe, as a preparation of the surface for his deeper operations**: As the infant grows, the thousand little creases on his face will disappear, and the face will become smooth, but as time passes, the smoothness will be replaced by wrinkles (Time's deeper operation).
6. **long-looked-for event**: Dombey had been expecting a son for a long time.
7. **jingled and jingled the heavy gold watch-chain**: a typical example of Dickens' mannerism; it shows Dombey's richness and pride.
8. **depended**: hung down.
9. **squaring at**: taking an attitude of offence or defence, as a boxer.
10. **appended**: added or joined.
11. **A. D. had no concern with anno Domini, but stood for anno Dombei—and Son**: This is a very famous passage in *Dombey and Son*. In this passage Dickens by means of exaggeration vividly portrays the self-aggrandizement of the English commercial capitalists in the middle of the 19th century.
12. **from Son to Dombey**: Mr. Dombey was first the son in "Dombey and Son" and after the death of his father, he became the Dombey in "Dombey and Son".
13. **idle talk**: nonsense.
14. **dealt in**: bought and sold. Dombey's cold-heartedness is brought into relief as "often dealt in hides" is contrasted with "but never in hearts".
15. **issue**: heir, child.
16. **base coin**: worthless coin.
17. **at variance with**: not in agreement with.
18. **simpering**: smiling in a silly, unnatural way.
19. **faded gentility**: The nurse had ancestors of noble blood in the distant past.
20. **apostrophised**: made a sudden and exclamatory address.
21. **compromise**: partial concession.

22. **muffled for the occasion, like the knocker**: Whenever there was some one fallen ill in a big house, the knocker would be wrapped up to deaden the sound of knocking. Here the doctor lowered his voice, as there was a dying person in the house.
23. **a valuable connexion**: The social status of Doctor Parker Peps, the court physician, was much higher than that of the family practitioner, who thought it was a very valuable connection ("connexion") to be acquainted with the court physician.
24. **Praise from Sir Hubert Stanley!**: a phrase from *A Cure for Heartache*, a comedy by Thomas Morton(1764? —1838).
25. **carriage**: the manner of holding one's head, limbs, and body when standing or walking.
26. **queer**: slightly ill.
27. **that tiddy ickle sing**: that very little thing; here Louisa is speaking of the newborn baby and is imitating baby talk.
28. **the very pink of general propitiation and politeness**: Miss Tox is described as the perfect example of a person who tries to be pleasing and polite to everybody. The word "pink" also means "pale red" and carries on the metaphor of colours in the previous sentence.
29. **the two ends were never on good terms**: The two ends would never match with each other.
30. **lockets**: a small ornamental case holding a portrait or lock of hair, etc., worn on a chain around the neck.
31. **with no approach to speculation in it**: There was no way to guess what was kept in the locket.
32. **compass**: due limits.
33. **pecuniary**: of money.
34. **Duke of York**: the title given to Frederick Augustus(1763—1827), second son of George Ⅲ.
35. **spar**: a strong pole used on a ship to support sails or ropes.

William Makepeace Thackeray (1811—1863)

Thackeray and Dickens were contemporaries. They were both novelists, and there are some similarities between them. They were both humourists, and they criticized the Victorian society satirically. Scholars always compare the merits and demerits of the two writers. Some critics regard Thackeray inferior to Dickens, a fact even Thackeray owned himself.

Unlike Dickens, Thackeray was born in a well-to-do family. His father was an officer in Calcutta and died when Thackeray was five. Thackeray did not lack education. He studied at a public school in London and attended Cambridge University but left in 1830 without taking a degree. Then he became a comic illustrator and journalist. His first major novel, *Vanity Fair*, was published in 1848. Among his other works are *The School of Snobs* (1846—1847), *The Newcomes* (1853—1855), and *Henry Esmond* (1852).

Though there are similarities between Thackeray and Dickens, their writings are distinguishable by the differences below:

(1) The world described by Thackeray was a different one from that of Dickens. Thackeray mainly described the lives of aristocrats and rich businessmen, that is, people of the upper and middle classes, whereas Dickens' chief contribution was his description of the underdogs and the unprivileged, like the orphan in *Oliver Twist*, the criminals in *Great Expectations*, and the debtors in *Little Dorrit*.

(2) Dickens was a sentimentalist. He liked to avail himself of every opportunity to arouse the emotions of his readers. He was noted for his pathetic scenes. Thackeray was a cynic who saw no good in anything and doubted the goodness of human nature. Indeed, Thackeray also showed anger and indignation at hypocrisy, vanity, snobbery, and all pervading selfishness which lay behind the charming masks of the socially successful, but he was "as has often been remarked, a spectator of the battle of life, not a combatant therein," as pointed out by Baker, author of *The History of the English Novel* (1936,1937). On the whole he preserved detachment, and he always held himself under control. Even in pathetic scenes, he was seldom sentimental, being usually quiet and effective. In this, he is reflective of the 18th century classicists, aiming "to scan the human spectacle from the same serene stand

point." Unlike Dickens, who enthusiastically advocated bringing about reforms, Thackeray was not a crusader for good causes.

(3) Whereas Dickens was a romantist in many aspects by letting loose his imagination, Thackeray was against affectation, Byronic attitudes, and all romantic conventions that were still popular among the Victorian writers. He says of himself, "I have no brains above my eyes; and I describe what I see." His satire is never personal like Pope's or brutal like Swift's and is tempered by humour. Thackeray presented his characters as they are real in life. He recorded the failings of his characters, as well as their merits and capacities. His cynical attitude towards life explains the fact that most of his clever people are rogues and most of his virtuous people are fools. The novel *Vanity Fair* is subtitled "A Novel without a Hero". For example, Amelia Sedley is a fool; her husband has slept with Becky Sharp, but she is loyal to him and keeps the doting Dobbin waiting for her hand. Thackeray described his characters through constrast. His main characters always come in pairs as Amelia Sedley and Becky Sharp in *Vanity Fair*. Some critics thought that Thackeray's characterization is more subtile than Dickens'. The former's creations are "round, entire, and quite alive and convincing."

Vanity Fair

The title *Vanity Fair* is taken from John Bunyan's *The Pilgrim's Progress*, in which the protagonist Christian passes a Vanity Fair, where are sold all sorts of vanity. In the novel, the Victorian egoistic, hypocritical, and money-grabbing aristocratic and commercial society is a vanity fair, where everything is sold in terms of money. The central character, Becky Sharp, is an orphan of poor parentage. In order to climb up into the upper class, she tries to marry the fat brother of her schoolmate Amelia Sedley, a kind-hearted, weakly sentimental girl, daughter of a rich merchant. Frustrated in her plan to entrap her target, Becky Sharp becomes a governess in the house of the mean and avaricious Sir Pitt Crawley. She secretly marries the second son of Sir Crawley, Captain Rawdon, who is a gallant but ignorant and dissolute man. Her husband, however, is disinherited by his rich old aunt for marrying a poor penniless girl. Then Becky and her husband spend their time in Paris and London, living comfortably on nothing a year. After many vicissitudes, though her ambitions are defeated, she ends up as a "respected" member of society. Thackeray's attitude towards Becky Sharp is sardonic. Though Becky Sharp is unscrupulous, the other members of the upper class are not a whit better than she. The subtitle "A Novel without a Hero" is significant. It not only shows Thackeray's cynical view toward life but also declares that the epoch in which capitalists, or aristocrats, posed themselves as heroes is over.

Chapter XXXVI

How to Live Well on Nothing a Year

On nothing per annum[1], then, and during a course of some two of three years, of which we can afford to give but a very brief history, Crawley and his wife lived very happily and comfortably at Paris. It was in this period that he quitted the Guards[2], and sold out of the army.[3] When we find him again, his mustachios[4] and the title of Colonel on his card[5] are the only relics of his military profession.

It has been mentioned that Rebecca, soon after her arrival in Paris, took a very smart and leading position in the society of that capital, and was welcomed at some of the most distinguished houses of the restored French nobility[6]. The English men of fashion in Paris courted her, too, to the disgust of the ladies their wives, who could not bear the parvenue[7]. For some months the salons of the Faubourg St. Germain[8], in which her place was secured, and the splendours of the new Court, where she was received with much distinction, delighted, and perhaps a little intoxicated Mrs. Crawley, who may have been disposed during this period of elation to slight the people[9]—honest young military men mostly—who formed her husband's chief society.

But the Colonel yawned sadly among the duchesses and great ladies of the Court. The old women who played écarté[10] made such a noise about a five-franc piece[11], that it was not worth Colonel Crawley's while to sit down at a card-table. The wit of their conversation he could not appreciate, being ignorant of their language. And what good could his wife get, he urged, by making curtsies every night to a whole circle of Princesses? He left Rebecca presently to frequent these parties alone; resuming his own simple pursuits and amusements amongst the amiable friends of his own choice[12].

The truth is, when we say of a gentleman that he lives elegantly on nothing a year, we use the word "nothing" to signify something unknown; meaning, simply, that we don't know how the gentleman in question[13] defrays the expenses of his establishment[14]. Now, our friend the Colonel had a great aptitude for all games of chance[15], and exercising himself, as he continually did, with[16] the cards, the dicebox, or the cue[17], it is natural to suppose that he attained a much greater skill in the use of these articles than men can possess who only occasionally handle them. To use a cue at billiards well is like using a pencil, or a German flute, or a small-sword—you cannot master any one of these implements at first, and it is only by repeated study and perseverance, joined to a natural taste[18], that a man can excel in the handling of either. Now Crawley, from being only a brilliant amateur had grown to be a consummate[19] master of billiards. Like a great general, his genius used to rise with the danger, and when the luck had been unfavourable to him for a whole game, and the bets were consequently against him, he would, with consummate skill and boldness, make some prodigious hits[20] which would restore the battle, and come in a victor at the end, to the astonishment of everybody—of everybody, that is, who was a stranger to his play.[21] Those who were accustomed to see it were cautious how they staked their money against a man of such sudden resources[22], and brilliant and overpowering skill.

At games of cards he was equally skilful; for though he would constantly lose money at the commencement of an evening, playing so carelessly and making such blunders, that new-comers were often inclined to think meanly of his talent[23]; yet, when roused to action, and awakened to caution by repeated small losses, it was remarked that Crawley's play became quite different, and that he was pretty sure of beating his enemy thoroughly before the night was over. Indeed, very few men could say that they ever had the better of him[24].

His successes were so repeated that no wonder the envious and the vanquished spoke sometimes with bitterness regarding them. And as the French say of the Duke of Wellington[25], who never suffered a defeat, that only an astonishing series of lucky accidents enabled him to be an invariable[26] winner; yet even they allow that he cheated at Waterloo, and was enabled to win the last great trick[27]: so it was hinted at headquarters in England, that some foul play[28] must have taken place in order to account for the continuous successes of Colonel Crawley.

Though Frascati's and the Salon[29] were open at that time in Paris, the mania for play was so widely spread, that the public gambling-rooms did not suffice for the general ardour, and gambling went on in private houses as much as if there had been no public means for gratifying the passion.[30] At Crawley's charming little reunions[31] of an evening this fatal amusement commonly was practiced much to good-natured little Mrs. Crawley's annoyance.[32] She spoke about her husband's passion for dice with the deepest grief; she bewailed it to everybody who came to her house. She besought[33] the young fellows never, never to touch a box[34], and when young Green of the Rifles[35], lost a very considerable sum of money, Rebecca passed a whole night in tears as the servant told the unfortunate young gentleman, and actually went on her knees to her husband to beseech him to remit the debt[36] and burn the acknowledgment[37]. How could he? He had lost just as much himself to Blackstone of the Hussars[38], and Count Punter of the Hanoverian Cavalry[39]. Green might have any decent time[40]; but pay? —of course he must pay;—to talk of burning IOU's[41] was child's play[42].

Other officers, chiefly young—for the young fellows gathered round Mrs. Crawley—came from her parties with long faces, having dropped more or less money at her fatal card-tables. Her house began to have an unfortunate reputation. The old hands warned the less experienced of their danger. Colonel O'Dowd, of the—the regiment, one of those occupying in Paris, warned Lieutenant Spooney of that corps. Aloud and violent fracas[43] took place between the infantry Colonel and his lady, who were dining at the Cafe de Paris, and Colonel and Mrs. Crawley, who were also taking their meal there. The ladies engaged on both sides. Mrs. O'Dowd snapped her fingers in Mrs. Crawley's face[44] and called her husband "no better than a blackleg." Colonel Crawley challenged Colonel O'Dowd, C. B.[45] The Commander-in-chief hearing of the dispute sent for Colonel Crawley, who was getting ready the same pistols "which he shot Captain Marker," and had such a conversation with him that no duel took place. If Rebecca had not gone on her knees to General Tufto[46], Crawley would have been sent back to England; and he did not play, except with civilians, for some weeks after.

But in spite of Rawdon's undoubted skill and constant successes, it became evident to Rebecca, considering these things, that their position was but a precarious[47] one, and that even, although they paid scarcely anybody, their little capital would end one day by dwindling into zero. "Gambling," she would say, "dear, is good to help your income, but not as an income itself. Some day people may be tired of play, and then where are we?" Rawdon acquiesced in the justice of her opinion[48]; and in truth he had remarked that after a few nights of his little suppers, etc., gentlemen were tired of play with him, and, in spite of Rebecca's charms, did not present themselves very eagerly.

Easy and pleasant as their life at Paris was, it was after all only an idle dalliance[49] and amiable trifling; and Rebecca saw that she must push Rawdon's fortune in their own country. She must get him a place or appointment at home or in the colonies; and she determined to make a move upon England as soon as the way could be cleared for her. As a first step she had made Crawley sell out of the Guards, and go on half-pay. His function as aide-de-camp[50] to General Tufto had ceased previously. Rebecca laughed in all companies at that officer, at his toupee[51] (which he mounted on coming to Paris), at his waistband, at his false teeth, at his pretensions to be a lady-killer above all, and his absurd vanity in fancying every woman whom he came near was in love with him. It was Mrs. Brent, the beetle-browed[52] wife of Mr. Commissary Brent, to whom the general transferred his attentions now—his bouquets, his dinners at the restaurateur's, his opera-boxes, and his knickknacks[53]. Poor Mrs. Tufto was no more happy than before, and had still to pass long evenings alone with her daughters, knowing that her General was gone off scented and curled to stand behind Mrs. Brent's chair at the play. Becky had a dozen admirers in his place, to be sure; and could cut her rival to pieces with her wit.[54] But as we have said, she was growing tired of this idle social life; opera-boxes and restaurateur-dinners palled upon her; nose-gays could not be laid by as a provision for future years; and she could not live upon knick-knacks, laced handkerchiefs and kid gloves. She felt the frivolity of pleasure, and longed for more substantial benefits.

At this juncture nows arrived which was spread among the many creditors of the Colonel at Paris, and which caused them great satisfaction. Miss Crawley, the rich aunt from whom he expected his immense inheritance, was dying; the Colonel must haste to her bedside, Mrs. Crawley and her child would remain behind until he came to

reclaim them. He departed for Calais[55], and having reached that place in safety, it might have been supposed that he went to Dover[56]; but instead he took the diligence[57] to Dunkirk[58], and thence travelled to Brussels, for which place he had a former predilection. The fact is, he owed more money at London than at Paris; and he preferred the quiet little Belgian city to either of the more noisy capitals.

Her aunt was dead. Mrs. Crawley ordered the most intense mourning for herself and little Rawdon. The Colonel was busy arranging the affairs of the inheritance. They could take the premier[59] now, instead of the little entresol[60] of the hotel which they occupied. Mrs. Crawley and the landlord had a consultation about the new hangings, an amicable wrangle about the carpets, and a final adjustment of everything except the bill. She went off in one of his carriages; her French bonne[61] with her; the child by her side; the admirable landlord and landlady smiling farewell to her from the gate. General Tufto was furious when he heard she was gone, and Mrs. Brent furious with him for being furious; Lieutenant Spooney was cut to the heart; and the landlord got ready his best apartments previous to the return of the fascinating little woman and her husband. He serré'd[62] the trunks which she left in his charge with the greatest care. They were not, however, found to be particularly valuable when opened some time after.

But before she went to join her husband in the Belgic[63] capital, Mrs. Crawley made an expedition into England, leaving behind her little son upon the Continent, under the care of her French maid.

The parting between Rebecca and the little Rawdon did not cause either party much pain. She had not, to say truth, seen much of the young gentleman since his birth. After the amiable fashion of French mothers, she had placed him out at nurse in a village in the neighbourhood of Paris, where little Rawdon passed the first months of his life, not unhappily, with a numerous family of fosterbrothers in wooden shoes. His father would ride over many a time to see him here, and the elder Rawdon's paternal heart glowed to see him rosy and dirty, shouting lustily, and happy in the making of mudpies under the superintendence of the gardener's wife, his nurse.

Rebecca did not care much to go and see the son and heir. Once he spoiled a new dove-coloured pelisse[64] of hers. He preferred his nurse's caresses to his mamma's, and when finally he quitted that jolly nurse and almost parent, he cried loudly for hours. He was only consoled by his mother's promise that he should return to his nurse the next day; indeed the nurse herself, who probably would have been pained at the parting too, was told that the child would immediately be restored to her, and for some time awaited quite anxiously his return.

In fact, our friends may be said to have been among the first of that brood of hardy English adventurers who have subsequently invaded the Continent, and swindled in all the capitals of Europe. The respect, in those happy days of 1817—1818, was very great, for the wealth and honour of Britons. They had not then learned, as I am told, to haggle for bargains with the pertinacity which now distinguishes them. The great cities of Europe had not been as yet open to the enterprise of our rascals. And whereas there is now hardly a town of France of Italy in which you shall not see some noble countryman of our own, with that happy swagger and insolence of demeanour which we carry everywhere, swindling inn-landlords, passing fictitious cheques upon credulous bankers, robbing coachmakers of their carriages, goldsmiths of their trinkets, easy travellers of their money at cards—even public libraries of their books; thirty years ago you needed but to be a Milor Anglais[65] travelling in a private carriage, and credit was at your hand[66] wherever you chose to seek it, and gentlemen, instead of cheating, were cheated. It was not for some weeks after Crawleys' departure that the landlord of the hotel, which they occupied during their residence at Paris, found out the losses which he had sustained; not until Madame Marabou, the milliner, made repeated visits with her little bill for articles supplied to Madame Crawley: not until Monsieur Didelot from the Boule d'Or[67] in the Palais Royal[68] had asked half a dozen times whether cette charmante Miladi[69], who had bought watches and bracelets of him, was de retour[70]. It is a fact that even the poor gardener's wife, who had nursed

Madame's child, was never paid after the first six months for that supply of the milk of human kindness with which she had furnished the lusty and healthy little Rawdon. No, not even the nurse was paid—the Crawleys were in too great a hurry to remember their trifling debt to her. As for the landlord of the hotel, his curses against the English nation were violent for the rest of his natural life. He asked all travellers whether they knew a certain Colonel Lor Crawley—avec sa femme[71]—une petite dame, tres spirituelle[72]. "Ah, Monsieur!" he would add,—"ils m'ont affreusement volé."[73] It was melancholy to hear his accents as he spoke of that catastrophe.

Rebecca's object in her journey to London was to effect a kind of compromise with her husband's numerous creditors, and by offering them a dividend of ninepence or a shilling in the pound, to secure a return for him into his own country. It does not become us to trace the steps which she took in the conduct of this most difficult negotiation; but, having shown them to their satisfaction, that the sum which she was empowered to offer was all her husband's available capital, and having convinced them that Colonel Crawley would prefer a perpetual retirement on the Continent to a residence in this country with his debts unsettled; having proved to them that there was no possibility of money accruing to him from other quarters and no earthly chance of their getting a larger dividend than that which she was empowered to offer, she brought the Colonel's creditors unanimously to accept their proposals, and purchased with fifteen hundred pounds of ready money, more than ten times that amount of debts.

Mrs. Crawley employed no lawyers in the transaction. The matter was so simple, to have or to leave, as she justly observed, that she made the lawyers of the creditors themselves do the business. And Mr. Lewis representing Mr. Davids of Red Lion Square, and Mr. Moss acting for Mr. Manasseh of Cursitor Street (chief creditors of the Colonel's), complimented his lady upon the brilliant way in which she did business, and declared that there was no professional man who could beat her.

Rebecca received their congratulations with perfect modesty; ordered a bottle of sherry and a bread cake to the little dingy lodgings where she dwelt while conducting the business, to treat the enemy's lawyers; shook hands with them at parting, in excellent good-humour, and returned straightway to the Continent, to rejoin her husband and son, and acquaint the former with the glad news of his entire liberation. As for the latter, he had been considerably neglected during his mother's absence by Mademoiselle Genevieve, her French maid: for that young woman, contracting an attachment for a soldier in the garrison of Calais, forgot her charge in the society of this militaire, and little Rawdon very narrowly escaped drowning on Calais sands at this period, where the absent Genevieve had left and lost him.

And so, Colonel and Mrs. Crawley came to London; and it is at their house in Curzon Street, Mayfair, that they really showed the skill which must be possessed by those who would live on the resources above named.

Notes

1. **per annum**: per year.
2. **the Guards**: troops attached to the person of a ruler (卫队).
3. **sold out of the army**: left the army by selling the commission.
4. **mustachios**: a large moustache.
5. **card**: calling card.
6. **restored French nobility**: After the defeat of Napoleon in 1815, the French aristocrats were restored to power.
7. **parvenue** [ˈpɑːvənjuː]: (*French*) a person of obscure origin who has gained wealth or position; an upstart.
8. **Faubourg St. Germain**: a residential district for aristocrats.
9. **who may have been disposed during this period of elation to slight the people**: Notice the satirical tone in this sentence. "Disposed to" means "inclined to"; "slight" means "to treat someone as not worth one's attention".
10. **écarté**: a French card game.
11. **made such a noise about a five-franc piece**: complained about losing a five-franc piece.
12. **friends of his own choice**: friends of his own selection.
13. **the gentleman in question**: the gentleman as mentioned above.
14. **defrays the expenses of his establishment**: pays the expenses of his household.
15. **a great aptitude for all games of chance**: readiness to master all kinds of gambling games.
16. **exercising himself... with** : Notice the satirical tone in the sentence.
17. **cue**: a long rod for striking the ball in Billiards(台球,桌球).
18. **joined to a natural taste**: together with natural aptitudes. Notice the satirical tone in this sentence.

19. **consummate**: supremely skilled.
20. **prodigious hits**: marvelous hits at the ball.
21. **who was a stranger to his play**: who was unfamiliar with the way he played.
22. **resources**: quick wit.
23. **think meanly of his talent**: think he was not talented in the act of gambling.
24. **had the better of him**: defeated him.
25. **Duke of Wellington**: Duke of Wellington(1769—1852) was the commander-in-chief of the allied army and defeated Napoleon at the Battle of Waterloo in 1815.
26. **invariable**: unalterable.
27. **the last great trick**: Here refers to the Battle of Waterloo.
28. **foul play**: unfair means in any game or contest.
29. **Frascati's and the Salon**: two gambling houses in Paris.
30. **passion**: an enthusiastic interest in gambling.
31. **reunions**: social gatherings.
32. **much to good-natured little Mrs. Crawley's annoyance**: Notice the hypocritical tone of the sentence. It also suggests the trick Becky played to cheat people out of their money.
33. **besought**: prayed earnestly.
34. **box**: dice-box.
35. **young Green of the Rifles**: a certain young officer named Green in the infantry.
36. **to remit the debt**: to cancel the debt.
37. **acknowledgement**: a statement that recognizes money owed to the holder of the statement.
38. **Blackstone of Hussars**: an officer named Blackstone in the regiment of Black Hussars(Hussars: soldiers of a light cavalry regiment).
39. **Count Punter of the Hanoverian Cavalry**: Count Punter, an officer in the regiment of Hanoverian Cavalry.
40. **Green might have any decent time**: Here implies that Green was not strictly bound by the terms in the IOU as to the date of payment. The date due may be postponed.
41. **IOU**: initials for "I owe you", a receipt for a loan.
42. **child's play**: as foolish as child's play.
43. **fracas**: a French word for "a noisy quarrel".
44. **snapped her fingers in Mrs. Crawley's face**: a sign of contempt.
45. **C. B.** : abbreviations for "Companion of the Bath", an order of knighthood.
46. **General Tufto**: Captain Rawdon's superior who flirted with Becky.
47. **precarious**: not secure.
48. **Rawdon acquiesced in the justice of her opinion**: Rawdon agreed with his wife in her judgment.
49. **dalliance**: losing time by idleness or trifling.
50. **aide-de-camp**: (*French*) an officer who carries the order of a general and acts as secretary.

51. **toupee**: a wig with a top-knot.
52. **beetle-browed**: with overhanging or prominent brows.
53. **knickknacks**: small, trifling ornamental articles.
54. **cut her rival to pieces with her wit**: hurt her rival with witty retort.
55. **Calais**: a seaport in northern France.
56. **Dovel**: an English seaport, opposite to Calais across the English Channel. The Dover-Calais route to the Continent is very popular, as it is the shortest sea crossing.
57. **diligence**: a French or Continental stage-coach.
58. **Dunkirk**: a seaport town in northern France.
59. **the premier**: (*French*) the first floor in a hotel.
60. **entresol**: (*French*) a low-ceilinged story between two main stories.
61. **bonne**: (*French*) maidservant.
62. **serré'd**: (*French*) stowed away.
63. **Belgic**: Belgium.
64. **pelisse**: (*French*) a lady's long mantle.
65. **Milor Anglais**: (*French*) my English lord.
66. **credit was at your hand**: You can easily gain the trust of the merchants and buy things on credit.
67. **Boule d'Or**: the name of a jeweller's shop (Boule d'Or=gold ball).
68. **Palais Royal**: a large building with shops on the ground floor in Paris.
69. **cette charmante Miladi**: (*French*) that charming lady.
70. **de retour**: (*French*) to return.
71. **avec sa femme**: (*French*) with his wife.
72. **une petite dame, tres spirituelle**: (*French*) a very small lady, very lively.
73. **"ils m'ont affreusement volé"**: (*French*) "they have robbed me dreadfully."

The Brontë Sisters

When G. K. Chesterton said, "The novel of the 19th century was female", he must have been referring to the emergence of a number of brilliant woman writers whose works gave voice to the feelings and aspirations of the educated women of their age.

By "the Brontë sisters" we are referring to Charlotte Brontë (1816—1855), the authoress of *Jane Eyre* (1847), Emily Brontë (1818—1848), the authoress of *Wuthering Heights* (1847), and Anne Brontë (1820—1849), the authoress of *Agnes Grey* (1847).

How the Brontë sisters became writers is a mystery to western scholars. Except for short visits to Brussel by Charlotte and Emily and their brief stay at a boarding school for clergymen's daughters (the likeness of which was described by Charlotte in *Jane Eyre*) where two of their elder sisters contracted tuberculosis and died like Helen Burns in the novel, the sisters were practically living in isolation, in a distant village of Haworth, a lonely village set in the wild moors of Yorkshire. A moor is a wild open, often raised area, covered with heather, rough grass, or low bushes and is not farmed because of its bad soil.

Some critics said that the Brontës inherited their strong emotion from their parents. For their father was an Irishman who was born into a peasant family and by working hard managed to enter Cambridge and became a clergyman. Their mother was born in Cornwall, a place where most of the population are of Celtic origin. The Celtic blood explains their strong emotions and their audacity in the search for spiritual integrity.

Another factor was the moorland, which was not yet corrupted by the evils of society. Surrounded by moorland and innumerable steep hills, the place was cut off in the thirties from inroading industrialism. The only communication with the outside world was by walking or by cart. Lacking amusements, the children could play only in wild nature, roaming on the moors; the moors nurtured their imagination, for from their childhood they would imagine fairy kingdoms and invented stories about them.

The third factor that explains their writing career was the fact that they were greatly influenced by the Romantic poets. They read works by Wordsworth, Coleridge, Byron, and Shelley. Charlotte and her brother Patrick Branwell Brontë

(1317—1848) in their early twenties even wrote to Wordsworth and Southey, begging opinions on their writings.

The works of Charlotte and Emily Brontë are different from those of other Victorian writers in the aspects below:

The Brontë Sisters' living and writing place—Parsonage

(1) Their works are marked by strong romantic elements. While the majority of novelists were writing about moral problems and relations between man and man in consequence of the growth of industrial capitalism, the Brontë sisters turned to fiction to express their private passions and personal emotions. Take *Jane Eyre* for example. It is infused with romantic spirit: the emphasis on the sensitiveness of the mind and the intense sensibility to changing nature (as in Wordsworth's poetry); the longing for adventure and the insistence on liberty, independence, and the right of the individual soul and self fulfillment (as in Byron's and Shelley's poetry); and the love of the mysterious (as in Coleridge's poetry). Other incidents and characters also point to the influences of romantic poetry. For example, Rochester was an incarnation of the spirit of Byronic hero; the mad woman story and the mysterious call that brought Jane back to Thornfield are also romantic elements.

(2) The role of nature is especially important in the works of the Brontë sisters. In nature one finds comfort and peace. Worthworth's philosophy that nature never did betray the heart that loved her was taken over by the Brontë siters. The most evident proof of the influence of Wordsworth is Chapter 28 in *Jane Eyre* when Jane, after her wedding has been interrupted by a stranger, reaches a cross road near a village. Exhausted and penniless, she finds comfort in nature, when she spends the night

resting on the heath. She thinks of nature as the "universal mother". Also, the readers are familiar with the violent storm and the lightning that rent the great horse-chestnut tree the night Rochester told Jane that he loved her.

(3) Their works are also marked by a new conception of women as heroines of vital strength and passionate feelings. In Victorian times women did not have any status. The Brontë sisters were long before Nora Helmer in Ibsen's *The Doll House* (1879) and Bella Rokesmith in Dickens' *Our Mutual Friend* (1864—1865); the latter told her husband, "I want to be much worthier than the doll in the doll's house." Although women's colleges were established at Cambridge in 1869 and at Oxford in 1879, women could not take degrees at the universities until 1920—1921. Until the last decade of the 19th century, almost the only occupation open to women of good families but reduced circumstances was teaching as schoolmistress or more likely serving as governess in a private family. The Victorian moral code for women was that they should remain ignorant and uneducated. It was regarded as preposterous that women should aspire to be writers. So when the Brontës had their books published, they had to use pseudonyms, pretending they were male writers, Currer Bell for Charlotte, Ellis Bell for Emily, and Acton Bell for Ann.

In *Jane Eyre*, it is Jane's rebelliousness, her dislike for servility, and her insistence on equality that make the book unique. The whole book is about Jane's struggle for spiritual liberty. What Jane claims is the triumph of spiritual values over material ones. *Jane Eyre* is the first English novel, even the most powerful and popular novel, which represents the modern view of women's position in society.

Emily Brontë (1818—1848)

Wuthering Heights

The story of *Wuthering Heights* is concerned with two symmetrical families and an intruding stranger. The Earnshaws, rough in manner, include Mr. Earnshaw, his son Hindley, and his daughter Catherine. They live in their old house, Wuthering Heights, up in the folds of the moor. The Linton family, richer and more genteel, includes Mr. Linton, his wife, his son Edgar, and his daughter Isabella, and they live down in a neighbouring valley at Thrushcross Grange. One day Mr. Earnshaw brings home a gypsy looking little boy he has found in the streets of Liverpool. He calls the boy Heathcliff. The children grow up together. Catherine loves Heathcliff, while Hindley hates him, being jealous of his father's fondness for the stranger. After the death of Mr. Earnshaw, Hindley degrades Heathcliff in every way he can. Heathcliff grows brutal and sullen, and Catherine turns from him to the mild Edgar Linton. Heathcliff runs away and returns when Catherine has become Edgar's wife. Heathcliff is now rich and is determined to take revenge on Hindley and the Lintons. Between Heathcliff and Edgar, Catherine becomes distracted. She gives birth to Edgar's daughter and dies. Heathcliff turns Hindley into a drunkard and gambler and wins all his possessions so that Hindley's son Hareton becomes a pauper in his house. Moreover, he contrives to marry Edgar Linton's vain and silly sister Isabella, and marry Linton's daughter, the young Catherine, to his own peevish ailing son, Linton Heathcliff. But all his revenge is foiled by Catherine and Hareton, who love each other. Heathcliff dies a defeated man. After his death people see the ghosts of Heathcliff and Catherine Earnshaw roam on the moor.

Except for Satan in Milton's *Paradise Lost*, the tempestuous and revengeful Heathcliff has no equal in English literature. His intense love for Catherine, his relentless revenge on his enemy, and his frantic restlessness after Catherine's death mark him a unique figure. In Heathcliff's conflict with Hindley and the Lintons, Emily Brontë portrays the conflict between the privileged and the underdog, between the master and the hired hand.

The excerpt is Chapter Ⅸ of the book. It describes how Catherine tells Mrs. Ellen Dean, the housekeeper at Wuthering Heights, her decision to marry Edgar Linton, but in the depth of her heart she loves Heathcliff. On that stormy night

Heatheliff, having eavesdropped on the conversation, leaves Wuthering Heights.

Chapter IX[1]

He[2] entered, vociferating oaths dreadful to hear; and caught me[3] in the act of stowing his son away in the kitchen cupboard. Hareton[4] was impressed with a wholesome terror of encountering either his wild beast's fondness or his madman's rage; for in one he ran a chance of being squeezed and kissed to death, and in the other of being flung into the fire, or dashed against the wall; and the poor thing remained perfectly quiet wherever I chose to put him.

"There, I've found it out at last!" cried Hindley, pulling me back by the skin of the neck, like a dog. "By heaven and hell, you've sworn between you to murder that child! I know how it is, now, that he is always out of my way. But, with the help of Satan, I shall make you swallow the carving knife, Nelly! You needn't laugh; for I've just crammed Kenneth, head-downmost, in the Blackhorse marsh; and two is the same as one[5]—and I want to kill some of you, I shall have no rest till I do!"

"But I don't like the carving knife, Mr. Hindley," I answered; "it has been cutting red herrings. I'd rather be shot, if you please."

"You'd rather be damned!" he said, "and so you shall. No law in England can hinder a man from keeping his house decent, and mine's abominable! open your mouth."

He held the knife in his hand, and pushed its point between my teeth: but, for my part, I was never much afraid of his vagaries. I spat out, and affirmed it tasted detestably—I would not take it on any account.

"Oh!" said he, releasing me, "I see that hideous little villain is not Hareton: I beg your pardon, Nell. If it be,[6] he deserves flaying alive for not running to welcome me, and for screaming as if I were a goblin. Unnatural cub, come hither! I'll teach thee to impose on a good-hearted, deluded father.[7] Now, don't you think the lad would be handsomer cropped? It makes a dog fiercer, and I love something fierce—get me a scissors—something fierce and trim! Besides, it's infernal affectation—devilish conceit it is—to cherish our ears: we're asses enough without them[8]. Hush, child, hush! well, then, it is my darling! wisht[9], dry thy eyes—there's a joy; kiss me; what! it won't? kiss me, Hareton! Damn thee, kiss me! By God, as if I would rear such a monster! As sure as I'm living, I'll break the brat's neck."

Poor Hareton was squalling and kicking in his father's arms with all his might, and redoubled his yells when he carried him upstairs and lifted him over the banister. I cried out that he would frighten the child into fits, and ran to rescue him.

As I reached them, Hindley leant forward on the rails to listen to a noise below, almost forgetting what he had in his hands.

"Who is that?" he asked, hearing some one approaching the stair's foot.

I leant forward also, for the purpose of signing to Heathcliff, whose step I recognized, not to come further; and, at the instant when my eye quitted Hareton, he gave a sudden spring, delivered himself from the careless grasp that held him, and fell.

There was scarcely time to experience a thrill of horror before we saw that the little wretch was safe. Heathcliff arrived underneath just at the critical moment; by a natural impulse, he arrested his descent,[10] and setting him on his feet, looked up to discover the author of the accident.

A miser who has parted with a lucky lottery ticket for five shillings, and finds next day he has lost in the bargain five thousand pounds, could not show a blanker countenance than he did on beholding the figure of Mr. Earnshsw above. It expressed, plainer than words could do, the intensest anguish at having made himself the instrument of thwarting his own revenge. Had it been dark, I dare say, he would have tried to remedy the mistake by smashing Hareton's skull on the steps; but we witnessed his salvation; and I was presently below with my precious charge pressed to my heart.

Hindley descended more leisurely, sobered and abashed.

"It is your fault, Ellen," he said, "you should have kept him out of sight; you should have taken him from me! Is he injured anywhere?"

"Injured!" I cried angrily, "If he's not killed, he'll be an idiot! Oh! I wonder his mother does not rise from her grave to see how you use him. You're worse than a heathen—treating your own flesh and blood in that manner!"

He attempted to touch the child, who, on finding himself with me, sobbed off his terror directly. At the first finger his father laid on him, however, he shrieked again louder than before, and struggled as if he would go into convulsions.

"You shall not meddle with him!" I continued, "He hates you—they all hate you—that's the truth! A happy family you have; and a pretty state you're come to![11]"

"I shall come to a prettier, yet, Nelly!" laughed the misguided man, recovering his hardness, "At present, convey yourself and him away. And, hark you, Heathcliff! clear you too, quite from my reach and hearing. I wouldn't murder you to-night, unless, perhaps, I set the house on fire; but that's as my fancy goes—"

While saying this he took a pint bottle of brandy from the dresser, and poured some into a tumbler.

"Nay, don't!"I entreated, "Mr. Hindley, do take warning. Have mercy on this unfortunate boy, if you care nothing for yourself!"

"Any one will do better for him than I shall,"he answered.

"Have mercy on your own soul!" I said, endeavouring to snatch the glass from his hand.

"Not I! on the contrary, I shall have great pleasure in sending it to perdition, to punish its Maker,"[12] exclaimed the blasphemer. "Here's to its hearty damnation!"

He drank the spirits, and impatiently bade us go; terminating his command with a sequel of horrid imprecations, too bad to repeat or remember.

"It's a pity he cannot kill himself with drink," observed

Heathcliff, muttering an echo of curses back when the door was shut. "He's doing his very utmost; but his constitution defies him. Mr. Kenneth says he would wager his mare, that he'll outlive any man on this side Gimmerton[13], and go to the grave a hoary sinner; unless some happy chance out of the common course befall him."

I went into the kitchen and sat down to lull my little lamb to sleep. Heathcliff, as I thought, walked through to the barn. It turned out, afterwards, that he only got as far as the other side the settle, when he flung himself on a bench by the wall, removed from the fire, and remained silent.

I was rocking Hareton on my knee, and humming a song that began—

"It was far in the night, and the bairnies grat[14],
The mither beneath the mools heard that,"[15]

when Miss Cathy, who had listened to the hubbub from her room, put her head in, and whispered—

"Are you alone, Nelly?"

"Yes, Miss," I replied.

She entered and approached the hearth. I, supposing she was going to say something, looked up. The expression of her face seemed disturbed and anxious. Her lips were half asunder as if she meant to speak; and she drew a breath, but it escaped in a sigh, instead of a sentence.

I resumed my song, not having forgotten her recent behaviour.

"Where's Heathcliff?" she said, interrupting me.

"About his work in the stable," was my answer.

He did not contradict me; perhaps he had fallen into a doze.

There followed another long pause, during which I perceived a drop or two trickle from Catherine's cheek to the flags.

Is she sorry for her shameful conduct? I asked myself. That will be a novelty, but she may come to the point as she will—I shan't help her!

No, she felt small trouble regarding any subject, save her own concerns.

"Oh, dear!" she cried at last. "I'm very unhappy!"

"A pity," observed I. "You're hard to please—so many friends and so few cares, and can't make yourself content!"

"Nelly, will you keep a secret for me?" she pursued kneeling down by me, and lifting her winsome eyes to my face with that sort of look which turns off bad temper, even when one has all the right in the world to indulge it[16].

"Is it worth keeping?" I inquired, less sulkily.

"Yes, and it worries me, and I must let it out! I want to know what I should do. Today, Edgar Linton has asked me to marry him, and I've given him an answer. Now, before I tell you whether it was a consent, or denial, you tell me which it ought to have been."

"Really, Miss Catherine, how can I know?" I replied. "To be sure, considering the exhibition you performed in his presence this afternoon, I might say it would be wise to refuse him: since he asked you after that, he must either be hopelessly stupid or a venturesome fool."

"If you talk so, I won't tell you any more," she returned, peevishly, rising to her feet, "I accepted him, Nelly. Be quick, and say whether I was wrong!"

"You accepted him? then, what good is it discussing the matter? You have pledged your word, and cannot retract."

"But, say whether I should have done so—do!" she exclaimed in an irritated tone, chafing her hands together, and frowning.

"There are many things to be considered before that question can be answered properly," I said sententiously. "First and foremost, do you love Mr. Edgar?"

"Who can help it? Of course I do," she answered.

Then I put her through the following catechism: for a girl of twenty-two, it was not injudicious.

"Why do you love him, Miss Cathy?"

"Nonsense, I do—that's sufficient."

"By no means; you must say why."

"Well, because he is handsome, and pleasant to be with."

"Bad," was my commentary.

"And because he is young and cheerful."

"Bad, still."

"And because he loves me."

"Indifferent, coming there."[17]

"And he will be rich, and I shall like to be the greatest woman of the neighbourhood, and I shall be proud of having such a husband."

"Worst of all! And now, say how you love him."

"As everybody loves—You're silly, Nelly."

"Not at all—Answer."

"I love the ground under his feet, and the air over his head, and everything he touches, and every word he says—I love all his looks, and all his actions, and him entirely, and altogether. There now!"

"And why?"

"Nay—you are making a jest of it; it is exceedingly ill-na-tured! It's no jest to me!" said the young lady, scowling, and turning her face to the fire.

"I'm very far from jesting, Miss Catherine," I replied. "You love Mr. Edgar, because he is handsome, and young, and cheerful. and rich, and loves you. The last, however, goes for nothing. You would love him without that, probably; and with it, you wouldn't, unless he possessed the four former attractions."

"No, to be sure not: I should only pity him—hate him, perhaps, if he were ugly, and a clown."

"But there are several other handsome, rich young men in the world; handsomer, possibly, and richer than he is. What should hinder you from loving them?"

"If there be any, they are out of my way. I've seen none like Edgar."

"You may see some; and he won't always be handsome, and young, and may not always be rich."

"He is now; and I have only to do with the present. I wish you would speak rationally."

"Well, that settles it—if you have only to do with the present, marry Mr. Linton."

"I don't want your permission for that—I *shall* marry him; and yet you have not told me whether I'm right."

"Perfectly right; if people be right to marry only for the present. And now, let us hear what you are unhappy about. Your brother will be pleased; the old lady and gentleman will not object, I think; you will escape from a disorderly, comfortless home into a wealthy, respectable one; and you love Edgar, and Edgar loves you. All seems smooth and easy—where is the obstacle?"

"*Here*! and *here*!" replied Catherine, striking one hand on her forehead, and the other on her breast. "In whichever place the soul lives—in my soul, and in my heart, I'm convinced I'm wrong!"

"That's very strange! I cannot make it out."

"It's my secret; but if you will not mock at me. I'll explain it; I can't do it distinctly, but I'll give you a feeling of how I feel."

She seated herself by me again: her countenance grew sadder and graver, and her clasped hands trembled.

"Nelly, do you never dream queer dreams?" she said, suddenly, after some minutes' reflection.

"Yes, now and then," I answered.

"And so do I. I've dreamt in my life dreams that have stayed with me ever after, and changed my ideas; they've gone through and through me, like wine through water, and altered the colour of my mind. And this is one—I'm going to tell it —but take care not to smile at any part of it."

"Oh! don't, Miss Catherine!" I cried. "We're dismal enough without conjuring up ghosts and visions to perplex us. Come, come, be merry, and like yourself! Look at little Hareton—*he's* dreaming nothing dreary. How sweetly he smiles in his sleep!"

"Yes; and how sweetly his father curses in his solitude! You remember him, I dare say, when he[18] was just such another as that chubby thing[19]—nearly as young and innocent. However, Nelly, I shall oblige you to listen—it's not long; and I've no power to be merry to-night."

"I won't hear it, I won't hear it!" I repeated, hastily.

I was superstitious about dreams then, and am still; and Catherine had an unusual gloom in her aspect, that made me dread something from which I might shape a prophecy, and foresee a fearful catastrophe.

She was vexed, but she did not proceed. Apparently taking up another subject, she recommenced in a short time.

"If I were in heaven, Nelly, I should be extremely miserable."

"Because you are not fit to go there," I answered. "All sinners would be miserable in heaven."

"But it is not for that. I dreamt, once, that I was there."

"I tell you I won't harken to your dreams, Miss Catherine! I'll go to bed," I interrupted again.

She laughed, and held me down, for I made a motion to leave my chair.

"This is nothing." cried she; "I was only going to say that heaven did not seem to be my home; and I broke my heart with weeping to come back to earth; and the angels were so angry that they flung me out, into the middle of the heath on the top of Wuthering Heights; where I woke sobbing for joy. That will do to explain my secret, as well as the other. I've no more business to marry Edgar Linton than I have to be in heaven; and if the wicked man in there[20] had not brought Heathcliff so low, I shouldn't have thought of it. [21] It would degrade me to marry Heathcliff now; so he shall never know how I love him; and that, not because he's handsome, Nelly, but because he's more myself than I am. Whatever our souls are made of, his and mine are the same, and Linton's is as different as a moonbeam from lightning, or frost from fire."

Ere this speech ended, I became sensible of Heathcliff's presence. Having noticed a slight movement, I turned my head, and saw him rise from the bench, and steal out, noiselessly. He had listened till he heard Catherine say it would degrade her to marry him, and then he stayed to hear no farther.

My companion, sitting on the ground, was prevented by the back of the settle from remarking his presence or departure; but I started, and bade her hush!

"Why?" she asked, gazing nervously round.

"Joseph is here," I answered, catching, opportunely, the roll of his cartwheels up the road; "and Heathcliff will come in with him. I'm not sure whether he were not at the door this moment."

"Oh, he couldn't overhear me at the door!" said she. "Give me Hareton, while you get the supper, and when it is ready ask me to sup with you. I want to cheat my uncomfortable conscience, and be convinced that Heathcliff has no notion of these things. He has not, has he? He does not know what being in love is?"

"I see no reason that he should not know, as well as you," I returned; "and if *you* are his choice, he'll be the most unfortunate creature that ever was born! As soon as you become Mrs. Linton, he loses friend, and love, and all! Have you considered how you'll bear the separation, and how he'll bear to be quite deserted in the world? Because, Miss Catherine—"

"He quite deserted! we separated!" she exclaimed, with an accent of indignation. "Who is to separate us, pray? They'll meet the fate of

Milo![22] Not as long as I live, Ellen—for no mortal creature. Every Linton on the face of the earth might melt into nothing, before I could consent to forsake Heathcliff. Oh, that's not what I intend—that's not what I mean! I shouldn't be Mrs. Linton were such a price demanded! He'll be as much to me as he has been all his lifetime. Edgar must shake off his antipathy, and tolerate him, at least. He will when he learns my true feelings towards him. Nelly, I see now, you think me a selfish wretch, but, did it never strike you that if Heathcliff and I married, we should be beggars? whereas, if I marry Linton, I can aid Heathcliff to rise, and place him out of my brother's power."

"With you husband's money, Miss Catherine?" I asked, "You'll find him not so pliable as you calculate upon: and, though I'm hardly a judge, I think that's the worst motive you've given yet for being the wife of young Linton."

"It is not," retorted she, "it is the best! The others were the satisfaction of my whims; and for Edgar's sake, too, to satisfy him. This is for the sake of one who comprehends in his person my feelings to Edgar and myself. I cannot express it; but surely you and everybody have a notion that there is, or should be, an existence of yours beyond you. What were the use of my creation if I were entirely contained here? My great miseries in this world have been Heathcliff's miseries, and I watched and felt each from the beginning; my great thought in living is himself. If all else perished, and *he* remained, I should still continue to be; and, if all else remained, and he were annihilated, the Universe would turn to a mighty stranger. I should not seem a part of it. My love for Linton is like the foliage in the woods. Time will change it, I'm well aware, as winter changes the trees. My love for Heathcliff resembles the eternal rocks beneath—a source of little visible delight, but necessary. Nelly, I *am* Heathcliff—he's always, always in my mind—not as a pleasure, any more than I am always a pleasure to myself—but as my own being—so, don't talk of our separation again—it is impracticable; and—"

She paused, and hid her face in the folds of my gown; but I jerked it forcibly away. I was out of patience with her folly!

"If I can make any sense of your nonsense, Miss," I said, "it only goes to convince me that you are ignorant of the duties you undertake in marrying; or else that you are a wicked, unprincipled girl. But trouble me with no more secrets. I'll not promise to keep them."

"You'll keep that?" she asked, eagerly.

"No, I'll not promise," I repeated.

She was about to insist, when the entrance of Joseph finished our conversation; and Catherine removed her seat to a corner, and nursed Hareton, while I made the supper.

After it was cooked, my fellow servant and I began to quarrel who should carry some to Mr. Hindley; and we didn't settle it till all was nearly cold. Then we came to the agreement that we would let him ask, if he wanted any, for we feared particularly to go into his presence when he had been some time alone.

"Und hah isn't that nowt comed in frough th'field, be this time?[23] What is he abaht?[24] girt eedle seeght!"[25] demanded the old man, looking round for Heathcliff.

"I'll call him," I replied. "He's in the barn, I've no doubt."

I went and called, but got no answer. On returning, I whispered to Catherine that he had heard a good part of what she said, I was sure; and told how I saw him quit the kitchen just as she complained of her brother's conduct regarding him.

She jumped up in a fine fright, flung Hareton onto the settle, and ran to seek for her friend herself, not taking leisure to consider why she was so flurried, or how her talk would have affected him.

She was absent such a while that Joseph proposed we should wait no longer. He cunningly conjectured they were staying away in order to avoid hearing his protracted blessing. They were "ill enough for ony fahl manners[26]," he affirmed. And, on their behalf, he added that night a special prayer to the usual quarter of an hour's supplication before meat, and would have tacked another to the end of the grace[27], had not his young mistress broken in upon him with a hurried command that he must run down the road, and, wherever Heathcliff had rambled, find and make him re-enter directly!

"I want to speak to him, and I *must*, before I go upstairs," she said. "And the gate is open, he is somewhere out of hearing; for he would not reply, though I shouted at the top of the fold as loud as I could."

Joseph objected at first; she was too much in earnest, however, to suffer contradiction; and at last he placed his hat on his head, and walked grumbling forth.

Meantime, Catherine paced up and down the floor, exclaiming—

"I wonder where he is— I wonder where he *can* be! What did I say, Nelly? I've forgotten. Was he vexed at my bad humour this afternoon? Dear! tell me what I've said to grieve him. I do wish he'd come. I do wish he would!"

"What a noise for nothing!" I cried, though rather uneasy myself. "What a trifle scares you! It's surely no great cause of alarm that Heathcliff should take a moonlight saunter on the moors, or even lie too sulky to speak to us, in the hay-loft. I'll engage he's lurking there. See if I don't ferret him out!"

I departed to renew my search; its result was disappointment, and Joseph's quest ended in the same.

"Yon lad gets war un war[28]!" observed he on re-entering. "He's left th' yate[29] ut t'full swing, and Miss's pony has trodden dahn two rigs uh corn, un plottered through, raight o'er intuh t'meadow![30] Hahsomdiver[31], t'maister 'ull play t'divil to-morn, [32] and he'll do weel. He's patience itsseln wi' sich careless, offald craters[33]—patience itsseln, he is! Bud he'll nut be soa allus—yah's see, all on ye![34] Yah mumn't drive him aht uf his heead fur nowt!"[35]

"Have you found Heathcliff, you ass?" interrupted Catherine. "Have you been looking for him, as I ordered?"

"Aw sud more likker look for th' horse,"[36] he replied. "It'ud be tuh more sense. [37] Bud Aw can look for norther horse, nur man uf a neeght loike this —as black as t'chimbley![38] und Hathecliff's noan t' chap tuh coom ut *maw* whistle—happen he'll be less hard uh hearing wi'*ye*!"[39]

It was a very dark evening for summer: the clouds appeared inclined to thunder, and I said we had better all sit down; the approaching rain would be certain to bring him home without further trouble.

However, Catherine would not be persuaded into tranquillity. She kept wandering to and fro, from the gate to the door, in a state of agitation which permitted no repose; and at length took up a permanent situation on one side of the wall, near the road, where, heedless of my expostulations, and the growling thunder, and the great drops that began to plash around her, she remained, calling at intervals, and then listening, and then crying outright. She beat Hareton, or any child, at a good, passionate fit of crying.

About midnight, while we still sat up, the storm came rattling over the Heights in full fury. There was a violent wind, as well as thunder, and either one or the other split a tree off at the corner of the building; a huge bough fell across the roof, and knocked down a portion of the east chimney-stack, sending a clatter of stones and soot into the kitchen fire.

We thought a bolt had fallen in the middle of us, and Joseph swung onto his knees, beseeching the Lord to remember the Patriarchs Noah and Lot[40]; and, as in former times, spare the righteous, though he smote the ungodly. I felt some sentiment that it must be a judgment on us also. The Jonah[41], in my mind, was Mr. Earnshaw, and I shook the handle of his den that I might ascertain if he were yet living. He replied audibly enough, in a fashion which made my companion vociferate more clamorously than before that a wide distinction might be drawn between saints like himself, and sinners like his master. But the uproar passed away in twenty minutes, leaving us all unharmed, excepting Cathy, who got thoroughly drenched for her obstinacy in refusing to take shelter, and standing bonnetless and shawlless to catch as much water as she could with her hair and clothes.

She came in and lay down on the settle, all soaked as she was, turning her face to the back, and putting her hands before it.

"Well, Miss!" I exclaimed, touching her shoulder; "you are not bent on getting your death, are you? Do you know what o'clock it is? Half-past twelve. Come! come to bed; there's no use waiting longer on that foolish boy—he'll be gone to Gimmerton, and he'll stay there now. He guesses we shouldn't wake[42] for him till this late hour: at least, he guesses that only Mr. Hindley would be up; and he'd rather avoid having the door opened by the master."

"Nay, nay, he's noan at Gimmerton!" said Joseph. "Aw's niver wonder, bud he's at t' bottom uf a bog-hoile[43]. This visitation worn't for nowt, und Aw wod hev ye tuh look aht, Miss—yahmuh be t' next. Thank Hivin for all![44] All warks togither for gooid tuh them as is chozzen and piked aht froo' th' rubbidge![45] Yah knaw whet t' Scripture ses—"[46]

And he began quoting several texts; referring us to the chapters and verses where we might find them.

I, having vainly begged the willful girl to rise and remove her wet things, left him preaching and her shivering, and betook myself to bed with little Hareton, who slept as fast as if every one had been sleeping round him.

I heard Joseph read on a while afterwards; then I distinguished his slow step on the ladder, and then I dropt asleep.

Coming down somewhat later than usual, I saw, by the sunbeams piercing the chinks of the shutters, Miss Catherine still seated near the fire-place. The house door was ajar, too; light entered from its unclosed windows; Hindley had come out, and stood on the kitchen hearth, haggard and drowsy.

"What ails you, Cathy?" he was saying when I entered; "you look as dismal as a drowned whelp. Why are you so damp and pale, child?"

"I've been wet," she answered reluctantly, "and I'm cold, that's all."

"Oh, she is naughty!" I cried, perceiving the master to be tolerably sober. "She got steeped in the shower of yesterday evening, and there she has sat the night through, and I couldn't prevail on her to stir."

Mr. Earnshaw stared at us in surprise. "The night through," he repeated. "What kept her up, not fear of the thunder, surely? That was over, hours since."

Neither of us wished to mention Heathcliff's absence, as long as we could conceal it; so I replied, I didn't know how she took it into her head to sit up; and she said nothing.

The morning was fresh and cool; I threw back the lattice, and presently the room filled with sweet scents from the garden; but Catherine called peevishly to me—

"Ellen, shut the window. I'm starving!" And her teeth chattered as she shrunk closer to the almost extinguished embers.

"She's ill," said Hindley, taking her wrist, "I suppose that's the reason she would not go to bed. Damn it! I don't want to be troubled with more sickness here. What took you into the rain?"

"Running after t' lads, as usuald!" croaked Joseph, catching an opportunity, from our hesitation, to thrust in his evil tongue.

"If Aw wur yah, maister, Aw'd just slam t' boards i' their faces all on'em, gentle and simple! Never a day ut yah're off, but yon cat uh

Linton comes sneaking hither; and Miss Nelly shoo's a fine lass! shoo sits watching for ye i' t' kitchen; and as yah're in at one door, he's aht at t' other; und, then, wer grand lady goes a coorting uf hor side! It's bonny behaviour, lurking amang t' flields, after twelve ut' night, wi that fahl, flaysome divil uf a gipsy, Heathcliff! They think *Aw'm* blind; but Aw'm noan, nowt ut t'soart! Aw seed young Linton, boath coming and going, and Aw *seed yah*" (directing his discourse to me), "yah gooid fur nowt, slattenly witch! nip up und bolt intuh th' hahs, t' minute yah heard t'maister's horse fit clatter up t'road."[47]

"Silence, eavesdropper!" cried Catherine. "None of your insolence before me! Edgar Linton came yesterday, by chance, Hindley; and it was *I* who told him to be off, because I knew you would not like to have met him as you were."

"You lie, Cathy, no doubt," answered her brother, "and you are a confounded simpleton! But never mind Linton, at present. Tell me, were you not with Heathcliff last night? Speak the truth, now. You need not be afraid of harming him: though I hate him as much as ever, he did me a good turn a short time since, that will make my conscience tender of breaking his neck. To prevent it, I shall send him about his business this very morning; and after he's gone, I'd advise you all to look sharp, I shall only have the more humour[48] for you!"

"I never saw Heathcliff last night," answered Catherine, beginning to sob bitterly: "and if you do turn him out of doors, I'll go with him. But perhaps, you'll never have an opportunity—perhaps, he's gone." Here she burst into uncontrollable grief, and the remainder of her words were inarticulate.

Hindley lavished on her a torrent of scornful abuse, and bid her get to her room immediately, or she shouldn't cry for nothing! I obliged her to obey; and I shall never forget what a scene she acted, when we reached her chamber. It terrified me. I thought she was going mad, and I begged Joseph to run for the doctor.

It proved the commencement of delirium; Mr. Kenneth, as soon as he saw her, pronounced her dangerously ill; she had a fever.

He bled her, and he told me to let her live on whey and water-gruel, and take care she did not throw herself downstairs, or out of the window; and then he left, for he had enough to do in the parish where two or three miles was the ordinary distance between cottage and cottage.

Though I cannot say I made a gentle nurse, and Joseph and the master were no better; and though our patient was as wearisome and headstrong as a patient could be, she weathered it through.

Old Mrs. Linton paid us several visits, to be sure, and set things to rights, and scolded and ordered us all; and when Catherine was convalescent, she insisted on conveying her to Thrushcross Grange: for which deliverance we were very grateful. But the poor dame had reason to repent of her kindness; she and her husband both took the fever, and died within a few days of each other.

Our young lady returned to us, saucier and more passionate, and haughtier than ever. Heathcliff had never been heard of since the evening of the thunder-storm, and, one day, I had the misfortune, when she had provoked me exceedingly, to lay the blame of his disappearance on her (where indeed it belonged, as she well knew). From that period, for several months, she ceased to hold any communication with me, save in the relation of a mere servant. Joseph fell under a ban also; he *would* speak his mind, and lecture her all the same as if she were a little girl; and she esteemed herself a woman, and our mistress, and thought that her recent illness gave her a claim to be treated with consideration. Then the doctor had said that she would not bear crossing much, she ought to have her own way; and it was nothing less than murder, in her eyes, for any one to presume to stand up and contradict her.

From Mr. Earnshaw and his companions she kept aloof; and tutored by Kenneth, and serious threats of a fit that often attended her rages, her brother allowed her whatever she pleased to demand, and generally avoided aggravating her fiery temper. He was rather *too* indulgent in humouring her caprices; not from affection, but from pride, he wished earnestly to see her bring honour to the family by an alliance with the Lintons, and, as long as she let him alone, she might trample us like slaves for ought he cared!

Edgar Linton, as multitudes have been before and will be after him, was infatuated; and believed himself the happiest man alive on the day he led her to Gimmerton chapel, three years subsequent to his father's death.

Much against my inclination, I was persuaded to leave Wuthering

Heights and accompany her here. Little Hareton was nearly five years old, and I had just begun to teach him his letters. We made a sad parting, but Catherine's tears were more powerful than ours. When I refused to go, and when she found her entreaties did not move me, she went lamenting to her husband and brother. The former offered me munificent wages; the latter ordered me to pack up. He wanted no women in the house, he said, now that there was no mistress; and as to Hareton, the curate should take him in hand, by and by. And so I had but one choice left, to do as I was ordered. I told the master he got rid of all decent people only to run to ruin a little faster; I kissed Hareton good-bye; and, since then, he has been a stranger, and it's very queer to think it, but I've no doubt he has completely forgotten all about Ellen Dean and that he was ever more than all the world to her, and she to him!

At this point of the housekeeper's story, she chanced to glance towards the time-piece over the chimney; and was in amazement on seeing the minute-hand measure half-past one. She would not hear of staying a second longer. In truth, I[49] felt rather disposed to defer the sequel of her narrative myself: and now that she is vanished to her rest, and I have meditated for another hour or two, I shall summon courage to go, also, in spite of aching laziness of head and limbs.

1. The events of this chapter took place in the summer of 1780. It is part of the diary of Mr. Lockwood, a stranger who came to stay at Thrushcross Grange at the end of 1801 and the beginning of 1802. He paid visits to Wuthering Heights on several occasions. There he met Ellen Dean, who told him about the story of the two families two decades earlier.
2. **He**: Hindley Earnshaw.
3. **me**: Ellen Dean, as she was telling the story to Mr. Lockwood.
4. **Hareton**: Hindley's own son.
5. **two is the same as one**: Cramming (pressing down with force) two people is the same as cramming one person.
6. **If it be**: If it were him.
7. **I'll teach thee to impose on a good-hearted, deluded father**: I'll teach you a lesson as you are cheating your kind-hearted, deceived father.
8. **them**: ears.

9. **wisht**: be quiet.
10. **he arrested his descent**: he caught hold of Hareton who fell down.
11. **a pretty state you're come to**: "Pretty" here is used ironically.
12. **in sending it to perdition, to punish its Maker**: in sending my soul to Hell, to punish God.
13. **Gimmerton**: a town not far from Wuthering Heights.
14. **bairnies grat**: little ones wept.
15. **The mither beneath the mools heard that**: The mother in the grave heard that ("mools"= "earth of a grave").
16. **to indulge it**: to give way to bad temper.
17. **Indifferent, coming there**: Unimportant, as to that.
18. **he**: Hindley.
19. **chubby thing**: round and plump child, here referring to Hareton.
20. **the wicked man in there**: Here refers to Hindley.
21. **I shouldn't have thought of it**: I shouldn't have thought of marrying Edgar.
22. **Milo**: a Greek athlete who flourished in the later part of the 6th century B. C., born at Crotona, Italy. Caught by the tree he was trying to split, he was eaten up by wild beasts.
23. **Und hah isn't that nowt comed in frough th' field, be this time?**: And how isn't that nothing come in from the field by this time?
24. **abaht**: about.
25. **girt eedle seeght**: great idle sight, referring to Heathcliff.
26. **ill enough for ony fahl manners**: ill enough for only foul manners.
27. **grace**: prayer before a meal.
28. **war un war**: worse and worse.
29. **yate**: gate.
30. **Miss's pony has trodden dahn two rigs uh corn, un plottered through, raight o'er intuh t' meadow**: Miss's pony has trodden the two ridges of corn, and scrambled through right over into the meadow.
31. **Hahsomdiver**: Howsoever.
32. **t' maister 'ull play t' divil to-morn**: the master will play the devil tomorrow morning.
33. **He's patience itsseln wi' sich careless, offald craters**: He is patience itself with such careless, worthless creatures.
34. **Bud he'll nut be soa allus—yah's see, all on ye**: But he will not be so always—you will see, all of you.
35. **Yah mumn't drive him aht uf his heead fur nowt**: You must not drive him out of his head for nothing.
36. **Aw sud more likker look for th' horse**: I should more likely look for the horse.
37. **It 'ud be tuh more sense**: It would be the more sensible thing.
38. **Bud Aw can look for norther horse, nur man uf a neeght loike this—as black as t' chimbley**: But I can look for neither horse, nor man of a night like this—as black

as the chimney.

39. **und Hathecliff's noan t'chap tuh coom ut *maw* whistle—happen he'll be less hard uh hearing wi'*ye*:** and Heathcliff is none the chap to come at my whistle—happen he'll be less hard of hearing with you.

40. **Patriarchs Noah and Lot:** "Patriarch"(族长) means one of the early heads of families from Adam downwards to Abraham, Jacob, and his sons in the *Bible*. Both Noah and Lot were patriarchs.

41. **Jonah:** In "The Book of Jonah" in The Old Testament《圣经・旧约》"约拿书" Jonah acted against God's command and was thrown overboard by the sailors when the ship he was in was threatened by a hurricane. Jonah was punished by God. He was swallowed by a big fish and remained in its belly for three days and three nights.

42. **wake:** wait for.

43. **at t' bottom uf a bog-hoile:** at the bottom of a bog-hole.

44. **Thank Hivin for all:** Thank heaven for all.

45. **All warks togither for gooid tuh them as is chozzen and piked aht froo'th'rubbidge:** All works together for good to them as is chosen and picked out from the rubbish.

46. **Yah knaw whet t' Scripture ses:** You know what the Scripture says.

47. **If Aw wur yah, maister,... heard t'maister's horse fit clatter up t'road:** If I were you, master, I'd just slam the doors in their faces all of them, gentle or simple! Never a day if you are off, but you cat of Linton comes sneaking hither; and Miss Nelly she's a fine lass! she sits watching for you in the kitchen and as you are in at one door, she's out at the other; and then our grand lady goes a courting of her side! It's bonny behaviour, lurking among the fields after twelve at night with that foul, flaysome devil of a Gypsy, Heathcliff! They think I'm blind, but I'm none, not of the sort! I seed young Linton, both coming and going, and I seed you... you good for nothing, slovenly witch! nip up and bolt into the house, the minute you heard the master's horse's feet clatter up the road.

48. **humour:** temper.

49. **I:** Mr. Lockwood.

George Eliot (1819—1880)

Mary Ann Evans, more well-known by her pen name George Eliot, was an English novelist, journalist, translator and a leading intellectual of the Victorian era. Despite the strong social conventions of her times, she lived unmarried with fellow writer George Henry Lewes for over 20 years. She is the author of seven novels, including *Adam Bede* (1859), *The Mill on the Floss* (1860), *Silas Marner* (1861) and *Middlemarch* (1871—1872), most of them set in provincial England and known for their intense moral concern and psychological realism.

Adam Bede

Book Four

CHAPTER IV

It was beyond the middle of August—nearly three weeks after the birthday feast. The reaping of the wheat had begun in our north midland county of Loamshire[1], but the harvest was likely still to be retarded by the heavy rains, which were causing inundations and much damage throughout the country. From this last trouble the Broxton and Hayslope[2] farmers, on their pleasant uplands and in their brook-watered valleys, had not suffered, and as I cannot pretend that they were such exceptional farmers as to love the general good better than their own, you will infer that they were not in very low spirits about the rapid rise in the price of bread, so long as there was hope of gathering in their own corn undamaged; and occasional days of sunshine and drying winds flattered this hope.

The eighteenth of August was one of these days when the sunshine looked brighter in all eyes for the gloom that went before. Grand masses of cloud were hurried across the blue, and the great round hills behind the Chase[3] seemed alive with their flying shadows; the sun was hidden for a moment, and then shone out warm again like a recovered joy; the leaves, still green, were tossed off the hedgerow trees by the wind; around the farmhouses there was a sound of clapping doors; the apples fell in the orchards; and the stray horses on the green sides of the lanes and on the common had their manes blown about their faces. And yet the wind seemed only part of the general gladness because the sun was shining. A merry day for the children, who ran and shouted to see if they could top the wind with their voices; and the grown-up people too were in good spirits, inclined to believe in yet finer days, when the wind had fallen. If only the corn were not ripe enough to be blown out of the husk and scattered as untimely seed!

And yet a day on which a blighting sorrow may fall upon a man. For if it be true that Nature at certain moments seems charged with a presentiment of one individual lot must it not also be true that she seems unmindful uncon-scious of another? For there is no hour that has not its births of gladness and despair, no morning brightness that does not bring new sickness to desolation as well as new forces to genius and love. There are so many of us, and our lots are so different, what wonder that Nature's mood is often in harsh contrast with the great crisis of our lives? We are children of a large family, and must learn, as such children do, not to expect that our hurts will be made much of—to be content with little nurture and caressing, and help each other the more.

It was a busy day with Adam, who of late had done almost double work, for he was continuing to act as foreman for Jonathan Burge,[4] until some satisfactory person could be found to supply his place, and Jonathan was slow to find that person. But he had done the extra work cheerfully, for his hopes were buoyant again about Hetty. Every time she had seen him since the birthday, she had seemed to make an effort to behave all the more kindly to him, that she might make him understand she had forgiven his silence and coldness during the dance. He had never mentioned the locket to her again; too happy that she smiled at him—still happier because he observed in her a more subdued air, something that he interpreted as the growth of womanly tenderness and seriousness. "Ah!" he thought, again and again, "she's only seventeen; she'll be thoughtful enough after a while. And her aunt allays says how clever she is at the work. She'll make a wife as Mother'll have no occasion to grumble at, after all." To be sure, he had only seen her at home twice since the birthday; for one Sunday, when he was intending to go from church to the Hall Farm,[5] Hetty had joined the party of upper servants from the Chase and had gone home with them—almost as if she were inclined to encourage Mr. Craig.[6] "She's takin' too much likin' to them folks i' the house keeper's room," Mrs. Poyser[7] remarked. "For my part, I was never overfond o'gentlefolks's servants—they're mostly like the fine ladies' fat dogs, nayther good for barking nor butcher's meat, but on'y for show." And another evening she was gone to Treddleston[8] to buy some things; though, to his great surprise, as he was returning home, he saw her at a distance getting over a stile quite out of the Treddleston road. But, when he hastened to her, she was very kind, and asked him to go in again when he had taken her to the yard gate. She had gone a little farther into the fields after coming from Treddleston because she didn't want to go in, she said: it was so nice to be out of doors, and her aunt always made such a fuss about it if she wanted to go out. "Oh, do come in with me!" she said, as he was going to shake hands with her at the gate, and he could not resist that. So he went in, and Mrs. Poyser was contented with only a slight remark on Hetty's being later than was expected; while Hetty, who had looked out of spirits when he met her, smiled and talked and waited on them all with unusual promptitude.

That was the last time he had seen her; but he meant to make leisure for going to the Farm tomorrow. Today, he knew, was her day for going to the Chase to sew with the lady's maid, so he would get as much work done as possible this evening, that the next might be clear.

One piece of work that Adam was superintending was some slight repairs at the Chase Farm, which had been hitherto occupied by Satchell,[9] as bailiff, but which it was now rumoured that the old squire was going to let to a smart man in top-boots, who had been seen to ride over it one day. Nothing but the desire to get a tenant could account for the squire's undertaking repairs, though the Saturday-evening party at Mr. Casson's[10] agreed over their pipes that no man in his senses would take the Chase Farm unless there was a bit more ploughland laid to it. However that might be, the repairs were ordered to be executed with all dispatch, and Adam, acting for Mr. Burge, was carrying out the order with his usual energy. But today, having been occupied elsewhere, he had not been able to arrive at the Chase Farm till late in the afternoon, and he then discovered that some old roofing, which he had calculated on preserving, had given way. There was clearly no good to be done with this part of the building without pulling it all down, and Adam immediately saw in his mind a plan for building it up again, so as to make the most convenient of cow-sheds and calf-pens, with a hovel for implements; and all without any great expense for materials. So, when the workmen were gone, he sat down, took out his pocket-book, and busied himself with sketching a plan, and making a specification of the expenses that he might show it to Burge the next morning, and set him on persuading the squire to consent. To "make a good job" of anything, however small, was always a pleasure to Adam, and he sat on a block, with his book resting on a planing-table, whistling low every now and then and turning his head on one side with a just perceptible smile of gratification—of pride, too, for if Adam loved a bit of good work, he loved also to think, "I did it!" And I believe the only people who are free from that weakness are those who have no work to call their own. It was nearly seven before he had finished and put on his jacket again; and on giving a last look round, he observed that Seth, who had been working here today, had left his basket of tools behind him. "Why, th' lad's forgot his tools," thought Adam, "and he's got to work up at the shop tomorrow. There never was such a chap for wool-gathering; he'd leave his head behind him, if it was loose. However, it's lucky I've seen 'em; I'll carry 'em home."

The buildings of the Chase Farm lay at one extremity of the Chase, at about ten minutes' walking distance from the Abbey. Adam had come thither on his pony, intending to ride to the stables and put up his nag on his way home. At the stables he encountered Mr. Craig, who had come to look at the captain's new horse, on which he was to ride away the day after tomorrow; and Mr. Craig detained him to tell how all the servants were to collect at the gate of the courtyard to wish the young squire luck as he rode out; so that by the time Adam had got into the Chase, and was striding along with the basket of tools over his shoulder, the sun was on the point of setting, and was sending level crimson rays among the great trunks of the old oaks, and touching every bare patch of ground with a transient glory that made it look like a jewel dropt upon the grass. The wind had fallen now, and there was only enough breeze to stir the delicate-stemmed leaves. Any one who had been sitting in the house all day would have been glad to walk now; but Adam had been quite enough in the open air to wish to shorten his way home, and he bethought himself that he might do so by striking across the Chase and going through the Grove[11], where he had never been for years. He hurried on across the Chase, stalking along the narrow paths between the fern, with Gyp[12] at his heels, not lingering to watch the magnificent changes of the light—hardly once thinking of it—yet feeling its presence in a certain calm happy awe which mingled itself with his busy working-day thoughts. How could he help feeling it? The very deer felt it, and were more timid.

Presently Adam's thoughts recurred to what Mr. Craig had said about Arthur Donnithorne, and pictured his going away, and the changes that might take place before he came back; then they travelled back affectionately over the old scenes of boyish companionship, and dwelt on Arthur's good qualities, which Adam had a pride in, as we all have in the virtues of the superior who honours us. A nature like Adam's, with a great need of love and reverence in it, depends for so much of its happiness on what it can believe and feel about others! And he had no ideal world of dead heroes; he knew little of the life of men in the past; he must find the beings to whom he could cling with loving admiration among those who came within speech of him. These pleasant thoughts about Arthur brought a milder expression than usual into his keen rough face: perhaps they were the reason why, when he opened the old green gate leading into the Grove, he paused to pat Gyp and say a kind word to him.

After that pause, he strode on again along the broad winding path through the Grove. What grand beeches! Adam delighted in a fine tree of all things; as the fisherman's sight is keenest on the sea, so Adam's perceptions were more at home with trees than with other objects. He kept them in his memory, as a painter does, with all the flecks and knots in their bark, all the curves and angles of their boughs, and had often calculated the height and contents of a trunk to a nicety, as he stood looking at it. No wonder that, not-withstanding his desire to get on, he could not help pausing to look at a curious large beech which he had seen standing before him at a turning in the road, and convince himself that it was not two trees wedded together, but only one. For the rest of his life he remembered that moment when he was calmly examining the beech, as a man remembers his last glimpse of the home where his youth was passed, before the road turned, and he saw it no more. The beech stood at the last turning before the Grove ended in an archway of boughs that let in the eastern light; and as Adam stepped away from the tree to continue his walk, his eyes fell on two figures about twenty yards before him.

He remained as motionless as a statue, and turned almost as pale. The two figures were standing opposite to each other, with clasped hands about to part; and while they were bending to kiss, Gyp, who had been running among the brushwood, came out, caught sight of them, and gave a sharp bark. They separated with a start-one hurried through the gate out of the Grove, and the other, turning round, walked slowly, with a sort of saunter, towards Adam who still stood transfixed and pale, clutching tighter the stick with which he held the basket of tools over his shoulder, and looking at the approaching figure with eyes in which amazement was fast turning to fierceness.

Arthur Donnithorne looked flushed and excited; he had tried to make unpleasant feelings more bearable by drinking a little more wine than usual at dinner today, and was still enough under its flattering influence to think more lightly of this unwished-for rencontre with Adam than he would otherwise have done. After all, Adam was the best person who could have happened to see him and Hetty together: he was a sensible fellow, and would not babble about it to other people. Arthur felt confident that he could laugh the thing off and explain it away. And so he sauntered forward with elaborate carelessness—his flushed face, his evening dress of fine cloth and fine linen, his hands half thrust into his waistcoat-pockets, all shone upon by the strange evening light which the light clouds had caught up even to the zenith, and were now shedding down between the topmost branches above him.

Adam was still motionless, looking at him as he came up. He understood it all now—the locket and everything else that had been doubtful to him: a terrible scorching light showed him the hidden letters that changed the meaning of the past. If he had moved a muscle, he must inevitably have sprung upon Arthur like a tiger; and in the conflicting emotions that filled those long moments, he had told himself that he would not give loose to passion, he would only speak the right thing. He stood as if petrified by an unseen force, but the force was his own strong will.

"Well, Adam," said Arthur, "you've been looking at the fine old beeches, eh? They're not to be come near by the hatchet, though; this is a sacred grove. I overtook pretty little Hetty Sorrel as I was coming to my den—the Hermitage,[13] there. She ought not to come home this way so late. So I took care of her to the gate, and asked for a kiss for my pains. But I must get back now, for this road is confoundedly damp. Good-night, Adam. I shall see you tomorrow—to say goodbye, you know."

Arthur was too much preoccupied with the part he was playing himself to be thoroughly aware of the expression in Adam's face. He did not look directly at Adam, but glanced carelessly round at the trees and then lifted up one foot to look at the sole of his boot. He cared to say no more; he had thrown quite dust enough into honest Adam's eyes; and as he spoke the last words, he walked on.

"Stop a bit, sir," said Adam, in a hard peremptory voice, without turning round. "I've got a word to say to you."

Arthur paused in surprise. Susceptible persons are more affected by a change of tone than by unexpected words, and Arthur had the susceptibility of a nature at once affectionate and vain. He was still more surprised when he saw that Adam had not moved, but stood with his back to him, as if summoning him to return. What did he mean? He was going to make a serious business of this affair. Arthur felt his temper rising. A patronising disposition always has its meaner side, and in the confusion of his irritation and alarm there entered the feeling that a man to whom he had shown so much favour as to Adam was not in a position to criticize his conduct. And yet he was dominated, as one who feels himself in the wrong always is, by the man whose good opinion he cares for. In spite of pride and temper, there was as much deprecation as anger in his voice when he said, "What do you mean, Adam?"

"I mean, sir," answered Adam, in the same harsh voice, still without turning round—"I mean, sir, that you don't deceive me by your light words. This is not the first time you've met Hetty Sorrel in this grove, and this is not the first time you've kissed her."

Arthur felt a startled uncertainty how far Adam was speaking from knowledge, and how far from mere inference. And this uncertainty, which prevented him from contriving a prudent answer, heightened his irritation. He said, in a high sharp tone, "Well, sir, what then?"

"Why, then, instead of acting like th' upright, honourable man we've all believed you to be, you've been acting the part of a selfish light-minded scoundrel. You know as well as I do what it's to lead to when a gentleman like you kisses and makes love to a young woman like Hetty, and gives her presents as she's frightened for other folks to see. And I say it again, you're acting the part of a selfish light-minded scoundrel though it cuts me to th' heart to say so, and I'd rather ha' lost my right hand."

"Let me tell you, Adam," said Arthur, bridling his growing anger and trying to recur to his careless tone, "you're not only devilishly impertinent, but you're talking nonsense. Every pretty girl is not such a fool as you, to suppose that when a gentleman admires her beauty and pays her a little attention, he must mean something particular. Every man likes to flirt with a pretty girl, and every pretty girl likes to be flirted with. The wider the distance between them, the less harm there is, for then she's not likely to deceive herself."

"I don't know what you mean by flirting," said Adam, "but if you mean behaving to a woman as if you loved her, and yet not loving her all the while, I say that's not th' action of an honest man, and what isn't honest does come t' harm. I'm not a fool, and you're not a fool, and you know better than what you're saying. You know it couldn't be made public as you've behaved to Hetty as y' have done without her losing her character and bringing shame and trouble on her and her relations. What if you meant nothing by your kissing and your presents? Other folks won't believe as you've meant nothing; and don't tell me about her not deceiving herself. I tell you as you've filled her mind so with the thought of you as it'll mayhap poison her life, and she'll never love another man as 'ud make her a good husband."

Arthur had felt a sudden relief while Adam was speaking; he perceived that Adam had no positive knowledge of the past, and that there was no irrevocable damage done by this evening's unfortunate rencontre. Adam could still be deceived. The candid Arthur had brought himself into a position in which successful lying was his only hope. The hope allayed his anger a little.

"Well, Adam," he said, in a tone of friendly concession, "you're perhaps right. Perhaps I've gone a little too far in taking notice of the pretty little thing and stealing a kiss now and then. You're such a grave, steady fellow, you don't understand the temptation to such trifling. I'm sure I wouldn't bring any trouble or annoyance on her and the good Poysers on any account if I could help it. But I think you look a little too seriously at it. You know I'm going away immediately, so I shan't make any more mistakes of the kind. But let us say good-night"—Arthur here turned round to walk on—"and talk no more about the matter. The whole thing will soon be forgotten."

"No, by God!" Adam burst out with rage that could be controlled no longer, throwing down the basket of tools and striding forward till he was right in front of Arthur. All his jealousy and sense of personal injury, which he had been hitherto trying to keep under, had leaped up and mastered him. What man of us, in the first moments of a sharp agony, could ever feel that the fellow-man who has been the medium of inflicting it did not mean to hurt us? In our instinctive rebellion against pain, we are children again, and demand an active will to wreak our vengeance on. Adam at this moment could only feel that he had been robbed of Hetty—robbed treacherously by the man in whom he had trusted, and he stood close in front of Arthur, with fierce eyes glaring at him, with pale lips and clenched hands, the hard tones in which he had hitherto been constraining himself to express no more than a just indignation giving way to a deep agitated voice that seemed to shake him as he spoke.

"No, it'll not be soon forgot, as you've come in between her and me, when she might ha' loved me—it'll not soon be forgot as you've robbed me o' my happiness, while I thought you was my best friend, and a noble-minded man, as I was proud to work for. And you've been kissing her, and meaning nothing, have you? And I never kissed her i' my life—but I'd ha' worked hard for years for the right to kiss her. And you make light of it. You think little o' doing what may damage other folks, so as you get your bit o' trifling, as means nothing. I throw back your favours, for you're not the man I took you for. I'll never count you my friend any more. I'd rather you'd act as my enemy, and fight me where I stand—it's all th' amends you can make me."

Poor Adam, possessed by rage that could find no other vent, began to throw off his coat and his cap, too blind with passion to notice the change that had taken place in Arthur while he was speaking. Arthur's lips were now as pale as Adam's; his heart was beating violently. The discovery that Adam loved Hetty was a shock which made him for the moment see himself in the light of Adam's indignation, and regard Adam's suffering as not merely a consequence, but an element of his error. The words of hatred and contempt—the first he had ever heard in his life—seemed like scorching missiles that were making ineffaceable scars on him. All screening self-excuse, which rarely falls quite away while others respect us, forsook him for an instant, and he stood face to face with the first great irrevocable evil he had ever committed. He was only twenty-one, and three months ago—nay, much later—he had thought proudly that no man should ever be able to reproach him justly. His first impulse, if there had been time for it, would perhaps have been to utter words of propitiation; but Adam had no sooner thrown off his coat and cap than he became aware that Arthur was standing pale and motionless, with his hands still thrust in his waistcoat pockets.

"What!" he said, "won't you fight me like a man? You know I won't strike you while you stand so."

"Go away, Adam," said Arthur, "I don't want to fight you."

"No," said Adam, bitterly; "you don't want to fight me—you think I'm a common man, as you can injure without answering for it."

"I never meant to injure you," said Arthur, with returning anger. "I didn't know you loved her."

"But you've made her love you," said Adam. "You're a double-faced man—I'll never believe a word you say again."

"Go away, I tell you," said Arthur, angrily, "or we shall both repent."

"No," said Adam, with a convulsed voice, "I swear I won't go away without fighting you. Do you want provoking any more? I tell you you're a coward and a scoundrel, and I despise you."

The colour had all rushed back to Arthur's face; in a moment his right hand was clenched, and dealt a blow like lightning, which sent Adam staggering backward. His blood was as thoroughly up as Adam's now, and the two men, forgetting the emotions that had gone before, fought with the instinctive fierceness of panthers in the deepening twilight darkened by the trees. The delicate-handed gentleman was a match for the workman in everything but strength, and Arthur's skill enabled him to protract the struggle for some long moments. But between unarmed men the battle is to the strong, where the strong is no blunderer, and Arthur must sink under a well planted blow of Adam's as a steel rod is broken by an iron bar. The blow soon came, and Arthur fell, his head lying concealed in a tuft of fern, so that Adam could only discern his darkly clad body.

He stood still in the dim light waiting for Arthur to rise.

The blow had been given now, towards which he had been straining all the force of nerve and muscle—and what was the good of it? What had he done by fighting? Only satisfied his own passion, only wreaked his own vengeance. He had not rescued Hetty, nor changed the past—there it was just as it had been, and he sickened at the vanity of his own rage.

But why did not Arthur rise? He was perfectly motionless and the time seemed long to Adam... Good God! had the blow been too much for him? Adam shuddered at the thought of his own strength, as with the oncoming of this dread he knelt down by Arthur's side and lifted his head from among the fern. There was no sign of life: the eyes and teeth were set. The horror that rushed over Adam completely mastered him, and forced upon him its own belief. He could feel nothing but that death was in Arthur's face, and that he was helpless before it. He made not a single movement, but knelt like an image of despair gazing at an image of death.

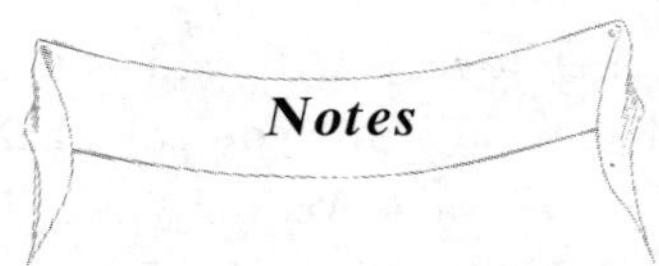

1. **Loamshire**: a fictional county in *Adam Bede* where most of its story takes place.
2. **Broxton and Hayslope**: both fictional communities in *Adam Bede*.
3. **the Chase**: name of the Donnithorne estate.
4. **Jonathan Burge**: Adam's employer at a carpentry workshop.
5. **the Hall Farm**: a place tenanted by the Poysers, Dinah's uncle and aunt.
6. **Mr. Craig**: the gardener at the Donnithorne estate.
7. **Mrs. Poyser**: one in a long tradition of English comic characters with rough exteriors but hearts of gold.
8. **Treddleston**: name of a place.
9. **Satchell**: the Squire's bailiff.
10. **Mr. Casson**: a butler for the Donnithornes for fifteen years.
11. **the Grove**: name of a place.
12. **Gyp**: Adam's dog.
13. **Hermitage**: name of a place.

Thomas Hardy (1840—1928)

Thomas Hardy was the last important novelist of the Victorian age. In his Wessex novels, he vividly and truthfully described the tragic lives of the tenants in the last decade of the 19th century.

Hardy was born in Dorsetshire, a county in the south of England. His birthplace, later used as the setting of his novels, he gave the name Wessex, which suggests the mysterious past of England during the Anglo-Saxon period, for it was here the Wessex kingdom once prospered under King Alfred and the prehistorical Stonehenge is located. The place is rich in its legend, folk customs and superstitions—all these would play their roles in Hardy's Wessex novels.

Born into an architect's family, he was expected to become an architect. He was an architect, but his real interest was in literature. His most famous novels are *Tess of the D'Urbervilles* (1891) and *Jude the Obscure* (1896).

Hardy was pessimistic in his view of life. His philosophy was that everything in the universe is determined by the Immanent Will, which is present in all parts of the universe and is impartially hostile towards human beings' desire for joy and happiness. The dominant theme of his novels is the futility of man's effort to struggle against cruel and unintelligible Fate, Chance, and Circumstances, which are all predestined by the Immanent Will. Although there is a humourous and attractive side to life, the prevailing mood in his novels is tragic. Since love is the most intense expression of human's desire for happiness, it is in love that the conflict between the efforts of human beings and the relentless force of the Immanenet Will is most acute.

From 1896 Hardy turned to poetry writing. He wrote altogether 918 poems, published in eight collections. Besides, he also wrote a great epic-drama, *The Dynasts*, which was published in three parts (1904, 1906, 1908).

Tess of the D'Urbervilles

The novel is about the tragic life of Tess Durbeyfield, the daughter of a poor foolish peasant, who believes that he is the descendant of an ancient aristocratic family, and who sends his daughter to work as a maid for a neighbouring family by the name of D'Urberville. Tess is seduced by Alec, the son of the family and gives birth to a child, which dies in infancy. Then Tess goes to work on a dairy farm, where she is engaged to Angel Clare, a man of liberal mind, and the son of a clergyman. On the wedding night, Tess confesses to Angel her seduction by Alec. On hearing her wife's tale, Angel's old-fashioned prejudice overcomes him and he abandons Tess. Then misfortunes fall upon Tess; finally, after a period of hard work on the Flintcomb Ash farm, she meets Alec again. When Angel repents and comes back to find Tess, it is too late. Tess murders Alec, and after hiding for a short period of time with Angel, is arrested, tried, and hanged. The book ends with the sentence: "Justice was done, and the President of the Immortals (in Aeschylean phrase) had ended his sport with Tess." The excerpts are selected from Chapters 42 and 43, when Tess is working in harsh conditions on the Flintcomb Ash farm.

XLII

She reached Chalk-Newton, and breakfasted at an inn, where several young men were troublesomely complimentary[1] to her good looks. Somehow she felt hopeful, for was it not possible that her husband also might say these same things to her even yet? She was bound to take care of herself on the chance of it, and keep off these casual lovers. To this end Tess resolved to run no further risks from her appearance. As soon as she got out of the village she entered a thicket and took from her basket one of the oldest field-gowns, which she had never put on even at the dairy—never since she had worked among the stubble at Marlott. She also, by a felicitous[2] thought, took a handkerchief from her bundle and tied it round her face under her bonnet, covering her chin and half her cheeks and temples, as if she were suffering from toothache. Then with her little scissors, by the aid of a pocket looking-glass, she mercilessly nipped her eyebrows off, and thus insured against aggressive admiration she went on her uneven way.

"What a mommet of a maid!"[3] said the next man who met her to a companion.

Tears came into her eyes for very pity of herself as she heard him.

"But I don't care!" she said. "O no—I don't care! I'll always be ugly now, because Angel is not here, and I have nobody to take care of me. My husband that was is gone away, and never will love me any more; but I love him just the same, and hate all other men, and like to make' em think scornfully of me!"

Thus Tess walks on; a figure which is part of the landscape; a fieldwoman pure and simple, in winter guise[4]; a gray serge cape, a red woollen cravat, a stuff skirt covered by a whitey-brown rough wrapper, and buff-leather gloves. Every thread of that old attire has become faded and thin under the stroke of raindrops, the burn of sunbeams, and the stress of winds. There is no sign of young passion in her now—

> The maiden's mouth is cold
> ......
> Fold over simple fold
> Binding her head.[5]

Inside this exterior, over which the eye might have roved as over a thing scarcely percipient[6], almost inorganic, there was the record of a pulsing life which had learnt too well, for its years, of the dust and ashes of things, of the cruelty of lust and the fragility of love.

Next day the weather was bad, but she trudged on, the honesty, directness, and impartiality of elemental enmity[7] disconcerting her but little. Her object being a winter's occupation and a winter's home, there was no time to lose. Her experience of short hirings[8] had been such that she was determined to accept no more.

Thus she went forward from farm to farm in the direction of the place whence Marian[9] had written to her, which she determined to make use of as a last shift only, its rumoured stringencies being the reverse of tempting. First she inquired for the lighter kinds of employment, and, as acceptance in any variety of these grew hopeless, applied next for the less light, till, beginning with the dairy and poultry tendance that she liked best, she ended with the heavy and coarse pursuits which she liked least—work on arable land: work of such roughness, indeed, as she would never have deliberately volunteered for.

Towards the second evening she reached the irregular chalk tableland or plateau, bosomed with semi-globular tumuli[10]—as if Cybele[11] the Many-breasted were supinely[12] extended there—which stretched between the valley of her birth and the valley of her love.

Here the air was dry and cold, and the long cart-roads were blown white and dusty within a few hours after rain. There were few trees, or none, those that would have grown in the hedges being mercilessly plashed[13] down with the quickset[14] by the tenant-farmers, the natural enemies of tree, bush, and brake[15]. In the middle distance ahead of her she could see the summits of Bulbarrow and of Nettlecombe Tout, and they seemed friendly. They had a low and unassuming aspect from this upland, though as approached on the other side from Blackmoor in her childhood they were as lofty bastions against the sky. Southerly, at many miles' distunce, and over the hills and ridges coastward, she could discern a surface like polished steel: it was the English Channel at a point far out towards France.

Before her, in a slight depression[16], were the remains of a village. She had, in fact, reached Flintcomb-Ash, the place of Marian's sojourn. There seemed to be no help for it; hither she was doomed to come. The stubborn soil around her showed plainly enough that the kind of labour in demand here was of the roughest kind; but it was time to rest from searching, and she resolved to stay, particularly as it began to rain. At the entrance to the village was a cottage whose gable jutted into the road, and before applying for a lodging she stood under its shelter, and watched the evening close in.

"Who would think I was Mrs. Angel Clare!" she said.

The wall felt warm to her back and shoulders, and she found that immediately within the gable was the cottage fireplace, the heat of which came through the bricks. She warmed her hands upon them, and also put her cheek—red and moist with the drizzle—against their comforting surface. The wall seemed to be the only friend she had. She had so little wish to leave it that she could have stayed there all night.

Tess could hear the occupants of the cottage—gathered together after their day's labour—talking to each other within, and the rattle of their supper-plates was also audible. But in the village-street she had seen no soul as yet. The solitude was at last broken by the approach of one feminine figure, who, though the evening was cold, wore the print gown and the tilt-bonnet of summer time. Tess instinctively thought it might be Marian, and when she came near enough to be distinguishable in the gloom surely enough it was she. Marian was even stouter and redder in the face than formerly, and decidedly shabbier in attire. At any previous period of her existence Tess would hardly have cared to renew the acquaintance in such conditions; but her loneliness was excessive, and she responded readily to Marian's greeting.

Marian was quite respectful in her inquiries, but seemed much moved by the fact that Tess should still continue in no better condition than at first; though she had dimly heard of the separation.

"Tess—Mrs. Clare—the dear wife of dear he! And is it really so bad as this, my child? Why is your comely face tied up in such a way? Anybody been beating 'ee ? Not *he*?"

"No, no, no! I merely did it not to be clipsed or colled[17], Marian."

She pulled off in disgust a bandage which could suggest such wild thoughts.

"And you've got no collar on." (Tess had been accustomed to wear a little white collar at the dairy.)

"I know it, Marian."

"You've lost it travelling."

"I've not lost it. The truth is, I don't care anything about my looks; and so I didn't put it on."

"And you don't wear your wedding-ring?"

"Yes, I do; but not in public. I wear it round my neck on a ribbon. I don't wish people to think who I am by marriage, or that I am married at all; it would be so awkward while I lead my present life."

Marian paused.

"But you *be* a gentleman's wife; and it seems hardly fair that you should live like this!"

"O yes it is, quite fair; though I am very unhappy."

"Well, well. *He* married you—and you can be unhappy!"

"Wives are unhappy sometimes; from no fault of their husbands—from their own."

"You've no faults, deary; that I'm sure of. And he's none. So it must be something outside ye both."

"Marian, dear Marian, will you do me a good turn without asking questions? My husband has gone abroad, and somehow I have overrun my allowance, so that I have to fall back upon my old work for a time. Do not call me Mrs. Clare, but Tess, as before. Do they want a hand here?"

"O yes; they'll take one always, because few care to come. 'Tis a starve-acre place[18]. Corn and swedes[19] are all they grow. Though I be here myself, I feel 'tis a pity for such as you to come."

"But you used to be as good a dairywoman as I."

"Yes; but I've got out o' that since I took to drink. Lord, that's the only comfort I've got now! If you engage, you'll be set swede-hacking. That's what I be doing; but you won't like it."

"O—anything! Will you speak for me?"

"You will do better by speaking for yourself."

"Very well. Now, Marian, remember—nothing about *him*, if I get the place. I don't wish to bring his name down to the dirt."

Marian, who was really a trustworthy girl though of coarser grain[20] than Tess, promised anything she asked.

"This is pay-night," she said, "and if you were to come with me you would know at once. I be real sorry that you are not happy; but 'tis because he's away, I know. You couldn't be unhappy if he were here, even if he gie'd ye no money—even if he used you like a drudge[21]."

"That's true; I could not!"

They walked on together, and soon reached the farmhouse, which was almost sublime in its dreariness. There was not a tree within sight; there was not, at this season, a green pasture—nothing but fallow and turnips everywhere; in large fields divided by hedges plashed to unrelieved levels.

Tess waited outside the door of the farmhouse till the group of workfolk had received their wages, and then Marian introduced her. The farmer himself, it appeared, was not at home, but his wife, who represented him this evening, made no objection to hiring Tess, on her agreeing to remain till Old Lady-Day[22]. Female field-labour was seldom offered now, and its cheapness made it profitable for tasks which women could perform as readily as men.

Having signed the agreement, there was nothing more for Tess to do at present than to get a lodging, and she found one in the house at whose gable-wall she had warmed herself. It was a poor subsistence that she had ensured, but it would afford a shelter for the winter at any rate.

That night she wrote to inform her parents of her new address, in case a letter should arrive at Marlott[23] from her husband. But she did not tell them of the sorriness of her situation: it might have brought reproach upon him.

XLIII

There was no exaggeration in Marian's definition of Flintcomb-Ash farm as a starve-acre place. The single fat thing on the soil was Marian herself; and she was an importation. Of the three classes of village, the village cared for by its lord, the village cared for by itself, and the village uncared for either by itself or by its lord (in other words, the village of a resident squire's tenantry[24], the village of free or copy-holders[25], and the absentee[26]-owner's village, farmed with the land) this place, Flintcomb-Ash, was the third.

But Tess set to work. Patience, that blending of moral courage with physical timidity, was now no longer a minor feature in Mrs. Angel Clare; and it sustained her.

The swede-field in which she and her companion were set hacking was a stretch of a hundred odd acres, in one patch, on the highest ground of the farm, rising above stony lanchets or lynchets[27]—the outcrop[28] of siliceous veins[29] in the chalk formation, composed of myriads of loose white flints in bulbous[30], cusped[31], and phallic shapes. The upper half of each turnip had been eaten off by the live-stock, and it was the business of the two women to grub up the lower or earthy half of the root with a hooked fork called a hacker, that it might be eaten also. Every leaf of the vegetable having already been consumed, the whole field was in colour a desolate drab; it was a complexion[32] without features, as if a face, from chin to brow, should be only an expanse of skin. The sky wore, in another colour, the same likeness; a white vacuity[33] of countenance with the lineaments[34] gone. So these two upper and nether visages confronted each other all day long, the white face looking down on the brown face, and the brown face looking up at the white face, without anything standing between them but the two girls crawling over the surface of the former like flies.

Nobody came near them, and their movements showed a mechanical regularity; their forms standing enshrouded in Hessian "wroppers"[35]—sleeved brown pinafores, tied behind to the bottom, to keep their gowns from blowing about—scant skirts revealing boots that reached high up the ankles, and yellow sheepskin gloves with gauntlets. The pensive character which the curtained hood lent to their bent heads would have reminded the observer of some early Italian conception of the two Marys[36].

They worked on hour after hour, unconscious of the forlorn aspect they bore in the landscape, not thinking of the justice or injustice of their lot. Even in such a position as theirs it was possible to exist in a dream. In the afternoon the rain came on again, and Marian said that they need not work any more. But if they did not work they would not be paid; so they worked on. It was so high a situation, this field, that the rain had no occasion to fall, but raced along horizontally upon the yelling wind, sticking into them like glass splinters till they were wet through. Tess had not known till now what was really meant by that. There are degrees of dampness, and a very little is called being wet through in common talk. But to stand working slowly in a field, and feel the creep of rainwater, first in legs and shoulders, then on hips and head, then at back, front, and sides, and yet to work on till the leaden light diminishes and marks that the sun is down, demands a distinct modicum[37] of stoicism[38], even of valour....

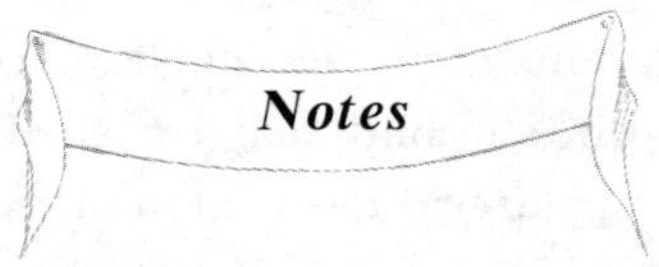

1. **troublesomely complimentary**: The compliments paid to her good looks may cause trouble to her.
2. **felicitous**: well chosen.
3. **What a mommet of a maid!**: What an ugly looking girl! (mommet=Maumet=an idol, or applied to a person as a term of abuse)
4. **guise**: dress.
5. **Binding her head**: quoted from Swinburne's "Fragoletta", "Ah sweet, the maiden's mouth is cold, /Her breast blossoms are simply red, /Her hair mere brown or gold, /Fold over simple fold /Binding her head."
6. **percipient**: perceptive.
7. **elemental enmity**: hostility of nature.
8. **short hirings**: hirings for a short period of time.
9. **Marian**: a girl who worked with her on the dairy farm and is now working at

Flintcomb Ash.

10. **tumuli**: plural form of "tumulus", which means "a burial mound".
11. **Cybele**: A goddess of ancient mythology, the mother of Zeus, Poseidon, and Hades, was worshipped as the mother of the gods.
12. **supinely**: lying face upward.
13. **plashed**: plash=to bend and interweave (branches and twigs) so as to form them into a hedge of fence.
14. **quickset**: a living plant, slip, or cutting set in the ground to grow for a hedge.
15. **brake**: a thicket.
16. **depression**: a low place.
17. **clipsed or colled**: embraced or hugged.
18. **a starve-acre place**: a wretched place.
19. **swedes**: a Swedish turnip.
20. **of coarser grain**: of a rough inborn character.
21. **drudge**: a slave, a menial servant.
22. **Old Lady-Day**: a holiday, the Feast of the Annunciation (圣母领报节), March 25th; on that day the angel Gabriel announced to Virgin Mary the birth of Christ.
23. **Marlott**: the name of the place where Tess's parents lived.
24. **a resident squire's tenantry**: the land on which the squire who owns the land lives.
25. **copy-holders**: a holder of land by copyhold (right of holding land, according to the custom of a manor, by copy of the roll originally made by the steward of the lord's court).
26. **absentee**: one who makes a habit of living away from his land.
27. **lynchets**: a slope or terrace along the face of a chalkdown(梯田崖).
28. **outcrop**: the part of a rock formation that appears at the surface of the ground.
29. **siliceous veins**: layers of silica(硅石)embedded in the rock.
30. **bulbous**: bulb-shaped(球茎状的).
31. **cusped**: pointed.
32. **complexion**: general appearance.
33. **vacuity**: lack of expression.
34. **lineaments**: distinctive features, esp. of the face.
35. **Hessian "wroppers"** : Wrappers (loose robes or gowns) made of strong coarse cloth (Hesse is a state in Germany).
36. **Marys**: Here refers to Virgin Mary.
37. **modicum**: a small amount.
38. **stoicism**: the philosophy of the Stoics, one school of Greek philosophers who practise repression of emotion, indifference to pleasure or pain, and patient endurance.

In Time of "The Breaking of Nations"[1,2]

The poem was written in 1915 during the First World War. In the poem Hardy indicates that nature would continue to exist despite the folly of the mankind.

I

Only a man harrowing clods[3]
    In a slow silent walk
With an old horse that stumbles[4] and nods
    Half asleep as they stalk[5].

II

Only thin smoke without flame
    From the heaps of couch-grass[6];
Yet this will go onward the same
    Through Dynasties pass.

III

Yonder a maid and her wight[7]
    Come whispering by:
War's annals will cloud into night
    Ere their story die.[8]

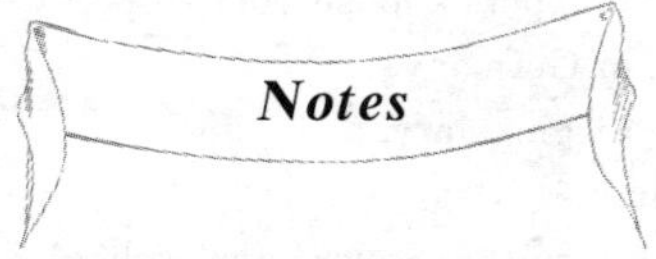

1. The metrical form of the poem is a combination of iambic and anapaestic feet. The rhyme scheme is abab.
2. **The breaking of nations**: Quoted from the "Book of Jeremiah", the *Bible* (《圣经·旧约》"耶利米书"). LI: 20: "Thou art my battle ax and weapons of war: for with thee will I break in pieces the nations." Here the quotation refers to the outbreak of the First World War.

3. **harrowing clods**: driving a harrow over the field (harrow: a farming instrument with sharp spikes or disks for breaking clods or covering sown seed with earth).
4. **stumbles**: to walk in an unsteady or clumsy manner.
5. **stalk**: walk in a stiff manner.
6. **couch-grass**: a grass akin to wheat, and a troublesome weed, owing to its creeping rootstock(匍匐冰草).
7. **wight** [waɪt]: a living being.
8. **War's annals will cloud into night/ Ere their story die**: Records of war will pass into oblivion, but the story of the maid and her lover will last forever.

Afterwards[1]

In this poem Hardy is imagining what people will think of him after his death.

When the Present[2] has latched[3] its postern[4] behind my tremulous stay,[5]
And the May month flaps its glad green leaves like wings,
Delicate-filmed as new-spun silk, will the neighbours say,
"He was a man who used to notice such things"?

If it be in the dusk when, like an eyelid's soundless blink,
The dewfall-hawk[6] comes crossing the shades to alight
Upon the wind-warped upland thorn, a gazer may think,
"To him this must have been a familiar sight."

If I pass during some nocturnal blackness, mothy and warm,
When the hedgehog travels furtively[7] over the lawn,
One may say, "He strove[8] that such innocent creatures should come to no harm,
But he could do little for them; and now he is gone"?

If, when hearing that I have been stilled[9] at last, they stand at the door,
Watching the full-starred heavens that winter sees,
Will this thought rise on those who will meet my face no more,
"He was one who had an eye for such mysteries"?

And will any say when my bell of quittance[10] is heard in the gloom,

And a crossing breeze cuts a pause in its outrollings,[11]
Till they rise again, as they were a new bell's boom,
"He hears it not now, but used to notice such things"?

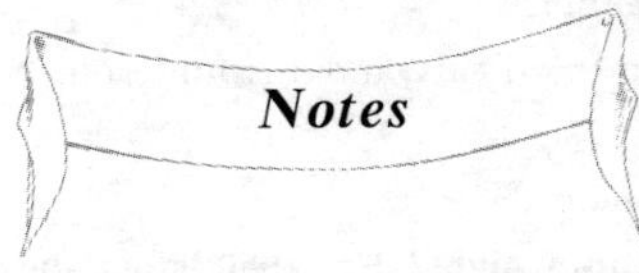

Notes

1. The metrical form of the poem is a combination of iambic and anapaestic feet, with a rhyme scheme of abab.
2. **Present**: Present time personified.
3. **latched**: fastened a door with a latch (latch: a small bar fastening a door or gate, lifted from its catch by a lever).
4. **postern**: a back door or gate.
5. **tremulous stay**: my short, timid and unconfident life.
6. **dewfall-hawk**: night-hawk.
7. **furtively**: stealthily.
8. **strove**: was contended.
9. **stilled**: here referring to "dead".
10. **my bell of quittance**: the bell tolls for my death.
11. **outrollings**: the sound of the bell rolling in the air.

Joseph Conrad (1857—1924)

Joseph Conrad was born in Ukraine, a part of Poland which was under the Russian rule. His father was an aristocrat with no land, and a translator of English and French literature. Because of his father's involvement in patriotic activities, his family were exiled to northern Russia where his mother fell ill of tuberculosis. Later both of his parents died of that disease. His maternal uncle supported his study and allowed him to go to the sea. After four years' work in the French merchant marine, he joined the British merchant navy for another 16 years. His marine life ended by 1894. He settled in England in 1893 and got married in 1896. During his marine life he visited many parts of the world, which provided him with an inexhaustible source for writing. Many universities had granted him honorary degrees but he declined. In 1924 he refused the offer of the order of Knighthood. Because of his long harsh life, he was physically fragile in his later years, and died of an heart attack on August 3, 1924. He was buried in Canterbury. Among his friends were H. G. Wells, and John Galsworthy. His influence can be seen in the works of many modern writers. Joseph Conrad's other novels include *Almayer's Folly* (1895), *The Nigger of "the Narcissus"*(1897), *Lord Jim* (1900), *Nostromo* (1904), *The Secret Agent* (1907).

The novel, *Heart of Darkness*, is based on his trip in Africa up to the Congo River in 1880. The story begins with Marlow telling his story to the other passengers while the ship is lying in anchor at the mouth of the Thames River. Marlow is applying for a job at a trading company with its headquarters at Brussels. He is sent by the Company to the Belgium Congo(present-day Zaire) to be a riverboat captain. When he gets there, he sees what the Company does is to grasp as much ivory as possible. The Europeans under the disguise of civilizing the natives, treat them brutally. There is a trader named Kurtz who is an agent in one of the Inner Stations and gathers as much ivory as all the other agents put together. He is praised by his fellow trader as "emissary of western ideals", but in fact he has degenerated into a "savage", and kills the natives in plundering ivory. On the fence posts in front of his hut are human skulls of the natives used for decoration. Marlow's mission is to get the seriously ill Kurtz out of the Inner Station. Kurtz dies on the way and his last words are "Horror! Horror!"

Marlow goes back to Belgium and meets Kurtz's fiancee. When asked what Kurtz's last word is, Marlow answers that he called her name.

Heart of Darkness

"I flew around like mad to get ready, and before forty-eight hours I was crossing the Channel[1] to show myself to my employers, and sign the contract. In a very few hours I arrived in a city that always makes me think of a whited sepulcher.[2] Prejudice no doubt. I had no difficulty in finding the Company's offices. It was the biggest thing in the town, and everybody I met was full of it. They were going to run an over-sea empire, and make no end of coin by trade.

"A narrow and deserted street in deep shadow, high houses, innumerable windows with venetian blinds, a dead silence, grass sprouting between the stones, imposing carriage archways right and left, immense double doors standing ponderously ajar. I slipped through one of these cracks, went up a swept and ungarnished staircase, as arid as a desert, and opened the first door I came to. Two women, one fat and the other slim, sat on straw-bottomed chairs, knitting black wool. The slim one got up and walked straight at me—still knitting with downcast eyes—and only just as I began to think of getting out of her way, as you would for a somnambulist, stood still, and looked up. Her dress was as plain as an umbrella-cover, and she turned round without a word and preceded me into a waiting-room. I gave my name, and looked about. Deal table in the middle, plain chairs all round the walls, on one end a large shining map, marked with all the colors of a rainbow. There was a vast amount of red—good to see at any time, because one knows that some real work is done in there, a deuce of a lot of blue, a little green, smears of orange, and, on the East Coast, a purple patch, to show where the jolly pioneers of progress drink the jolly lager-beer. However, I wasn't going into any of these. I was going into the yellow. Dead in the center. And the river was there—fascinating—deadly—like a snake. Ough! A door opened, a white-haired secretarial head, but wearing a compassionate expression, appeared, and a skinny forefinger beckoned me into the sanctuary. Its light was dim, and a heavy writing-desk squatted in the middle. From behind that structure came out an impression of pale plumpness in a frock-coat. The great man himself. He was five feet six, I should judge, and had his grip on the handle-end of ever so many millions. He shook hands, I fancy, murmured vaguely, was satisfied with my French. Bon voyage.

"In about forty-five seconds I found myself again in the waiting-room with the compassionate secretary, who, full of desolation and sympathy, made me sign some document. I believe I undertook amongst other things not to disclose any trade secrets. Well, I am not going to.

"I began to feel slightly uneasy. You know I am not used to such ceremonies, and there was something ominous in the atmosphere. It was just as though I had been let into some conspiracy—I don't know—something not quite right; and I was glad to get out. In the outer room the two women knitted black wool feverishly. People were arriving, and the younger one was walking back and forth introducing them. The old one sat on her chair. Her flat cloth slippers were propped up on a foot-warmer, and a cat reposed on her lap. She wore a starched white affair on her head, had a wart on one cheek, and silver-rimmed spectacles hung on the tip of her nose. She glanced at me above the glasses. The swift and indifferent placidity of that look troubled me. Two youths with foolish and cheery countenances were being piloted over, and she threw at them the same quick glance of unconcerned wisdom. She seemed to know all about them and about me too. An eerie feeling came over me. She seemed uncanny and fateful. Often far away there I thought of these two, guarding the door of Darkness, knitting black wool as for a warm pall, one introducing, introducing continuously to the unknown, the other scrutinizing the cheery and foolish faces with unconcerned old eyes. Ave! Old knitter of black wool. Morituri te salutant.[3] Not many of those she looked at ever saw her again—not half, by a long way.

"There was yet a visit to the doctor. 'A simple formality,' assured me the secretary, with an air of taking an immense part in all my sorrows. Accordingly a young chap wearing his hat over the left eyebrow, some clerk I suppose,—there must have been clerks in the business, though the house was as still as a house in a city of the dead,—came from somewhere up-stairs, and led me forth. He was shabby and careless, with ink-stains on the sleeves of his jacket, and his cravat was large and billowy, under a chin shaped like the toe of an old boot. It was a little too early for the doctor, so I proposed a drink, and thereupon he developed a vein of joviality. As we sat over our vermouths he glorified the Company's business, and by-and-by I expressed casually my surprise at him not going out there. He became very cool and collected all at once. 'I am not such a fool as I look, quoth Plato to his disciples,' he said sententiously, emptied his glass with great resolution, and we rose.

"The old doctor felt my pulse, evidently thinking of something else the while. 'Good, good for there,' he mumbled, and then with a certain eagerness asked me whether I would let him measure my head. Rather surprised, I said Yes, when he produced a thing like calipers and got the dimensions back and front and every way, taking notes carefully. He was an unshaven little man in a threadbare coat like a gaberdine, with his feet in slippers, and I thought him a harmless fool. 'I always ask leave, in the interests of science, to measure the crania of those going out there,' he said. 'And when they come back, too?' I asked. 'Oh, I never see them,' he remarked; 'and, moreover, the changes take place inside, you know.' He smiled, as if at some quiet joke. 'So you are going out there. Famous. Interesting too.' He gave me a searching glance, and made another note. 'Ever any madness in your family?' he asked, in a matter-of-fact tone. I felt very annoyed. 'Is that question in the interests of science too?' 'It would be,' he said, without taking notice of my irritation, 'interesting for science to watch the mental changes of individuals, on the spot, but...' 'Are you an alienist?' I interrupted. 'Every doctor should be—a little,' answered that original, imperturbably. 'I have a little theory which you Messieurs who go out there must help me to prove. This is my share in the advantages my country shall reap from the possession of such a magnificent dependency. The mere wealth I leave to others. Pardon my questions, but you are the first Englishman coming under my observation....' I hastened to assure him I was not in the least typical. 'If I were,' said I, 'I wouldn't be talking like this with you.' 'What you say is rather profound, and probably erroneous,' he said, with a laugh. 'Avoid irritation more than exposure to the sun. Adieu. How do you English say, eh? Good-by. Ah! Good-by. Adieu. In the tropics one must before everything keep calm.' ... He lifted a warning forefinger.... 'Du calme, du calme.[4] Adieu.'

"One thing more remained to do—say good-bye to my excellent aunt. I found her triumphant. I had a cup of tea—the last decent cup of tea for many days—and in a room that most soothingly looked just as you would expect a lady's drawing-room to look, we had a long quiet chat by the fireside. In the course of these confidences it became quite plain to me I had been represented to the wife of the high dignitary, and goodness knows to how many more people besides, as an exceptional and gifted creature—a piece of good fortune for the Company—a man you don't get hold of every day. Good heavens! and I was going to take charge of a two-penny-halfpenny river-steamboat with a penny whistle attached! It appeared, however, I was also one of the workers, with a capital—you know. Something like an emissary of light, something like a lower sort of apostle. There had been a lot of such rot let loose in print and talk just about that time, and the excellent woman, living right in the rush of all that humbug, got carried off her feet. She talked about 'weaning those ignorant millions from their horrid ways,' till, upon my word, she made me quite uncomfortable. I ventured to hint that the Company was run for profit.

"'You forget, dear Charlie, that the laborer is worthy of his hire,' she said, brightly. It's queer how out of touch with truth women are. They live in a world of their own, and there had never been anything like it, and never can be. It is too beautiful altogether, and if they were to set it up it would go to pieces before the first sunset. Some confounded fact we men have been living contentedly with ever since the day of creation would start up and knock the whole thing over.

"After this I got embraced, told to wear flannel, be sure to write often, and so on—and I left. In the street—I don't know why—a queer feeling came to me that I was an impostor. Odd thing that I, who used to clear out for any part of the world at twenty-four hours' notice, with less thought than most men give to the crossing of a street, had a moment—I won't say of hesitation, but of startled pause, before this commonplace affair. The best way I can explain it to you is by saying that, for a second or two, I felt as though, instead of going to the center of a continent, I were about to set off for the center of the earth.

"I left in a French steamer, and she called in every blamed port they have out there, for, as far as I could see, the sole purpose of landing soldiers and custom-house officers. I watched the coast.

Watching a coast as it slips by the ship is like thinking about an enigma. There it is before you—smiling, frowning, inviting, grand, mean, insipid, or savage, and always mute with an air of whispering, 'Come and find out.' This one was almost featureless, as if still in the making, with an aspect of monotonous grimness. The edge of a colossal jungle, so dark-green as to be almost black, fringed with white surf, ran straight, like a ruled line, far, far away along a blue sea whose glitter was blurred by a creeping mist. The sun was fierce, the land seemed to glisten and drip with steam. Here and there grayish-whitish specks showed up, clustered inside the white surf, with a flag flying above them perhaps. Settlements some centuries old, and still no bigger than pin-heads on the untouched expanse of their background. We pounded along, stopped, landed soldiers; went on, landed custom-house clerks to levy toll in what looked like a God-forsaken wilderness, with a tin shed and a flag-pole lost in it; landed more soldiers—to take care of the custom-house clerks, presumably. Some, I heard, got drowned in the surf; but whether they did or not, nobody seemed particularly to care. They were just flung out there, and on we went. Every day the coast looked the same, as though we had not moved; but we passed various places—trading places—with names like Gran' Bassam Little Popo, names that seemed to belong to some sordid farce acted in front of a sinister backcloth. The idleness of a passenger, my isolation amongst all these men with whom I had no point of contact, the oily and languid sea, the uniform somberness of the coast, seemed to keep me away from the truth of things, within the toil of a mournful and senseless delusion. The voice of the surf heard now and then was a positive pleasure, like the speech of a brother. It was something natural, that had its reason, that had a meaning. Now and then a boat from the shore gave one a momentary contact with reality. It was paddled by black fellows. You could see from afar the white of their eyeballs glistening. They shouted, sang; their bodies streamed with perspiration; they had faces like grotesque masks—these chaps; but they had bone, muscle, a wild vitality,[5] an intense energy of movement, that was as natural and true as the surf along their coast. They wanted no excuse for being there. They were a great comfort to look at. For a time I would feel I belonged still to a world of straightforward facts; but the feeling would not last long. Something would turn up to scare it away. Once, I remember, we came upon a man-of-war anchored off the coast. There wasn't even a shed there, and she was shelling the bush. It appears the French had one of their wars going on thereabouts. Her ensign dropped limp like a rag; the muzzles of the long eight-inch guns stuck out all over the low hull; the greasy, slimy swell swung her up lazily and let her down, swaying her thin masts. In the empty immensity of earth, sky, and water, there she was, incomprehensible, firing into a continent. Pop, would go one of the eight-inch guns; a small flame would dart and vanish, a little white smoke would disappear, a tiny projectile would give a feeble screech—and nothing happened. Nothing could happen. There was a touch of insanity in the proceeding, a sense of lugubrious drollery in the sight; and it was not dissipated by somebody on board assuring me earnestly there was a camp of natives—he called them enemies! —hidden out of sight somewhere.

"We gave her her letters (I heard the men in that lonely ship were dying of fever at the rate of three a day) and went on. We called at some more places with farcical names, where the merry dance of death and trade goes on in a still and earthy atmosphere as of an overheated catacomb;[6] all along the formless coast bordered by dangerous surf, as if Nature herself had tried to ward off intruders; in and out of rivers, streams of death in life, whose banks were rotting into mud, whose waters, thickened into slime, invaded the contorted mangroves, that seemed to writhe at us in the extremity of an impotent despair. Nowhere did we stop long enough to get a particularized impression, but the general sense of vague and oppressive wonder grew upon me. It was like a weary pilgrimage amongst hints for nightmares.

"It was upward of thirty days before I saw the mouth of the big river. We anchored off the seat of the government. But my work would not begin till some two hundred miles farther on. So as soon as I could I made a start for a place thirty miles higher up.

"I had my passage on a little sea-going steamer. Her captain was a Swede, and knowing me for a seaman, invited me on the bridge. He was a young man, lean, fair, and morose, with lanky hair and a shuffling gait. As we left the miserable little wharf, he tossed his head contemptuously at the shore. 'Been living there?' he asked. I said, 'Yes.' 'Fine lot these government chaps—are they not?' he went on, speaking English with great precision and considerable bitterness. 'It is funny what some people will do for a few francs a month. I wonder what becomes of that kind when it goes up country?' I said to him I expected to see that soon. 'So-o-o!' he exclaimed. He shuffled athwart, keeping one eye ahead vigilantly. 'Don't be too sure,' he continued. 'The other day I took up a man who hanged himself on the road. He was a Swede, too.' 'Hanged himself! Why, in God's name?' I cried. He kept on looking out watchfully. 'Who knows? The sun too much for him, or the country perhaps.'

"At last we opened a reach. A rocky cliff appeared, mounds of turned-up earth by the shore, houses on a hill, others, with iron roofs, amongst a waste of excavations, or hanging to the declivity. A continuous noise of the rapids above hovered over this scene of inhabited devastation. A lot of people, mostly black and naked, moved about like ants. A jetty projected into the river. A blinding sunlight drowned all this at times in a sudden recrudescence of glare. 'There's your Company's station,' said the Swede, pointing to three wooden barrack-like structures on the rocky slope. 'I will send your things up. Four boxes did you say? So. Farewell.'

"I came upon a boiler wallowing in the grass, then found a path leading up the hill. It turned aside for the boulders, and also for an undersized railway-truck lying there on its back with its wheels in the air. One was off. The thing looked as dead as the carcass of some animal. I came upon more pieces of decaying machinery, a stack of rusty rails. To the left a clump of trees made a shady spot, where dark things seemed to stir feebly. I blinked, the path was steep. A horn tooted to the right, and I saw the black people run. A heavy and dull detonation shook the ground, a puff of smoke came out of the cliff, and that was all. No change appeared on the face of the rock. They were building a railway. The cliff was not in the way or anything; but this objectless blasting was all the work going on.

"A slight clinking behind me made me turn my head. Six black men advanced in a file, toiling up the path. They walked erect and slow, balancing small baskets full of earth on their heads, and the clink kept time with their footsteps. Black rags were wound round their loins, and the short ends behind wagged to and fro like tails. I could see every rib, the joints of their limbs were like knots in a rope; each had an iron collar on his neck, and all were connected together with a chain whose bights swung between them, rhythmically clinking. Another report from the cliff made me think suddenly of that ship of war I had seen firing into a continent. It was the same kind of ominous voice; but these men could by no stretch of imagination be called enemies. They were called criminals, and the outraged law, like the bursting shells, had come to them, an insoluble mystery from over the sea. All their meager breasts panted together, the violently dilated nostrils quivered, the eyes stared stonily uphill. They passed me within six inches, without a glance, with that complete, deathlike indifference of unhappy savages. Behind this raw matter one of the reclaimed,[7] the product of the new forces at work, strolled despondently, carrying a rifle by its middle. He had a uniform jacket with one button off, and seeing a white man on the path, hoisted his weapon to his shoulder with alacrity. This was simple prudence, white men being so much alike at a distance that he could not tell who I might be. He was speedily reassured, and with a large, white, rascally grin, and a glance at his charge, seemed to take me into partnership in his exalted trust. After all, I also was a part of the great cause of these high and just proceedings.

"Instead of going up, I turned and descended to the left. My idea was to let that chain-gang get out of sight before I climbed the hill. You know I am not particularly tender; I've had to strike and to fend off. I've had to resist and to attack sometimes—that's only one way of resisting—without counting the exact cost, according to the demands of such sort of life as I had blundered into. I've seen the devil of violence, and the devil of greed, and the devil of hot desire; but, by all the stars! these were strong, lusty, red-eyed devils, that swayed and drove men—men, I tell you. But as I stood on this hillside, I foresaw that in the blinding sunshine of that land I would become acquainted with a flabby, pretending, weak-eyed devil of a rapacious and pitiless folly.[8] How insidious he could be, too, I was only to find out several months later and a thousand miles farther. For a moment I stood appalled, as though by a warning. Finally I descended the hill, obliquely, towards the trees I had seen.

"I avoided a vast artificial hole somebody had been digging on the slope, the purpose of which I found it impossible to divine. It wasn't a quarry or a sandpit, anyhow. It was just a hole. It might have been connected with the philanthropic desire of giving the criminals something to do. I don't know. Then I nearly fell into a very narrow ravine, almost no more than a scar in the hillside. I discovered that a lot of imported drainage-pipes for the settlement had been tumbled in there. There wasn't one that was not broken. It was a wanton smash-up. At last I got under the trees. My purpose was to stroll into the shade for a moment; but no sooner within than it seemed to me I had stepped into a gloomy circle of some Inferno.[9] The rapids were near, and an uninterrupted, uniform, headlong, rushing noise filled the mournful stillness of the grove, where not a breath stirred, not a leaf moved, with a mysterious sound—as though the tearing pace of the launched earth had suddenly become audible.

"Black shapes crouched, lay, sat between the trees, leaning against the trunks, clinging to the earth, half coming out, half effaced within the dim light, in all the attitudes of pain, abandonment, and despair. Another mine on the cliff went off, followed by a slight shudder of the soil under my feet. The work was going on. The work! And this was the place where some of the helpers had withdrawn to die.

"They were dying slowly—it was very clear. They were not enemies, they were not criminals, they were nothing earthly now,—nothing but black shadows of disease and starvation, lying confusedly in the greenish gloom. Brought from all the recesses of the coast in all the legality of time contracts, lost in uncongenial surroundings, fed on unfamiliar food, they sickened, became inefficient, and were then allowed to crawl away and rest. These moribund shapes were free as air—and nearly as thin. I began to distinguish the gleam of eyes under the trees. Then, glancing down, I saw a face near my hand. The black bones reclined at full length with one shoulder against the tree, and slowly the eyelids rose and the sunken eyes looked up at me, enormous and vacant, a kind of blind, white flicker in the depths of the orbs, which died out slowly. The man seemed young—almost a boy—but you know with them it's hard to tell. I found nothing else to do but to offer him one of my good Swede's ship's biscuits I had in my pocket. The fingers closed slowly on it and held—there was no other movement and no other glance. He had tied a bit of white worsted round his neck—Why? Where did he get it? Was it a badge—an ornament—a charm—a propitiatory act? Was there any idea at all connected with it? It looked startling round his black neck, this bit of white thread from beyond the seas.

"Near the same tree two more bundles of acute angles sat with their legs drawn up. One, with his chin propped on his knees, stared at nothing, in an intolerable and appalling manner: his brother phantom rested its forehead, as if overcome with a great weariness; and all about others were scattered in every pose of contorted collapse, as in some picture of a massacre or a pestilence. While I stood horror-struck, one of these creatures rose to his hands and knees, and went off on all-fours towards the river to drink. He lapped out of his hand, then sat up in the sunlight, crossing his shins in front of him, and after a time let his woolly head fall on his breastbone.

"I didn't want any more loitering in the shade, and I made haste towards the station. When near the buildings I met a white man, in such an unexpected elegance of get-up that in the first moment I took him for a sort of vision. I saw a high starched collar, white cuffs, a light alpaca jacket, snowy trousers, a clear necktie, and varnished boots. No hat. Hair parted, brushed, oiled, under a green-lined parasol held in a big white hand. He was amazing, and had a penholder behind his ear.[10]

"I shook hands with this miracle, and I learned he was the Company's chief accountant, and that all the bookkeeping was done at this station. He had come out for a moment, he said, 'to get a breath of fresh air.' The expression sounded wonderfully odd, with its suggestion of sedentary desk-life. I wouldn't have mentioned the fellow to you at all, only it was from his lips that I first heard the name of the man who is so indissolubly connected with the memories of that time. Moreover, I respected the fellow. Yes; I respected his collars, his vast cuffs, his brushed hair. His appearance was certainly that of a hairdresser's dummy; but in the great demoralization of the land he kept up his appearance. That's backbone. His starched collars and got-up shirt-fronts were achievements of character. He had been out nearly three years; and, later on, I could not help asking him how he managed to sport such linen. He had just the faintest blush, and said modestly, 'I've been teaching one of the native women about the station. It was difficult. She had a distaste for the work.' This man had verily accomplished something. And he was devoted to his books, which were in apple-pie order.

"Everything else in the station was in a muddle—heads, things, buildings. Strings of dusty niggers with splay feet arrived and departed; a stream of manufactured goods, rubbishy cottons, beads, and brass-wire set into the depths of darkness, and in return came a precious trickle of ivory.

"I had to wait in the station for ten days—an eternity. I lived in a hut in the yard, but to be out of the chaos I would sometimes get into the accountant's office. It was built of horizontal planks, and so badly put together that, as he bent over his high desk, he was barred from neck to heels with narrow strips of sunlight. There was no need to open the big shutter to see. It was hot there too; big flies buzzed fiendishly, and did not sting, but stabbed. I sat generally on the floor, while, of faultless appearance (and even slightly scented), perching on a high stool, he wrote, he wrote. Sometimes he stood up for exercise. When a truckle-bed with a sick man (some invalided agent from up-country) was put in there, he exhibited a gentle annoyance. 'The groans of this sick person,' he said, distracting my attention. And without that it is extremely difficult to guard against clerical errors in this climate.'

"One day he remarked, without lifting his head, 'In the interior you will no doubt meet Mr. Kurtz.' On my asking who Mr. Kurtz was, he said he was a first-class agent; and seeing my disappointment at this information, he added slowly, laying down his pen, 'He is a very remarkable person.' Further questions elicited from him that Mr. Kurtz was at present in charge of a trading post, a very important one, in the true ivory-country, at 'the very bottom of there. Sends in as much ivory as all the others put together....' He began to write again. The sick man was too ill to groan. The flies buzzed in a great peace.
"Suddenly there was a growing murmur of voices and a great tramping of feet. A caravan had come in. A violent babble of uncouth sounds burst out on the other side of the planks. All the carriers were speaking together, and in the midst of the uproar the lamentable voice of the chief agent was heard 'giving it up' tearfully for the twentieth time that day.... He rose slowly. 'What a frightful row,' he said. He crossed the room gently to look at the sick man, and returning, said to me, 'He does not hear.' 'What! Dead?' I asked, startled. 'No, not yet,' he answered, with great composure. Then, alluding with a toss of the head to the tumult in the station-yard, 'When one has got to make

correct entries, one comes to hate those savages—hate them to the death.' He remained thoughtful for a moment. 'When you see Mr. Kurtz,' he went on, 'tell him from me that everything here'—he glanced at the desk—'is very satisfactory. I don't like to write to him—with those messengers of ours you never know who may get hold of your letter—at that Central Station.' He stared at me for a moment with his mild, bulging eyes. 'Oh, he will go far, very far,' he began again. 'He will be a somebody in the Administration before long. They, above—the Council in Europe, you know—mean him to be.'"

1. **Channel**: the English Channel.
2. **a whited sepulcher**: which appears beautiful outward, but is within full of... uncleanness—Mattbew xxiii 27.
3. **Morituri te salutant**: when the Roman gladiators entered the arena, they saluted the Emperor by shouting: "Hail! Those who are about to die salute you!"
4. **Du calme, du calme**: Be calm, be calm.
5. **these chaps; but they had bone, muscle, a wild vitality**: Notice how Marlow compares the natives with the white traders.
6. **where the merry dance of death and trade goes on... as of an overheated catacomb**: Notice the image of death is again repeated here and is related with "trade".
7. **one of the reclaimed**: a native who has been turned into Christian.
8. **a flabby, pretending, weak-eyed devil of a rapacious ad pitiless folly**: Here Kurtz is referred to.
9. **Inferno**: Hell, the place where the sickened natives are brought to die.
10. **I saw a high starched collar... a penholder behind his ear**: Notice the contrast between the natives and the Company's chief accountant.

3. The Victorian poets

Although the novel was the predominating genre of literature in the Victorian age, it does not follow that there were no prominent poets after the deaths of major romantic poets. In fact, poets like Alfred Tennyson (1809—1892), Robert Browning (1812—1889), Elizabeth Barrett Browning (1806—1861), and Matthew Arnold (1822—1888) were important in the sense not only that they wrote highly lyrical poems as the romantists did, but also that they in their poetry reflected the spiritual search which was characteristic of the age.

The Victorian poets were living in a time of spiritual unrest that was the result of the increasingly sharpening of the class struggle between the wealthy and the poor, the rapid progress of science and technology, and the discovery of new theories of social science. All these greatly shook the religious faith that had been the mainstay of people's spiritual life for centuries. Hence the Victorian age was marked throughout by the prominence of the spirit of inquiry and criticism, by scepticism and religious uncertainty, and by spiritual struggle and unrest. All these were echoed in the poetry written in the Victorian age.

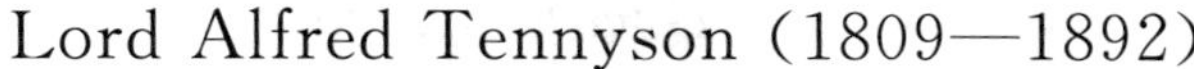

Lord Alfred Tennyson (1809—1892)

Tennyson lived almost through the Victorian age and was the leading poet of his age. Some historians even called the period from 1832 to the death of Tennyson "the Age of Tennyson". Tennyson was born into a clergyman's family. He lived a very quiet life in his early years. He attended Cambridge but had to leave in 1831 because of financial need. He fell in love in 1836 but had to postpone his marriage until 1850 because of poverty.

Tennyson's first collection of poems was *Poems by Two Brothers* (1827), on which he collaborated with his brother. The volume is a slight one, but in it we can see Tennyson's metrical aptitude and descriptive power. His first important work *Poems* (1833), was a collection of his early poems. It was the two volumes of *Poems* (1842) that secured his position as the leading poet of the time. In this collection there are his famous poems such as "The Lady of Shalott", "Morte d'Arthur", and "Ulysses".

In 1850 Tennyson published *In Memoriam* and succeeded Wordsworth as poet laureate. In 1854 he published *Maud.* In 1859 he published *Idylls of the King*, which was a sequence of tales based on the legend of King Arthur. In 1884 he was knighted. He died in 1892 and was buried in Westminster Abbey.

Break, Break, Break[1]

The poem is one of many lyrics that Tennyson wrote in memory of his friend Arthur Hallam. Sorrow strikes him just as the breakers strike against the shore. Everything goes on as usual but his friend is no longer there.

Break, break, break,
    On thy cold gray stones, O sea!
And I would[2] that my tongue could utter
    The thoughts that arise in me.

O, well for[3] the fisherman's boy,
    That he shouts with his sister at play!
O, well for the sailor lad,
    That he sings in his boat on the bay!
And the stately ships go on
    To their haven under the hill;
But O for the touch of a vanish'd hand[4],
    And the sound of a voice that is still![5]

Break, break, break,
    At the foot of thy crags, O Sea!
But the tender grace of a day[6] that is dead
    Will never come back to me.

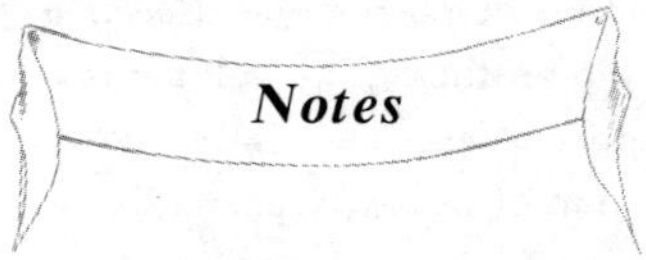

Notes

1. The poem is written in irregular meter. The prevailing foot is anapaestic. In the first line two unaccented syllables of each foot are omitted, but the time is preserved by the three long pauses.
2. **I would**: I wish.
3. **O, well for**: O, it would be well for.
4. **a vanish'd hand**: the hand of his friend who has vanished.
5. **a voice that is still**: the voice of his friend can no longer be heard.
6. **tender grace of a day**: the loving kindness of the day when I was enjoying your company.

Ulysses[1]

Tennyson's two comments on the poem help us to understand the meaning of this poem. First, "The poem was written soon after Arthur Hallam's death, and it gives the feeling about the need of going forward and braving the struggle of life perhaps more simply than anything *In Memoriam*." Second, "There is more about myself in *Ulysses*, which was written under the sense of loss and that all had gone by, but that still life must be fought out to the end." Ulysses is the Roman name for the Greek hero Odysseus in Homer's *Odyssey*, king of Ithaca, husband of Penelope and father of Telemachus. After the Greeks' victory over the Trojans, Ulysses wanders at sea for ten years before he returns home. In the poem, despite his old age, Ulysses is planning to put out to sea again.

It little profits[2] that an idle king,
By this still hearth[3], among these barren crags[4],
Match'd with an agèd wife,[5] I mete[6] and dole[7]
Unequal laws[8] unto a savage race[9],
That hoard, and sleep, and feed, and know not me.[10]
I cannot rest from travel: I will drink
Life to the lees:[11] all times I have enjoy'd
Greatly, have suffer'd greatly, both with those
That loved me, and alone; on shore, and when[12]
Thro' scudding drifts[13] the rainy Hyades[14]
Vext the dim sea; I am become a name;[15]
For always roaming with a hungry heart
Much have I seen and known; cities of men,
And manners, climates, councils, governments,
Myself not least, but honour'd of them all;[16]
And drunk delight of battle with my peers[17],
Far on the ringing plains[18] of windy Troy.
I am a part of all that I have met.[19]
Yet all experience is an arch where-thro'[20]
Gleams that untravell'd world,[21] whose margin[22] fades
Forever and forever when I move.
How dull it is to pause,[23] to make an end,

To rust unburnish'd,[24] not to shine in use!
As tho' to breathe were life, Life piled on life[25]
Were all too little, and of one to me
Little remains[26]: but every hour is saved
From that eternal silence[27], something more[28],
A bringer of new things; and vile it were[29]
For some three suns[30] to store and hoard myself[31],
And this grey spirit[32] yearning in desire
To follow knowledge like a sinking star,
Beyond the utmost bound of human thought.

This is my son, mine own Telemachus,
To whom I leave the sceptre and the isle—
Well-loved of me[33], discerning[34] to fulfil
This labour, by slow prudence to make mild
A rugged people[35], and thro' soft degrees
Subdue them to the useful and the good.
Most blameless is he, centred in the sphere
Of common duties, decent not to fail
In offices[36] of tenderness, and pay
Meet adoration[37] to my household gods,
When I am gone. He works his work, I mine.

There lies the port; the vessel[38] puffs her sail:
There gloom the dark broad seas. My mariners,
Souls that have toil'd, and wrought, and thought with me—
That ever with a frolic welcome took
The thunder and the sunshine, and opposed[39]
Free hearts, free foreheads[40]—you and I are old;
Old age hath yet his honour and his toil; so
Death closes all: but something ere the end,
Some work of noble note, may yet be done,
Not unbecoming men[41] that strove with Gods.
The lights begin to twinkle from the rocks:
The long day wanes: the slow moon climbs: the deep[42]
Moans round with many voices. Come, my friends,
'Tis not too late to seek a newer world,
Push off, and sitting well in order smite
The sounding furrows[43]; for my purpose holds

To sail beyond the sunset, and the baths
Of all the western stars[44], until I die.
It may be that the gulfs will wash us down:
It may be we shall touch the Happy Isles[45],
And see the great Achilles[46], whom we knew.
Tho' much is taken, much abides[47]; and tho'
We are not now that strength which in old days
Moved earth and heaven; that which we are, we are[48];
One equal temper of heroic hearts,[49]
Made weak by time and fate, but strong in will
To strive, to seek, to find, and not to yield.

1. The poem is written in blank verse.
2. **It little profits**: It is of no use. "It"here is an introductory subject.
3. **still hearth**: calm family.
4. **barren crags**: Here refers to the unproductive rocky island of Ithaca.
5. **aged wife**: here refers to Penelope.
6. **mete**: measure.
7. **dole**: deal out.
8. **Unequal laws**: not "unjust", but "not affecting all in the same manner or degree".
9. **a savage race**: referring to the people of Ithaca. Ulysses looks down on his people contemptuously.
10. **That hoard, and sleep, and feed, and know not me**: The people of Ithaca only know how to hide money and live like beasts; they don't know me.
11. **I will drink/Life to the lees**: Here life is compared to a cup of wine; "lees" means "dregs". I will experience life until the last breath.
12. **on shore, and when...**: I have suffered much both on shore and at sea when...
13. **scudding drifts**: showers of rain driven quickly by the wind.
14. **rainy Hyades**: Hyades(毕宿星团)is a group of seven stars in the constellation Tarus, the rising of which was thought to bring storm.
15. **I am become a name**: I have become a name, because of my long absence in my native country.
16. **Myself not least, but honour'd of them all**: I am not the least important, but honoured by them all.
17. **peers**: companions.
18. **ringing plains**: plains ringing with war cry.
19. **I am a part of all that I have met**: I have become a part of all that I have met.

20. **where-thro'**: through which.
21. **that untravell'd world**: that world which I have not visited.
22. **margin**: boundary.
23. **How dull it is to pause**: How dull it is not to take action.
24. **unburnish'd**: not to be polished by rubbing.
25. **Life piled on life/Were all too little**: Even if I should live more than one life, I would still not be satisfied.
26. **and of one to me/Little remains**: and little of the life of mine remains.
27. **that eternal silence**: death.
28. **something more**: if it (every hour) is something more.
29. **vile it were**: It would be vile... to store and hoard myself.
30. **some three suns**: three years or so.
31. **to store and hoard myself**: not to take action; the idea of this line repeats what is said above.
32. **this grey spirit**: Here refers to Ulysses himself.
33. **of me**: by me.
34. **discerning**: understanding.
35. **A rugged people**: again referring to the people of Ithaca.
36. **offices**: duties.
37. **Meet adoration**: Proper worship.
38. **the vessel**: The ship is ready to sail.
39. **and opposed**: The objects are "the thunder and the sunshine".
40. **Free hearts, free foreheads**: Here refers to Ulysses' companions who will sail with him.
41. **Not unbecoming men**: Not unsuitable to men.
42. **the deep**: the sea.
43. **in order smite/The sounding furrows**: in order to beat the roaring waves vigorously.
44. **To sail beyond... the baths/Of all the western stars**: To sail beyond the place where all the western stars take their baths.
45. **the Happy Isles**: The Islands of the Blest are the abodes of just men after their deaths.
46. **Achilles**: the hero of Homer's *Iliad*.
47. **Tho'much is taken, much abides**: Though much is taken from us, much remains.
48. **that which we are, we are**: We are still what we were.
49. **One equal temper of heroic hearts**: Our hearts are tempered by the same heroic spirit.

In Memoriam A. H. H.[1]

In Memoriam is a series of 131 lyrics brought together. It was an elegy, which was begun shortly after the death of his college friend Arthur Henry Hallam in 1833, but it was not published until 1850. In the seventeen years of brooding, it had grown from a personal lament over a particular loss to a philosophical poem on death and immortality, on doubt and faith. None of his poems is so representative of the mood of religious thinking in the middle of the century, and no English elegy deals so broadly and so deeply with the ultimate question of life and death.

Like so many men of his age, Tennyson was very much worried about God and nature and man, about modern science and its effect on belief, about Darwinism and the significance of Darwin's theory of evolution, and about the meaning of life.

7

Dark house[2], by which once more I stand
Here in the long unlovely street,
Doors, where my heart was used to beat
So quickly, waiting for a hand[3],

A hand that can be clasped no more—
Behold me, for I cannot sleep,
And like a guilty thing[4] I creep
At earliest morning to the door.

He is not here; but far away
The noise of life begins again,
And ghastly through the drizzling rain
On the bald street breaks the blank day.[5]

22

The path by which we[6] twain did go,
Which led by tracts[7] that pleased us well,
Through four sweet years[8] arose and fell,

From flower to flower, from snow to snow;

And we with singing cheered the way,
And, crowned with all the season lent,[9]
From April on to April went,
And glad at heart from May to May.

But where the path we walked began
To slant the fifth autumnal slope,[10]
As we descended following Hope,
There sat the Shadow[11] feared of man[12];

Who broke our fair companionship,
And spread his mantle dark and cold,
And wrapped thee formless in the fold,
And dulled the murmur on thy lip,

And bore thee where I could not see
Nor follow, though I walk in haste,
And think that somewhere in the waste
The Shadow sits and waits for me.

130

Thy voice is no the rolling air;
I hear thee where the waters run;
Thou standest in the rising sun,
And in the setting thou art fair.

What art thou then? I cannot guess;
But tho' I seem in star and flower
To feel thee some diffusive power,[13]
I do not therefore love thee less:

My love involves the love before;
My love is vaster passion now;
Tho'mix'd with God and Nature thou,[14]

I seem to love thee more and more.

Far off thou art, but ever nigh[15];
  I have thee still, and I rejoice;
  I prosper, circled with thy voice;
I shall not lose thee tho' I die.

Notes

1. The poem is written basically in iambic tetrameter, with a rhyme scheme abba. A. H. H. is the abbreviation of Arthur Henry Hallam.
2. **Dark house**: the house where Hallam lived.
3. **waiting for a hand**: When his friend was alive, he used to visit him. "A hand" refers to the hand of Hallam.
4. **a guilty thing**: a ghost.
5. **On the bald street breaks the blank day**: The plain, uninteresting day breaks on the empty street. Notice the disharmonious sound of this line.
6. **we**: Here refers to Tennyson and Hallam.
7. **tracts**: tracks.
8. **four sweet years**: Hallam and Tennyson were fellow students at Cambridge for four years.
9. **lent**: lend, given.
10. **the path we walked began/To slant the fifth autumnal slope**: The path we had walked happily for the past four years began to descend in the fifth autumn (Hallam died in early autumn in the fifth year of their friendship).
11. **the Shadow**: Death.
12. **feared of man**: feared by man.
13. **I seem in star and flower /To feel thee some diffusive power**: I seem to feel your power spreading in star and flower.
14. **Tho'mix'd with God and Nature thou**: Though you are now mixed with God and nature.
15. **ever nigh**: ever near.

Robert Browning (1812—1889)

Browning was the son of a clerk in the Bank of England, He did not attend school and was privately educated by his parents. In 1833 he published his first poem "Pauline", which was written under the influence of Shelley. Between 1841 and 1847, he published many other poems and seven plays. He married Elizabeth Barrett in 1846 and lived with her in Italy until her death in 1861. After the death of his wife, he spent the rest of his life in London. In contrast with Tennyson, Browning was bold and unconventional in matter and style. He is noteworthy for the dramatic monologue (戏剧独白诗), i, e. , a poem in which there is one imaginary speaker addressing an imaginary audience. In his dramatic monologues, he penetrates to depth the psychology of his characters and through their own speeches, he analyzes and dissects his characters and reveals the innermost secret of their lives.

Unlike Tennyson who felt melancholy in the process of his spiritual search, Browning was always optimistic. He, like Tennyson, also preached God and Immortality, but he looked boldly at the evils in human beings without losing faith.

The poem "My Last Duchess" is one of the most representative of his dramatic monologues. The speaker is Duke of Ferrara(a city in Italy), who is negotiating with the envoy sent by a count for the marriage of the count's daughter. He is showing the portrait of his late naive and beautiful wife whom he has killed. The nonchalance in his tone fully reveals the arrogance and cruelty of an Italian tyrant in the age of the Renaissance.

My Last Duchess[1]

That's my last Duchess painted on the wall,
Looking as if she were alive. I call
That piece a wonder, now: Frà Pandolf's hands
Worked busily a day, and there she stands.
Will't please you sit and look at her? I said
"Frà Pandolf"[2] by design[3], for never read
Strangers like you that pictured countenance,[4]
The depth and passion of its earnest glance,[5]
But to myself they turned[6] (since none puts by
The curtain I have drawn for you, but I)[7]
And seemed as they would ask me, if they durst[8],
How such a glance came there; so, not the first
Are you to turn and ask thus,[9] Sir, 't was not
Her husband's presence only, called that spot
Of joy[10] into the Duchess' cheek: perhaps
Frà Pandolf chanced to say "Her mantle laps[11]
Over my Lady's wrist too much, "or "Paint
Must never hope to reproduce the faint
Half-flush that dies along her throat:"[12] such stuff
Was courtesy[13], she thought, and cause enough
For calling up that spot of joy. She had
A heart—how shall I say? —too soon made glad,
Too easily impressed: she liked whate'er
She looked on, and her looks went everywhere.[14]
Sir, 't was all one![15] My favour at her breast[16],
The dropping of the daylight in the West,
The bough of cherries some officious[17] fool
Broke in the orchard for her, the white mule
She rode with round the terrace—all and each
Would draw from her alike the approving speech,
Or blush, at least. She thanked men. —good![18] but thanked
Somehow—I know not how—as if she ranked
My gift of a nine-hundred-year-old name

With anybody's gift.[19] Who'd stoop to blame
This sort of trifling?[20] Even had you skill
In speech—(which I have not)—to make your will
Quite clear to such an one[21], and say "Just this
Or that in you disgusts me; here you miss,
Or there exceed the mark"[22]—and if she let
Herself be lessoned so, nor plainly set
Her wits to yours,[23] forsooth, and made excuse[24],
—E'en then would be some stooping[25]; and I choose
Never to stoop. Oh, sir, she smiled, no doubt,
Whene'er I passed her; but who passed without
Much the same smile? This grew; I gave commands[26];
Then all smiles stopped together[27]. There she stands[28]
As if alive. Will't please you rise? We'll meet
The company below, then. I repeat,
The Count your master's known munificence[29]
Is ample warrant that no just pretense
Of mine[30] for dowry will be disallowed[31];
Though his fair daughter's self, as I avowed
At starting[32], is my object. Nay, we'll go
Together down, sir. Notice Neptune[33], though,
Taming a sea-horse, thought a rarity,
Which Claus of Innsbruck[34] cast in bronze for Me!

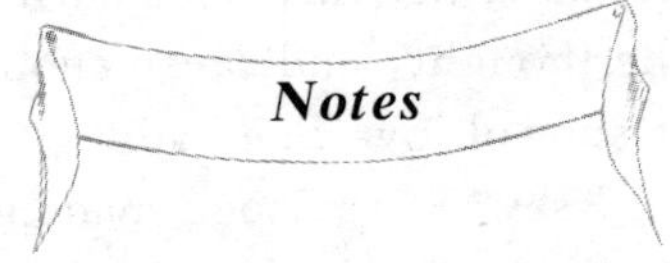

1. The poem is written in heroic couplets.
2. **Frà Pandolf**: Brother Pandolf is a fictitious painter who painted the portrait of the Duchess("fà" is an Italian word for "friar", meaning "brother"). In the age of the Renaissance, many painters and artists were friars.
3. **by design**: purposely.
4. **for never read/Strangers like you that pictured countenance**: for strangers like you never looked at that face in the picture.
5. **The depth and passion of its earnest glance**: the deep feelings showed on her face as she glanced in earnest.
6. **But to myself they turned**: Strangers always turned to me.
7. **since none puts by /The curtain I have drawn for you, but I**: since none but I have the right to draw the curtain behind which the portrait is hung.

8. **if they durst**: if they dare.
9. **not the first/ Are you to turn and ask thus**: You are not the first to turn to me and ask in the way you did.
10. **'t was not /Her husband's presence only, called that spot / Of joy**: It was not only her husband's presence that caused that blush to appear.
11. **laps**: wraps round.
12. **the faint/Half-flush that dies along her throat**: the dim reddish blush that gradually disappears along her throat.
13. **such stuff / Was courtesy**: Such foolish words were acts of politeness and respect.
14. **her looks went everywhere**: She loved to see everything.
15. **'t was all one**: All the following things meant the same to her.
16. **My favour at her breast**: the gift I gave her which she wore at her breast.
17. **officious**: over zealous.
18. **good!**: a parenthetical remark spoken by the Duke.
19. **she ranked/ My gift of a nine-hundred-year-old name/With anybody's gift**: She regarded the title of Duchess which I gave her and which has a history of nine hundred years to be of the same value as the gift given to her by some insignificant person.
20. **Who'd stoop to blame/ This sort of trifling?**: Who would lower himself to find fault with this kind of trivial things? Notice the haughty and hypocritical tone of the Duke.
21. **such an one**: Here refers to the Duchess.
22. **here you miss/ Or there exceed the mark**: In this matter you are not doing enough, in that matter you are doing too much(both "miss" and "exceed" take the object "mark").
23. **set /Her wits to yours**: set her mind against your mind.
24. **and made excuse**: and apologized.
25. **E'en then would be some stooping**: Even then I would be lowering myself.
26. **This grew; I gave commands**: These kind of things grew worse and worse; I gave orders. Notice the Duke does not explicitly say what his commands are, and he speaks these words nonchalantly.
27. **Then all smiles stopped together**: Then she died.
28. **There she stands**: Here refers to the portrait on the wall.
29. **munificence**: bountifulness.
30. **just pretense/ Of mine**: my well-grounded claim.
31. **disallowed**: rejected.
32. **At starting**: At the beginning of our conversation.
33. **Neptune**: Here refers to the statue of Neptune, the Greek sea-god, which the Duke is showing to the envoy as they are going downstairs to meet the people there.
34. **Claus of Innsbruck**: Claus is an imaginary sculptor; Innsbruck is a place in Austria, then the capital of Tyrol.

Meeting at Night[1]

This poem and the next one are a pair of love lyrics, which describe the meeting and parting of two lovers. Nature seems to be sharing in their happiness and reflects the excited mood of the lovers.

1

The gray sea and the long black land;
And the yellow half-moon large and low;
And the startled[2] little waves that leap
In fiery ringlets[3] from their sleep,
As I gain the cove with pushing prow,[4]
And quench its speed i' the slushy sand.[5]

2

Then a mile of warm sea-scented beach;
Three fields to cross till a farm appears;
A tap at the pane, the quick sharp scratch
And blue spurt of a lighted match,[6]
And a voice[7] less loud, through its[8] joys and fears,
Than the two hearts beating each to each!

1. The metrical form of this poem is a combination of iambic and anapaestic tetrameter. The rhyme scheme is abccba.
2. **startled**: Even the little waves cannot fall asleep but leap up with joy.
3. **fiery ringlets**: the water drops are like bright red curls of hair("fiery"also means "passionate").
4. **As I gain the cove with pushing prow**: As I reach the small bay with the front part of the boat pushing ahead.
5. **quench its speed i' the slushy sand**: put an end to its speed in the muddy sand. Notice the sound effect of the "s" sound.
6. **A tap at the pane, the quick sharp scratch / And blue spurt of a lighted match**: The

hurried actions show the eagerness of the lovers to see each other. Notice the effect of the sound and light in this line.

7. **a voice**: Here refers to the voice of the girl in the house.
8. **its**: Here refers to the voice.

Parting at Morning[1]

Round the cape[2] of a sudden came the sea,
And the sun looked over the mountain's rim:
And straight was a path of gold for him[3],
And the need of a world of men for me.[4]

1. The metrical form of this poem is a combination of iambic and anapaestic movement, with five stresses in the first two lines and four stresses in the next two lines. The rhyme scheme is abba.
2. **cape**: a piece of land projecting into a body of water.
3. **him**: Here refers to the sun.
4. **the need of a world of men for me**: Besides love, I must engage myself in the worldly affairs and do business with other men.

Matthew Arnold (1822—1888)

Matthew Arnold was born into a clergyman's family. His father was the headmaster of Rugby School, where Matthew was educated. After Matthew left Oxford, he became an inspector of schools, a post which he held from 1851 to 1883. He was professor of poetry at Oxford from 1857 to 1867.

Arnold was both a poet and a literary critic. He was an important figure in the intellectual field of 19th century England. In his poetry he reflects on the doubt of his age, and the conflict between science and religion.

The bulk of his literary criticism appeared after 1860, among which the most important ones are *Essays in Criticism* (1865 and 1888) and *Culture and Anarchy*(1889). As a literary critic, he attacked the barbarians, a term used to refer to the aristocrats, whom he thought to be essentially crude in soul, notwithstanding their good clothes and superficial graces. He also attacked "philistines", a term referring to the middle classes, whom he regarded as narrow-minded and self-conceited people. He stated that owing to the narrow-mindedness, the rule of the barbarians and the philistines, and the rise of individualism and democracy, England was in a state of anarchy. In his opinion, poetry should be "a criticism of life" and was destined to take the place of religion as man's principal moral guide. He believed that culture should be the antidote to anarchy and that through culture and liberal education modern man could avoid anarchy without abandoning liberty to some coercive external authority.

The chosen poem "Dover Beach" represents Arnold's view on the spiritual unrest of his time. On a moonlit night he enjoys a moment of calmness on the Dover Beach with his wife by his side. But the flinging in and flinging out of the pebbles makes him think of the rise and fall of humans' faith.

Dover Beach[1]

The sea is calm tonight.
The tide is full, the moon lies fair
Upon the straits[2]—on the French coast the light
Gleams and is gone; the cliffs[3] of England stand,
Glimmering and vast, out in the tranquil bay.
Come to the window, sweet is the night air!
Only, from the long line of spray
Where the sea meets the moon-blanched[4] land,
Listen! you hear the grating roar[5]
Of pebbles which the waves draw back, and fling,
At their return, up the high strand[6],
Begin, and cease, and then again begin,
With tremulous cadence slow, and bring
The eternal note of sadness in.[7]

Sophocles[8] long ago
Heard it on the Aegean,[9] and it brought
Into his mind the turbid[10] ebb and flow
Of human misery; we
Find also in the sound a thought,
Hearing it by this distant northern sea.

The Sea of Faith
Was once, too, at the full, and round earth's shore
Lay like the folds of a bright girdle furled.[11]
But now I only hear
Its melancholy, long, withdrawing roar,
Retreating, to the breath
Of the night wind, down the vast edges drear
And naked shingles[12] of the world.

Ah, love, let us be true
To one another! for the world, which seems

To lie before us like a land of dreams,
So various[13], so beautiful, so new,
Hath really neither joy, nor love, nor light,
Nor certitude, nor peace, nor help for pain;
And we are here as on a darkling plain
Swept with confused alarms of struggle and flight,
Where ignorant armies[14] clash by night.

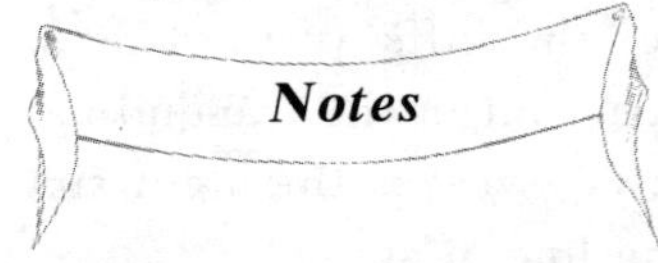

1. The poem is written in irregular metrical form and rhyme scheme.
2. **the straits**: Here refers to the Strait of Dover.
3. **cliffs**: shores.
4. **moon-blanched**: becomes white in the moon light.
5. **grating roar**: The rubbing pebbles give forth a rumbling sound.
6. **strand**: shore.
7. **bring/ The eternal note of sadness in**: The normal order of the sentence is "bring in the eternal note of sadness".
8. **Sophocles**: (ca. 496—405 B. C.) a Greek dramatist and poet, author of *Oedipus* and *Antigone*.
9. **Aegean**: the Aegean Sea, the name used by the Greeks and Romans for that part of the Mediterranean Sea between Asia Minor and Greece.
10. **turbid**: confused.
11. **like the folds of a bright girdle furled**: At high tide the water encircles the shore like the folds of bright clothing which have been compressed.
12. **shingles**: beaches covered with pebbles.
13. **various**: different.
14. **ignorant armies**: Some scholars think that it might refer to the revolutions of 1848.

Culture and Anarchy

CHAPTER IV

Hebraism and Hellenism

This fundamental ground is our preference of doing to thinking.

Now this preference is a main element in our nature, and as we study it we find ourselves opening up a number of large questions on every side.

Let me go back for a moment to Bishop Wilson,[1] who says:—'First, never go against the best light you have; secondly, take care that your light be not darkness.' We show, as a nation, laudable energy and persistence in walking according to the best light we have, but are not quite careful enough, perhaps, to see that our light be not darkness. This is only another version of the old story that energy is our strong point and favourable characteristic, rather than intelligence. But we may give to this idea a more general form still, in which it will have a yet larger range of application. We may regard this energy driving at practice, this paramount sense of the obligation of duty, self-control, and work, this earnestness in going manfully with the best light we have, as one force. And we may regard the intelligence driving at those ideas which are, after all, the basis of right practice, the ardent sense for all the new and changing combinations of them which man's development brings with it, the indomitable impulse to know and adjust them perfectly, as another force. And these two forces we may regard as in some sense rivals,—rivals not by the necessity of their own nature, but as exhibited in man and his history,—and rivals dividing the empire of the world between them. And to give these forces names from the two races of men who have supplied the most signal and splendid manifestations of them, we may call them respectively the forces of Hebraism and Hellenism. Hebraism and Hellenism,—between these two points of influence moves our world. At one time it feels more powerfully the attraction of one of them, at another time of the other; and it ought to be, though it never is, evenly and happily balanced between them.

The final aim of both Hellenism and Hebraism, as of all great spiritual disciplines, is no doubt the same: man's perfection or salvation. The very language which they both of them use in schooling us to reach this aim is often identical. Even when their language indicates by variation,—sometimes a broad variation, often a but slight and subtle variation,—the different courses of thought which are uppermost in each discipline, even then the unity of the final end and aim is still apparent. To employ the actual words of that discipline with which we ourselves are all of us most familiar, and the words of which, therefore, come most home to us, that final end and aim is 'that we might be partakers of the divine nature.' These are the words of a Hebrew apostle, but of Hellenism and Hebraism alike this is, I say, the aim. When the two are confronted, as they very often are confronted, it is nearly always with what I may call a rhetorical purpose; the speaker's whole design is to exalt and enthrone one of the two, and he uses the other only as a foil and to enable him the better to give effect to his purpose. Obviously, with us, it is usually Hellenism which is thus reduced to minister to the triumph of Hebraism. There is a sermon on Greece and the Greek spirit by a man never to be mentioned without interest and respect, Frederick Robertson,[2] in which this rhetorical use of Greece and the Greek spirit, and the inadequate exhibition of them necessarily consequent upon this, is almost ludicrous, and would be censurable if it were not to be explained by the exigencies of a sermon. On the other hand, Heinrich Heine,[3] and other writers of his sort, give us the spectacle of the tables completely turned, and of Hebraism brought in just as a foil and contrast to Hellenism, and to make the superiority of Hellenism more manifest. In both these cases there is injustice and misrepresentation. The aim and end of both Hebraism and Hellenism is, as I have said, one and the same, and this aim and end is august and admirable.

Still, they pursue this aim by very different courses. The uppermost idea with Hellenism is to see things as they really are; the uppermost idea with Hebraism is conduct and obedience. Nothing can do away with this ineffaceable difference. The Greek quarrel with the body and its desires is, that they hinder right thinking, the Hebrew quarrel with them is, that they hinder right acting. 'He that keepeth the law, happy is he;' 'Blessed is the man that feareth the Eternal, that delighteth greatly in his commandments;'—that is the Hebrew notion of felicity; and, pursued with passion and tenacity, this notion would not let the Hebrew rest till, as is well known, he had at last got out of the law a network of prescriptions to enwrap his whole life, to govern every moment of it, every impulse, every action. The Greek notion of felicity, on the other hand, is perfectly conveyed in these words of a great French moralist: '*C'est le bonheur des hommes*,'—when? when they abhor that which is evil? —no; when they exercise themselves in the law of the Lord day and night? —no; when they die daily? —no;

when they walk about the New Jerusalem with palms in their hands? — no; but when they think aright, when their thought hits: '*quand its pensent juste.*'[4] At the bottom of both the Greek and the Hebrew notion is the desire, native in man, for reason and the will of God, the feeling after the universal order,—in a word, the love of God. But, while Hebraism seizes upon certain plain, capital intimations of the universal order, and rivets itself, one may say, with unequalled grandeur of earnestness and intensity on the study and observance of them, the bent of Hellenism is to follow, with flexible activity, the whole play of the universal order, to be apprehensive of missing any part of it, of sacrificing one part to another, to slip away from resting in this or that intimation of it, however capital. An unclouded clearness of mind, an unimpeded play of thought, is what this bent drives at. The governing idea of Hellenism is *spontaneity of consciousness*; that of Hebraism, *strictness of conscience*.

Christianity changed nothing in this essential bent of Hebraism to set doing above knowing. Self-conquest, self-devotion, the following not our own individual will, but the will of God, *obedience*, is the fundamental idea of this form, also, of the discipline to which we have attached the general name of Hebraism. Only, as the old law and the network of prescriptions with which it enveloped human life were evidently a motive-power not driving and searching enough to produce the result aimed at,—patient continuance in well doing, self-conquest,—Christianity substituted for them boundless devotion to that inspiring and affecting pattern of self-conquest offered by Jesus Christ; and by the new motive-power, of which the essence was this, though the love and admiration of Christian churches have for centuries been employed in varying, amplifying, and adorning the plain description of it, Christianity, as St. Paul[5] truly says, 'establishes the law,' and in the strength of the ampler power which she has thus supplied to fulfil it, has accomplished the miracles, which we all see, of her history.

So long as we do not forget that both Hellenism and Hebraism are profound and admirable manifestations of man's life, tendencies, and powers, and that both of them aim at a like final result, we can hardly insist too strongly on the divergence of line and of operation with which they proceed. It is a divergence so great that it most truly, as the prophet Zechariah[6] says, 'has raised up thy sons, O Zion,[7] against thy sons, O Greece!' The difference whether it is by doing or by knowing that we set most store, and the practical consequences which follow from this difference, leave their mark on all the history of our race and of its development. Language may be abundantly quoted from both Hellenism and Hebraism to make it seem that one follows the same current as the other towards the same goal. They are, truly, borne towards the same goal; but the currents which bear them are infinitely different. It is true, Solomon[8] will praise knowing: 'Understanding is a well-spring of life unto him that hath it.' And in the New Testament, again, Jesus Christ is a 'light,' and 'truth makes us free.' It is true, Aristotle will undervalue knowing: 'In what concerns virtue,' says he, 'three things are necessary—knowledge, deliberate will, and perseverance; but, whereas the two last are all-important, the first is a matter of little importance.' It is true that with the same impatience with which St. James[9] enjoins a man to be not a forgetful hearer, but a *doer of the work*, Epictetus[10] exhorts us to *do* what we have demonstrated to ourselves we ought to do; or he taunts us with futility, for being armed at all points to prove that lying is wrong, yet all the time continuing to lie. It is true, Plato, in words which are almost the words of the New Testament or the Imitation, calls life a learning to die. But underneath the superficial agreement the fundamental divergence still subsists. The understanding of Solomon is 'the walking in the way of the commandments;' this is 'the way of peace,' and it is of this that blessedness comes. In the New Testament, the truth which gives us the peace of God and makes us free, is the love of Christ constraining us to crucify, as he did, and with a like purpose of moral regeneration, the flesh with its affections and lusts, and thus establishing, as we have seen, the law. The moral virtues, on the other hand, are with Aristotle but the porch and access to the intellectual, and with these last is blessedness. That partaking of the divine life, which both Hellenism and Hebraism, as we have said, fix as their crowning aim, Plato expressly denies to the man of practical virtue merely, of self-conquest with any other motive than that of perfect intellectual vision. He reserves it for the lover of pure knowledge, of seeing things as they really are,—the φιλομαθης. (philomathes)

Both Hellenism and Hebraism arise out of the wants of human nature, and address themselves to satisfying those wants. But their methods are so different, they lay stress on such different points, and call into being by their respective disciplines such different activities, that the face which human nature presents when it passes from the hands of one of them to those of the other, is no longer the same. To get rid of one's ignorance, to see things as they are, and by seeing them as they are to see them in their beauty, is the simple and attractive ideal which Hellenism holds out before human nature; and from the simplicity and charm of this ideal, Hellenism, and human life in the hands of Hellenism, is invested with a kind of aërial ease, clearness, and radiancy; they are full of what we call sweetness and light. Difficulties are kept out of view, and the beauty and rationalness of the ideal have all our thoughts. 'The best man is he who most tries to perfect himself, and the happiest man is he who most feels that he is perfecting himself,'—this account of the matter by Socrates, the true Socrates of the *Memorabilia*,[11] has something so simple, spontaneous, and unsophisticated about it, that it seems to fill us with clearness and hope when we hear it. But there is a saying which I have heard attributed to Mr. Carlyle[12] about Socrates,—a very happy saying, whether it is really Mr. Carlyle's or not,—which excellently marks the essential point in which Hebraism differs from Hellenism. 'Socrates,' this saying goes, 'is terribly *at ease in Zion*.' Hebraism,—and here is the source of its wonderful strength,—has always been severely pre-occupied with an awful sense of the impossibility of being at ease in Zion; of the difficulties which oppose themselves to man's pursuit or attainment of that perfection of which Socrates talks so hopefully, and, as from this point of view one might almost say, so glibly. It is all very well to talk of getting rid of one's ignorance, of seeing things in their reality, seeing them in their beauty; but how is this to be done when there is something which thwarts and spoils all our efforts?

This something is sin; and the space which sin fills in Hebraism, as compared with Hellenism, is indeed prodigious. This obstacle to perfection fills the whole scene, and perfection appears remote and rising away from earth, in the background. Under the name of sin, the difficulties of knowing oneself and conquering oneself which impede man's passage to perfection, become, for Hebraism, a positive, active entity hostile to man, a mysterious power which I heard Dr. Pusey[13] the other day, in one of his impressive sermons, compare to a hideous hunchback seated on our shoulders, and which it is the main business of our lives to hate and oppose. The discipline of the Old Testament may be summed up as a discipline teaching us to abhor and flee from sin; the discipline of the New Testament, as a discipline teaching us to die to it. As Hellenism speaks of thinking clearly, seeing things in their essence and beauty, as a grand and precious feat for man to achieve, so Hebraism speaks of becoming conscious of sin, of awakening to a sense of sin, as a feat of this kind. It is obvious to what wide divergence these differing tendencies, actively followed, must lead. As one passes and repasses from Hellenism to Hebraism, from Plato to St. Paul, one feels inclined to rub one's eyes and ask oneself whether man is indeed a gentle and simple being, showing the traces of a noble and divine nature; or an unhappy chained captive, labouring with groanings that cannot be uttered to free himself from the body of this death.

Apparently it was the Hellenic conception of human nature which was unsound, for the world could not live by it. Absolutely to call it unsound, however, is to fall into the common error of its Hebraising enemies; but it was unsound at that particular moment of man's development, it was premature. The indispensable basis of conduct and self-control, the platform upon which alone the perfection aimed at by Greece can come into bloom, was not to be reached by our race so easily; centuries of probation and discipline were needed to bring us to it. Therefore the bright promise of Hellenism faded, and Hebraism ruled the world. Then was seen that astonishing spectacle, so well marked by the often quoted words of the prophet Zechariah, when men of all languages and nations took hold of the skirt of him that was a Jew, saying:—'*We will go with you, for we have heard that God is with you.*' And the Hebraism which thus received and ruled a world all gone out of the way and altogether become unprofitable, was, and could not but be, the later, the more spiritual, the more attractive development of Hebraism. It was Christianity; that is to say, Hebraism aiming at self-conquest and rescue from the thrall of vile affections, not by obedience to the letter of a law, but by conformity to the image of a self-sacrificing example. To a world stricken with moral enervation Christianity offered its spectacle of an inspired self-sacrifice; to men who refused themselves nothing, it showed one who refused himself everything;—'*my Saviour banished joy*!' says George Herbert.[14]

When the *alma Venus*, the life-giving and joy-giving power of nature, so fondly cherished by the Pagan world, could not save her followers from self-dissatisfaction and ennui, the severe words of the apostle came bracingly and refreshingly: 'Let no man deceive you with vain words, for because of these things cometh the wrath of God upon the children of disobedience.' Through age after age and generation after generation, our race, or all that part of our race which was most living and progressive, was *baptized into a death*; and endeavoured, by suffering in the flesh, to cease from sin. Of this endeavour, the animating labours and afflictions of early Christianity, the touching asceticism of mediaeval Christianity, are the great historical manifestations. Literary monuments of it, each in its own way incomparable, remain in the Epistles of St. Paul, in St. Augustine's[15] Confessions, and in the two original and simplest books of the Imitation.

Of two disciplines laying their main stress, the one, on clear intelligence, the other, on firm obedience; the one, on comprehensively knowing the grounds of one's duty, the other, on diligently practicing it; the one, on taking all possible care (to use Bishop Wilson's words again) that the light we have be not darkness, the other, that according to the best light we have we diligently walk,—the priority naturally belongs to that discipline which braces all man's moral powers, and founds for him an indispensable basis of character. And, therefore, it is justly said of the Jewish people, who were charged with setting powerfully forth that side of the divine order to which the words *conscience* and *self-conquest* point, that they were 'entrusted with the oracles of God;' as it is justly said of Christianity, which followed Judaism and which set forth this side with a much deeper effectiveness and a much wider influence, that the wisdom of the old Pagan world was foolishness compared to it. No words of devotion and admiration can be too strong to render thanks to these beneficent forces which have so borne forward humanity in its appointed work of coming to the knowledge and possession of itself; above all, in those great moments when their action was the wholesomest and the most necessary.

But the evolution of these forces, separately and in themselves, is not the whole evolution of humanity,—their single history is not the whole history of man; whereas their admirers are always apt to make it stand for the whole history. Hebraism and Hellenism are, neither of them, the *law* of human development, as their admirers are prone to make them; they are, each of them, contributions to human development,—august contributions, invaluable contributions; and each showing itself to us more august, more invaluable, more preponderant over the other, according to the moment in which we take them, and the relation in which we stand to them. The nations of our modern world, children of that immense and salutary movement which broke up the Pagan world, inevitably stand to Hellenism in a relation which dwarfs it, and to Hebraism in a relation which magnifies it. They are inevitably prone to take Hebraism as the law of human development, and not as simply a contribution to it, however precious. And yet the lesson must perforce be learned, that the human spirit is wider than the most priceless of the forces which bear it onward, and that to the whole development of man Hebraism itself is, like Hellenism, but a contribution.

Perhaps we may help ourselves to see this clearer by an illustration drawn from the treatment of a single great idea which has profoundly engaged the human spirit, and has given it eminent opportunities for showing its nobleness and energy. It surely must be perceived that the idea of immortality, as this idea rises in its generality before the human spirit, is something grander, truer, and more satisfying, than it is in the particular forms by which St. Paul, in the famous fifteenth chapter of the Epistle to the Corinthians, and Plato, in the *Phaedo*, endeavour to develop and establish it. Surely we cannot but feel, that the argumentation with which the Hebrew apostle goes about to expound this great idea is, after all, confused and inconclusive; and that the reasoning, drawn from analogies of likeness and equality, which is employed upon it by the Greek philosopher, is over-subtle and sterile. Above and beyond the inadequate solutions which Hebraism and Hellenism here attempt, extends the immense and august problem itself, and the human spirit which gave birth to it. And this single illustration may suggest to us how the same thing happens in other cases also.

But meanwhile, by alternations of Hebraism and Hellenism, of a man's intellectual and moral impulses, of the effort to see things as they really are, and the effort to win peace by self-conquest, the human spirit proceeds; and each of these two forces has its appointed hours of culmination and seasons of rule. As the great movement of Christianity was a triumph of Hebraism and man's moral impulses, so the great movement which goes by the name of the Renascence[16] was an uprising and re-instatement of man's intellectual impulses and of Hellenism. We in England, the devoted children of Protestantism, chiefly know the Renascence by its subordinate and secondary side of the Reformation[17]. The Reformation has been often called a Hebraising revival, a return to the ardour and sincereness of primitive Christianity. No one, however, can study the development of Protestantism and of Protestant churches without feeling that into the Reformation too,—Hebraising child of the Renascence and offspring of its fervour, rather than its intelligence, as it undoubtedly was,—the subtle Hellenic leaven of the Renascence found its way, and that the exact respective parts, in the Reformation, of Hebraism and of Hellenism, are not easy to separate. But what we may with truth say is, that all which Protestantism was to itself clearly conscious of, all which it succeeded in clearly setting forth in words, had the characters of Hebraism rather than of Hellenism. The Reformation was strong, in that it was an earnest return to the Bible and to doing from the heart the will of God as there written. It was weak, in that it never consciously grasped or applied the central idea of the Renascence,—the Hellenic idea of pursuing, in all lines of activity, the law and science, to use Plato's words, of things as they really are. Whatever direct superiority, therefore, Protestantism had over Catholicism was a moral superiority, a superiority arising out of its greater sincerity and earnestness,—at the moment of its apparition at any rate,—in dealing with the heart and conscience. Its pretensions to an intellectual superiority are in general quite illusory. For Hellenism, for the thinking side in man as distinguished from the acting side, the attitude of mind of Protestantism towards the Bible in no respect differs from the attitude of mind of Catholicism towards the Church. The mental habit of him who imagines that Balaam's[18] ass spoke, in no respect differs from the mental habit of him who imagines that a Madonna[19] of wood or stone winked; and the one, who says that God's Church makes him believe what he believes, and the other, who says that God's Word makes him believe what he believes, are for the philosopher perfectly alike in not really and truly knowing, when they say *God's Church* and *God's Word*, what it is they say, or whereof they affirm.

In the sixteenth century, therefore, Hellenism re-entered the world, and again stood in presence of Hebraism,—a Hebraism renewed and purged. Now, it has not been enough observed, how, in the seventeenth century, a fate befell Hellenism in some respects analogous to that which befell it at the commencement of our era. The Renascence, that great re-awakening of Hellenism, that irresistible return of humanity to nature and to seeing things as they are, which in art, in literature, and in physics, produced such splendid fruits, had, like the anterior Hellenism of the Pagan world, a side of moral weakness, and of relaxation or insensibility of the moral fibre, which in Italy showed itself with the most startling plainness, but which in France, England, and other countries was very apparent too. Again this loss of spiritual balance, this exclusive preponderance given to man's perceiving and knowing side, this unnatural defect of his feeling and acting side, provoked a reaction. Let us trace that reaction where it most nearly concerns us.

Science has now made visible to everybody the great and pregnant elements of difference which lie in race, and in how signal a manner they make the genius and history of an Indo-European people vary from those of a Semitic people. Hellenism is of Indo-European growth, Hebraism is of Semitic growth; and we English, a nation of Indo-European stock, seem to belong naturally to the movement of Hellenism. But nothing more strongly marks the essential unity of man, than the affinities we can perceive, in this point or that, between members of one family of peoples and members of another. And no affinity of this kind is more strongly marked than that likeness in the strength and prominence of the moral fibre, which, notwithstanding immense elements of difference, knits in some special sort the genius and history of us English, and our American descendants across the Atlantic, to the genius and history of the Hebrew people. Puritanism, which has been so great a power in the English nation, and in the strongest part of the English nation, was originally the reaction in the seventeenth century of the conscience and moral sense of our race, against the moral indifference and lax rule of conduct which in the sixteenth century came in with the Renascence. It was a reaction of Hebraism against Hellenism; and it powerfully manifested itself, as was natural, in a people with much of what we call a Hebraising turn, with a signal affinity for the bent which was the master-bent of Hebrew life. Eminently Indo-European by its *humour*, by the power it shows, through this gift, of imaginatively acknowledging the multiform aspects of the problem of life, and of thus getting itself unfixed from its own over-certainty, of smiling at its own over-tenacity, our race has yet (and a great part of its strength lies here), in matters of practical life and moral conduct, a strong share of the assuredness, the tenacity, the intensity of the Hebrews. This turn manifested itself in Puritanism, and has had a great part in shaping our history for the last two hundred years. Undoubtedly it checked and changed amongst us that movement of the Renascence which we see producing in the reign of Elizabeth such wonderful fruits. Undoubtedly it stopped the prominent rule and direct development of that order of ideas which we call by the name of Hellenism, and gave the first rank to a different order of ideas. Apparently, too, as we said of the former defeat of Hellenism, if Hellenism was defeated, this shows that Hellenism was imperfect, and that its ascendancy at that moment would not have been for the world's good.

Yet there is a very important difference between the defeat inflicted on Hellenism by Christianity eighteen hundred years ago, and the check given to the Renascence by Puritanism. The greatness of the difference is well measured by the difference in force, beauty, significance and usefulness, between primitive Christianity and Protestantism. Eighteen hundred years ago it was altogether the hour of Hebraism. Primitive Christianity was legitimately and truly the ascendent force in the world at that time, and the way of mankind's progress lay through its full development. Another hour in man's development began in the fifteenth century, and the main road of his progress then lay for a time through Hellenism. Puritanism was no longer the central current of the world's progress, it was a side stream crossing the central current and checking it. The cross and the check may have been necessary and salutary, but that does not do away with the essential difference between the main stream of man's advance and a cross or side stream. For more than two hundred years the main stream of man's advance has moved towards knowing himself and the world, seeing things as they are, spontaneity of consciousness; the main impulse of a great part, and that the strongest part, of our nation has been towards strictness of conscience.

They have made the secondary the principal at the wrong moment, and the principal they have at the wrong moment treated as secondary. This contravention of the natural order has produced, as such contravention always must produce, a certain confusion and false movement, of which we are now beginning to feel, in almost every direction, the inconvenience. In all directions our habitual causes of action seem to be losing efficaciousness, credit, and control, both with others and even with ourselves. Everywhere we see the beginnings of confusion, and we want a clue to some sound order and authority. This we can only get by going back upon the actual instincts and forces which rule our life, seeing them as they really are, connecting them with other instincts and forces, and enlarging our whole view and rule of life.

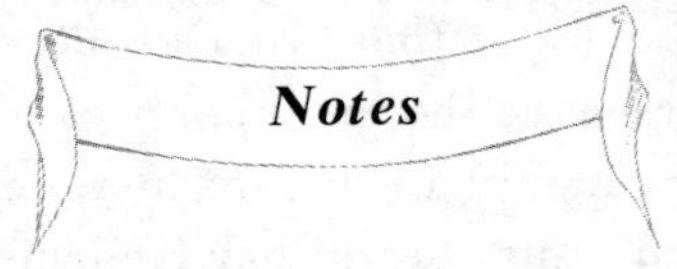

1. Bishop Wilson, i. e. , Thomas Wilson (20 December 1663—7 March 1755) , who was Anglican Bishop of Sodor and Man (the Isle of Man) between 1697 and 1755.
2. Frederick William Robertson (3 February 1816 — 15 August 1853), known as Robertson of Brighton, was an English theologian and preacher.
3. Heinrich Heine's complete name was Christian Johann Heinrich Heine (13 December 1797—17 February 1856) . He was a German poet, journalist, essayist, and literary critic.
4. Here Arnold is quoting from Sainte-Beuve, *Causeries du lundi* (Monday Conversations) (1862).
5. **St. Paul**: Paul the Apostle (c. 5—c. 67), originally known as Saul of Tarsus. He was an apostle (though not one of the Twelve Apostles) who taught the gospel of Christ to the first-century world. He is generally considered one of the most important figures of the Apostolic Age.
6. the prophet Zechariah was a person in the Hebrew Bible and traditionally considered the author of the Book of Zechariah of the Bible.
7. Zion (Hebrew: Siyyôn), also transliterated Sion, Syon, Tzion or Tsion, is a place name often used as a synonym for the Temple Mount in Jerusalem. It is the most holy place in the world for Jews, seen as the connection between God and humanity.
8. Solomon was, according to the Bible, a king of Israel and the son of David. The conventional dates of Solomon's reign are about 970 to 931 BC. He is described as the third king of the United Monarchy, which would break apart into the northern Kingdom of Israel and the southern Kingdom of Judah shortly after his death.

9. **St. James**: also called James the Just, brother of Jesus, considered the author of the Epistle of James in the New Testament, and the first bishop of Jerusalem.
10. Epictetus (c. 55—135 A. D.) was a Greek-speaking Stoic philosopher.
11. *Memorabilia* is a collection of Socratic dialogues by Xenophon, a student of Socrates. It is the lengthiest and most famous of Xenophon's Socratic writings.
12. **Mr. Carlyle**: Thomas Carlyle (4 December 1795—5 February 1881) was a Scottish philosopher, satirical writer, essayist, historian and teacher.
13. **Dr. Pusey**: Edward Bouverie Pusey (22 August 1800—16 September 1882). He was one of the leaders of the Oxford Movement, for more than fifty years Regius Professor of Hebrew at Christ Church College, Oxford.
14. George Herbert (3 April 1593—1 March 1633) was a Welsh-born English poet, orator and Anglican priest.
15. Augustine of Hippo (13 November 354 — 28 August 430), also known as Saint Augustine or Saint Austin, was an early Christian theologian and philosopher whose writings, among which *Confessions* was the best known, influenced the development of Western Christianity and Western philosophy.
16. **Renascence**: Renaissance.
17. "The Reformation" should be properly referred to as the Protestant Reformation. It was the schism within Western Christianity initiated by Martin Luther, John Calvin, Huldrych Zwingli and other early Protestant Reformers.
18. Balaam is a diviner in the Jewish sacred scripts.
19. A Madonna is a representation of Mary, either alone or with her child Jesus. Such an image is a central icon for both the Catholic and Orthodox churches. The word is from Italian *ma donna*, meaning "my lady". No image permeates Christian art as much as the image of the Madonna and child.

4. Thomas Carlyle (1795—1881)

Thomas Carlyle was an essayist, historian, and philosopher. He was one of the most influential man of letters in the mid-Victorian period. He was born into a peasant family in a little village in Scotland. At the age of 15 he entered Edinburgh University and left in 1813 without taking a degree. Against the wish of his parents who wanted their son to be a clergyman, Carlyle first taught mathematics in a school and then he studied law. In 1826 he married Jane Welsh, a Scottish lady of strong character, whose literary talent equaled that of Carlyle. The couple settled down on a farm which was property of Mrs Carlyle. They lived there for six years, and there Carlyle wrote his essays on German literature and completed *Sartor Resartus* (1833—1834). In 1834 the Carlyles moved to London and Carlyle devoted his time to writing. He made his fame by the publication of *History of the French Revolution* in 1837, which was followed by *German Literature* (1837), *Periods of European Culture* (1838), *Heroes and Hero Worship* (1841), *Past and Present* (1843) and other works. His reputation reached its height in 1866, when he was elected Lord Rector of Edinburgh University. While he was in Edinburgh to deliver his inaugural address, news reached him that his wife had died suddenly in London. For the next fifteen years, he lived in loneliness. His *Reminiscences*, published in 1881, was pervaded by his sorrow for his wife, who had shared his toil but not his triumph.

Thomas Carlyle denounces the privileged classes of England—the aristocrats and the new industrial rich. He attacks the aristocrats for their uselessness; they are idle and do not govern or govern only to protect their own interests. He also attacks the industrial bourgeoisie for their worship of money, that is, they believe that the chief business of their life is to buy cheap and sell dear. He calls for some spiritual force that will revitalize the spirit of man, which has been corrupted and benumbed by mercantilism. The spirit he desires is that of renunciation, duty, work, and reverence. And he wants some heroes who would reorganize society and govern it in an efficient way.

Past and Present gives an evocative account of Samson, an abbot of St. Edmundsbury, who brought order to a decaying monastery, as the end of the twelfth century. A contrast is made between the feudal society of the Middle Ages and modern society. In the following selection, Carlyle extols labour and calls for a Force to revitalize decadent capitalist society and a hero to lead the mass forward.

Past and Present

Book III

Chapter XI Labour

For there is a perennial nobleness, and even sacredness, in Work.[1] Were he never so benighted, forgetful of his high calling,[2] there is always hope in a man that actually and earnestly works: in Idleness alone is there perpetual despair. Work, never so Mammonish[3], mean, is in communication with Nature; the real desire to get Work done will itself lead one more and more to truth, to Nature's appointments and regulations, which are truth.

The latest Gospel in this world[4] is. Know thy work and do it. "Know thyself:" long enough has that poor "self" of thine tormented thee; thou wilt never get to "know" it, I believe! Think it not thy business, this of knowing thyself; thou art an unknowable individual: know what thou canst work at; and work at it, like a Hercules[5]. That will be thy better plan.

It has been written, "an endless significance lies in Work;" a man perfects himself by working. Foul jungles are cleared away, fair seedfields rise instead, and stately cities; and withal[6] the man himself first ceases to be a jungle and foul unwholesome desert thereby. Consider how, even in the meanest sorts of Labour, the whole soul of a man is composed into[7] a kind of real harmony, the instant he sets himself to work! Doubt, Desire, Sorrow, Remorse, Indignation, Despair itself, all these like helldogs lie beleaguering[8] the soul of the poor day-worker, as of every man: but he bends himself with free valour against his task, and all these are stilled, all these shrink murmuring far off into their caves. The man is now a man. The blessed glow of Labour in him, is it not as purifying fire, wherein[9] all poison is burnt up, and of sour smoke[10] itself there is made bright blessed flame!

Destiny, on the whole, has no other way of cultivating us. A formless Chaos[11], once set it revolving, grows round and ever rounder; ranges itself[12], by mere force of gravity, into strata, spherical courses; is no longer a Chaos, but a round-compacted World. What would become of the Earth, did she cease to revolve? In the poor old Earth, so long as she revolves, all inequalities, irregularities disperse themselves; all irregularities are incessantly becoming regular. Hast thou looked on the Potter's[13] wheel.[14]—one of the venerablest objects; old as the Prophet Ezechiel[15] and far older? Rude lumps of clay, how they spin themselves up, by mere quick whirling, into beautiful circular dishes. And fancy the most assiduous Potter, but without his wheel; reduced to[16] make dishes, or rather amorphous[17] botches,[18] by mere kneading and baking! Even Such a Potter were Destiny, with a human Soul that would rest and lie at ease, that would not work and spin! Of an idle unrevolving man[19] the kindest Destiny, like the most assiduous Potter without wheel, can bake and knead nothing other than a botch; let her spend on him what expensive colouring, what gilding and enamelling she will, he is but a botch. Not a dish; no, a bulging, kneaded, crooked, shambling[20], squint-cornered[21], amorphous botch, —a mere enamelled vessel of dishonour![22] Let the idle think of this.

Blessed is he who has found his work; let him ask no other blessedness. He has a work, a life-purpose; he has found it, and will follow it! How, as a free-flowing channel, dug and torn by noble force through the sour mud-swamp of one's existence, like an everdeepening river there, it runs and flows; —draining-off the sour festering[23] water, gradually from the root of the remotest grass-blade; making, instead of pestilential swamp, a green fruitful meadow with its clear-flowing stream. How blessed for the meadow itself, let the stream and its value be great or small! Labour is Life: from the inmost heart of the Worker rises his God-given Force, the sacred celestial Life-essence breathed into him by Almighty God; from his inmost heart awakens him to all nobleness, —to all knowledge, "selfknowledge" and such else, so soon as Work fitly begins. Knowledge? The knowledge that will hold good in working, cleave thou to that. for Nature herself accredits[24] that, says Yea to that. Properly thou hast no other knowledge but what thou hast got by working: the rest is yet all a hypothesis[25] of knowledge; a thing to be argued of in schools, a thing floating in the clouds, in endless logic-vortices[26], till we try it and fix it. "Doubt, of whatever kind, can be ended by Action alone."

And again, hast thou valued Patience, Courage, Perseverance, Openness to light; readiness to own thyself mistaken, to do better next time? All these, all virtues, in wrestling with the dim brute Powers of Fact, in ordering of thy fellows in such wrestle, there and elsewhere not at all, thou wilt continually learn. Set down a brave Sir Christopher[27] in the middle of black ruined Stone-heaps, of foolish unarchitectural Bishops, redtape[28] Officials, idle Nell-Gwyn Defenders of the Faith[29]; and see whether he will ever raise a Paul's Cathedral out of all that, yea or no! Rough, rude, contradictory are all things and persons, from the mutinous masons and Irish hodmen[30], up to the idle Nell-Gwyn Defenders, to blustering redtape Officials, foolish unarchitectural Bishops. All these things and persons are there not for Christopher's sake and his Cathedral's; they are there for their own sake mainly! Christopher will have to conquer and constrain[31] all these, —if he be able. All these are against him. Equitable[32] Nature herself, who carries her mathematics and architectonics[33] not on the face of her, but deep in the hidden heart of her, —Nature herself is but partially for him; will be wholly against him, if he constrain her not! His very money, where is it to come from? The pious munificence of England[34] lies far-scattered, distant, unable to speak, and say, "I am here;"—must be spoken to before it can speak. Pious munificence, and all help, is so silent, invisible like the gods; impediment, contradictions manifold are so loud and near! O brave Sir Christopher, trust thou in those notwithstanding, and front all these; understand all these; by valiant patience, noble effort, insight, by man's—strength, vanquish and compel all these, —and, on the whole, strike down victoriously the last topstone[35] of that Paul's Edifice; thy monument for certain centuries, the stamp "Great Man" impressed very legibly on Portland-stone[36] there! —

Yes, all manner of help, and pious response from Men or Nature, is always what we call silent; cannot speak or come to light, till it be seen, till it be spoken to. Every noble work is at first "impossible". In very truth, for every noble work the possibilities will lie diffused through Immensity; inarticulate, undiscoverable except to faith. Like Gideon[37] thou shalt spread out thy fleece at the door of thy tent; see whether under the wide arch of Heaven there be any bounteous moisture, or none. Thy heart and life-purpose shall be as a miraculous Gideon's fleece, spread out in silent appeal to Heaven: and from the kind Immensities, what from the poor unkind Localities[38] and town and country Parishes there never could, blessed dew-moisture to suffice thee shall have fallen!

Work is of a religious nature: —work is of a brave nature; which it is the aim of all religion to be. All work of man is as the swimmer's: a waste ocean threatens to devour him; if he front[39] it not bravely, it will keep its word. By incessant wise defiance of it, lusty rebuke[40] and buffet[41] of it, behold how it loyally supports him, bears him as its conqueror along. "It is so," says Goethe, "with all things that man undertakes in this world."

Brave Sea-captain, Norse Sea-king, —Columbus, my hero, royalest Sea-king of all! it is no friendly environment this of thine, in the waste deep waters; around thee mutinous discouraged souls, behind thee disgrace and ruin, before thee the unpenetrated veil of Night.

Brother, these wild water-mountains, bounding from their deep bases (ten miles deep, I am told), are not entirely there on thy behalf! Meseems[42] they have other work than floating thee forward:— and the huge Winds, that sweep from Ursa Major[43] to the Tropics and Equators, dancing their giant-waltz through the kingdoms of Chaos and Immensity, they care little about filling rightly or filling wrongly the small shoulder-of-mutton sails[44] in this cockleskiff of thine! Thou art not among articulate-speaking friends, my brother; thou art among immeasurable dumb monsters, tumbling, howling wide as the world here. Secret, far off, invisible to all hearts but thine, there lies a help in them: see how thou wilt get at that. Patiently thou wilt wait till the mad South-wester[45] spend itself, saving thyself by dexterous science of defence, the while. Valiantly, with swift decision, wilt thou strike in, when the favouring East, the Possible, springs up. Mutiny of men thou wilt sternly repress; weakness, despondency, thou wilt cheerily encourage: thou wilt swallow down complaint, unreason, weariness, weakness of others and thyself; —how much wilt thou swallow down. There shall be a depth of Silence in thee, deeper than this Sea, which is but ten miles deep: a Silence unsoundable; known to God only. There shalt be a Great Man. Yes, my World-Soldier, thou of the World Marine-service. Thou wilt have to be greater than this tumultuous unmeasured World here round thee is: thou, in thy strong soul, as with wrestler's arms, shalt embrace it, harness it down; and make it bear thee on, —to new Americas, or whither God wills!

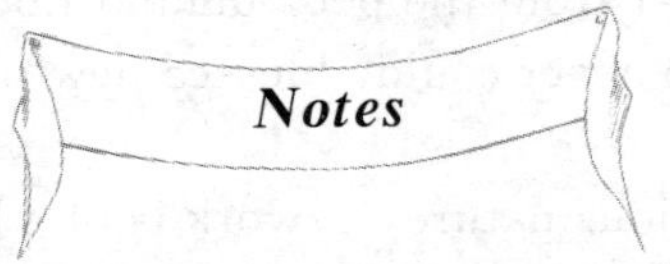

1. **For there is a perennial nobleness, and even sacredness, in Work**: Here Carlyle boldly expresses his thought that work is not only noble but is also sacred. This idea of the sacredness of labour has great influence in the modern world.
2. **Were he never so benighted, forgetful of his high calling**: No matter how ignorant he is, or how he neglects his lofty vocation.
3. **Mammonish**: devoted to money-getting ("Mammon" is wealth personified and regarded as an evil influence).
4. **The latest Gospel in this world**: the absolute truth recently held by people at large (Gospel: the teaching of Christ).
5. **Hercules**: son of Zeus in Geek mythology, noted for his great strength.
6. **withal**: in addition, at the same time.

7. **is compose into**: to be fashioned into.
8. **like helldogs lie beleaguering**: According to the ancient Greek belief, the gate of the hell was guarded by helldogs (beleaguering: besieging, surrounding).
9. **wherein**: in which.
10. **of sour smoke**: out of extremely distasteful smoke.
11. **Chaos**: the "formless void" of primordial matter.
12. **ranges itself**: arranges itself in a special way.
13. **Potter**: a person who makes earthenware dishes or ornaments, etc.
14. **Potter's wheel**: a rotating disk on which clay is shaped by a potter.
15. **Prophet Ezechiel**: Prophet Ezekiel, a prophet in The Old Testament (见《圣经·旧约》"以西结书").
16. **reduced to**: forced to.
17. **amorphous**: formless.
18. **botches**: pieces of clumsy work.
19. **Of an idle unrevolving man**: out of an idle man who does not work (revolve).
20. **shambling**: unable to stand upright.
21. **squint-cornered**: having oblique corners.
22. **a mere enamelled vessel of dishonour**: a biblical allusion to the Epistle to the Romans(《圣经·新约》"罗马书"),9:21: "Hath not the potter power over the clay, of the same lump to make one vessel unto honour, and another unto dishonour?"
23. **festering**: stagnant.
24. **accredits**: approves of officially.
25. **hypothesis**: supposition, conjecture.
26. **logic-vortices**: vortex=whirlpool; logic-vortices=in a whirlpool of logic, meaning in an endless confused state.
27. **Sir Christopher**: Christopher Wren (1632—1723), an architect, who was assigned the work of rebuilding the St. Paul's Cathedral in London after it had been burned down in the great fire in 1666.
28. **redtape**: tape of a pinkish red colour commonly used to secure legal and other documents.
29. **idle Nell-Gwyn Defenders of the Faith**: Here refers to the dissolute lives of the English ruling class such as Nell-Gwyn, the mistress of King Charles Ⅱ. "Defender of the Faith" is a title conferred by the Pope on Henry Ⅷ before he broke with the Church of Rome.
30. **hodmen**: hodman=a worker who carries mortar, etc., for a bricklayer or mason.
31. **constrain**: compel.
32. **Equitable**: Fair and just.
33. **architectonics**: the principle of building.
34. **The pious munificence of England**: men of great generosity and devoted to the Anglican Church.
35. **topstone**: a stone forming the top.

36. **Portland-stone**: The tombstone of Sir Christopher Wren's grave. Wren was buried in St Paul's Cathedral.
37. **Gideon**: a warrior judge of Israel. In "The Book of Judges"(《圣经·旧约》"士师记")God came upon Gideon and wanted him to lead the Israelites to defeat the Midianites. Gideon said to God, "Behold, I will put a fleece of wool in the floor; and if the dew be on the fleece only, and it be dry upon all the earth beside, then shall I know that thou will save Israel by mine hand, as thou hast said."
38. **Localities**: neighbourhood.
39. **front**: confront.
40. **rebuke**: beat down or force back.
41. **buffet**: blow with hand.
42. **Meseems**: (*archaic*) It seems to me.
43. **Ursa Major**: the Great Bear (大熊星座). The constellation is a useful guide to finding the Pole Star.
44. **shoulder-of-mutton sails**: triangular sails.
45. **South-wester**: a gale from the south west.

5. George Bernard Shaw (1856—1950)

Born in Dublin of Irish stock, Shaw did not receive much education. At the age of 15, he worked as a clerk in a land agent's office. He went to London in 1876 and became a music critic. In 1884 he read Marx's works and declared himself a socialist. In that year he founded the Fabian Society (费边社) with Sidney Webb and his wife. The Fabian Society attempted to attain socialism through peaceful and evolutionary means. It got its name from a Roman general by the name Fabius Maximums (died 203 B.C.), who defeated Hannibal (247 B.C. —183 B.C.) of Carthage by dilatory tactics and avoidance of direct engagement.

Shaw's main contribution to English literature is his dramas. Like Ibsen, he was much concerned about the social problems of his time. In 1892 he produced his first play *Widowers' Houses*, in which he exposes the relentless slum owner Sartoris and the respectable Trench, who would be his son-in-law. Trench, on finding out that Sartoris, his future father-in-law, is a notorious slum landlord, refuses to marry his daughter, but Trench surrenders when he finds out that his own income comes from the same source. This play was followed by *Mrs. Warren's Profession*, in which the respectability and pride of Vivie is maintained by her mother, who cooperates with a respectable aristocrat in owning a brothel. Shaw lived a long life and wrote altogether fifty-one plays. By means of witty remarks, surprise, and paradoxes, he tries to shock the conventional audience. Among his plays the best known ones are *Major Barbara*(1905), *Pygmalion* (1912), and *Heartbreak House* (1917).

Major Barbara is a play about two conflicting ideas. Major Barbara is the daughter of a millionaire named Andrew Undershaft, who was a foundling and a poor boy when young but has become a munition magnate. Barbara wants to save the souls of the poor, and she has joined the Salvation Army(救世军), a kind of religious faction, which is organized like the army. Her father is unashamed of his business, and he boasts that with his money the workers in his munition factory are living contentedly. He tells his daughter that with his money he can buy anything in the world, including the Salvation Army. Later it is found out that it is indeed the merchant of death who financially supports the Salvation Army. So the girl who tries to save people's souls is defeated by the merchant of death. At last she capitulates and withdraws from the Salvation Army. She thinks that the only thing for her to do is to let her future husband, who is also a foundling and is a professor of Greek, inherit the munition factory, and in this way she will convert the souls of the rich.

In the play Andrew Undershaft is a Shavian hero, who embodies Life Force, a kind of mysterious force advocated by Shaw. Undershaft believes that poverty breeds social discontent and thus constitutes a threat to capitalism, and he tries to use his immense power to eliminate poverty.

The excerpt is selected from Act Ⅲ, scene i, in which Lady Britomart, Undershaft's wife. Who lives separately from her husband, argues with Undershaft that he should let their son Stephen inherit the munition factory. But Stephen flatly refuses to succeed to his father's business. Through the character of Stephen, Shaw satirizes bitterly the English education, government, journalism, and moral values.

Major Barbara

ACT III

Scene 2

The dining room at Wilton Crescent[1] *next morning. Breakfast is ready. Morrison*[2] *in attendance. Lady Britomart comes in.*

LADY BRITOMART. Nobody down yet!

MORRISON. No, my lady.

LADY BRITOMART. Miss Barbara has gone, I suppose.

MORRISON. No, my lady. Miss Barbara is not up yet.

LADY BRITOMART. What! Are you sure?

MORRISON. Quite sure, my lady. Miss Barbara came in late last night and said she was not to be called.

LADY BRITOMART. Not to be called!!!

MORRISON. Yes, my lady. She said she was very tired and must have twelve hours sleep.

LADY BRITOMART. Was she quite well?

MORRISON. A little pale, my lady, and without her bonnet. I hadn't much time to notice; for she went straight upstairs, and left me to settle with the taxi and the policeman.

LADY BRITOMART. Policeman! What are you talking about, Morrison!

MORRISON. He came with her in the taxi. He asked questions, my lady. Was she Miss Undershaft? Was it all right? And an account to settle for the taxi, and for an ambulance, and some tea at the police station. I thought it best to pay and say nothing.

LADY BRITOMART. An ambulance! There must have been some accident. You are quite sure she was not hurt?

MORRISON. She seemed all right, my lady.

LADY BRITOMART. But you say she was brought home by a policeman.

MORRISON. I think he wanted to make sure who she was: whether he had her name and address all right, as it were.

LADY BRITOMART. Hm! What have you laid all those covers for? Have the young ladies invited anyone to breakfast?

MORRISON. You are expecting Mr Cusins[3] and Mr Lomax[4], my lady. The car is ordered for half-past ten to take the party to—to— to—

LADY BRITOMART. Well? To where?

MORRISON. To Mr Undershaft's premises[5], I think, my lady.

LADY BRITOMART. To the factory, you mean?

MORRISON. [*apologetically*] Well, yes, my lady.

LADY BRITOMART. The factory pays your wages, Morrison.

MORRISON. Yes, my lady. That is what factories are for. We must put up with them. Bacon and eggs, my lady, as usual?

LADY BRITOMART. No: I'll have a sausage this morning.

Morrison serves the sausage. Lomax comes in.

LADY BRITOMART. You are late, Charles. Where is Adolphus?

LOMAX [*taking a seat at the table*] He will be here soon. He was out all night. He wasn't quite himself when he came home. [*to Morrison*] Eggs and bacon, please. [*he is served.*]

LADY BRITOMART. When you say he wasn't quite himself, Charles, what exactly do you mean?

Cusins enters, in an ordinary lounge suit.

LADY BRITOMART. Good morning, Adolphus. Charles was just telling me that when you came home this morning you were not quite yourself. May I ask what was the matter with you?

CUSINS. [*taking his seat at the table*] Only a hangover[6]. [*to Morrison*] Coffee, please. Nothing to eat. [*to Lady Britomart*] I got blind drunk last night.

LADY BRITOMART. Blind drunk!!!

CUSINS. I went home with your husband. Have you ever tasted vodka, Lady Brit.?

LADY BRITOMART. Certainly not.

CUSINS. It looks exactly like spring water. The strongest spirits taste like milk after it.

Sarah bounces in, fresh from her morning toilet.

SARAH. Good morning. [*she kisses her mother, then kisses Lomax.*] Morning, Dolly[7]. [*to Morrison*] Buttermilk and kippers[8], please. [*she sits.*]

CUSINS. A new Spanish burgundy, warranted free from added alcohol: a Temperance[9] burgundy in fact, finished me. Its richness in natural alcohol made any addition superfluous.

LOMAX. You know, there is a certain amount of tosh[10] about alcohol. Burgundy is either burgundy or it isn't. If it is, it's hot stuff unless you are used to it.

CUSINS. Quite true. I've never been really drunk before. I rather liked it last night. I regret it now.

Barbara comes in, in ordinary dress, black and simple, contrasting with Sarah.

BARBARA. Good morning everybody. [*to Morrison*] Porridge: lots of porridge. And grape fruit. I'm as hungry as a hunter.

LOMAX. Oh, I say! You've chucked[11] the uniform.

LADY BRITOMART. You mean that Barbara has changed her dress, Charles. Why not say so?

LOMAX. No: I'm afraid I mean something more than that. I mean she has chucked her salvation things.

BARBARA. Cholly[12] means exactly what he says, mother. We are all going to the factory of money and gunpowder, death and destruction, on which we are living. The uniform would be out of place there. Tell us about the meeting. Dolly.

CUSINS. It was an amazing meeting. We prayed for Bodger: it was most touching. Then we prayed for the anonymous donor of the £5000. Your father would not let his name be given.

LOMAX. That was rather fine of the old man, you know. Most chaps would have wanted the advertisement.

CUSINS. He said all the charitable institutions would be down on him like vultures on a battlefield if he gave his name.

LADY BRITOMART. That is Andrew all over. He never does a proper thing without giving an improper reason for it.

CUSINS. I can't blame him. All my life I've been doing improper things for proper reasons.

BARBARA. Tell me the truth, Dolly. Were you really ever in earnest about the Army? Would you have joined if you had never seen me?

CUSINS. Well—er— Well, possibly as a collector of religions—

LOMAX. Not as a drummer though. You know, Dolly, you are a very clearheaded brainy chap; and you must have felt what even I feel, that there is a certain amount of tosh about the Salvation Army. Now the claims of the Church of England—

LADY BRITOMART. That's enough, Charles. Speak of something suited to your mental capacity.

LOMAX. But surely the Church of England is suited to all our capacities.

LADY BRITOMART. That is its worst fault: a thoroughly English one.

LOMAX. You are so awfully strongminded, Lady Brit.

LADY BRITOMART. Don't dare to say so. If there is one thing in the world that I am not, it is a strongminded woman.

Morrison returns.

LADY BRITOMART. What is it?

MORRISON. Mr Undershaft has just drove up to the door, my lady.

LADY BRITOMART. Well, let him in.

MORRISON. Shall I announce him, my lady? or is he at home here in a manner of speaking?

LADY BRITOMART. That is a very difficult question, Morrison. What do you advise, Adolphus? You are his friend; you got drunk with him.

CUSINS. I did not marry him. I tolerate him because he was the instrument of Barbara's birth; but to me he is the Prince of Darkness.

LADY BRITOMART. You are getting drunker and drunker, Adolphus. Finish your breakfast and stop talking.

LOMAX. Has the old man a latchkey?

LADY BRITOMART. Another word, Charles; and I'll box your ears. What do you say, Sarah?

SARAH. As Morrison has raised the question I should leave him to solve it.

BARBARA. Of course. Morrison knows better than anybody. Don't you, Morrison?

MORRISON. Well miss, the occasion is new to me. But as he has not come to breakfast, I could shew him into the library with your ladyship's leave.

LADY BRITOMART. Yes, do, Morrison.

Morrison goes.

LADY BRITOMART. Children: go and get ready.

BARBARA. I've not finished my porridge.

LADY BRITOMART. Take it with you.

Barbara does so and goes out with Sarah.

LADY BRITOMART. Charles: tell Stephen to come to the library in five minutes or so.

LOMAX. Righto. [*he goes*].

LADY BRITOMART. I wish Charles would not say righto: we shall have Morrison saying it next. Adolphus: are you sober enough to tell them to send round the carriage in fifteen minutes?

CUSINS [*rising*] I will try. I will take an emetic[13], I think.

LADY BRITOMART. Do, Adolphus: do.

He goes.

Meanwhile Morrison has gone down the grand stairs to the entrance hall and opened the hall door. Undershaft comes in.

UNDERSHAFT. Morning, Morrison. You quite well, eh?

MORRISON. [*taking Undershaft's overcoat and hat*] Quite well. thank you, sir. Glad to see you home again, sir.

UNDERSHAFT. Home again? Hm! You are more at home here than I am by this time, eh?

MORRISON. Oh, I am only part of house, sir.

UNDERSHAFT. Where is her ladyship?

MORRISON. In the library, sir.

UNDERSHAFT. I forget where the library is. Which door?

MORRISON. Where you were the night before last, sir. Shall I shew you?

UNDERSHAFT. [*following him*]Yes, yes. I am only a visitor here.

Morrison leads the way upstairs to the library.

MORRISON. I will tell her ladyship, sir. [*he closes the library door, leaving Undershaft alone*].

Undershaft examines the room like a stranger, making faces expressive of strong distaste. He hates the place.

Lady Britomart bounces in. Undershaft clears his countenance, and puts on his best husbandly manner.

UNDERSHAFT. Good morning, dear. How fortunate to find you alone!

LADY BRITOMART. Don't be sentimental, Andrew. Sit down.

They sit side by side on the settee.

LADY BRITOMART. [*attacking instantly*]Sarah must have £800 a year until Charles Lomax comes into his property. Barbara will need more, especially if she has a lot of children; and she will need it permanently, because Adolphus is only a professor and hasn't any property.

UNDERSHAFT. [*resignedly*]Yes, my dear: I will see to it. Anything else? for yourself, for instance?

LADY BRITOMART. I want to talk to you about Stephen.

UNDERSHAFT. [*rather wearily*]Don't, my dear. Stephen doesn't interest me.

LADY BRITOMART. He does interest me. He is our son.

UNDERSHAFT. Do you really think so? He has induced us to bring him into the world; but he chose his parents very incongruously, I think. I see nothing of myself in him, and less of you.

LADY BRITOMART. Andrew: Stephen is an excellent son, and a most steady, capable, highminded young man. You are simply trying to find an excuse for disinheriting him.

UNDERSHAFT. My dear Biddy: the Undershaft tradition disinherits him. It would be dishonest of me to leave the cannon foundry to my son.

LADY BRITOMART. It would be most unnatural and improper of you to leave it to anyone else, Andrew. Do you suppose this wicked and immoral tradition can be kept up for ever? Do you pretend that Stephen could not carry on the foundry just as well as all the other sons of the big business houses?

UNDERSHAFT. Yes: he could learn the office routine without understanding the business, like all the other sons; and the firm would go on by its own momentum until the real Undershaft—probably an Italian or a German—would invent something new, and cut him out.

LADY BRITOMART. There is nothing that any Italian or German could do that Stephen could not do. And Stephen at least has breeding.

UNDERSHAFT. The son of a foundling! Nonsense!

LADY BRITOMART. My son, Andrew! And even you may have good blood in your veins for all you know.

UNDERSHAFT. True. Probably I have. That is another argument in favor of a foundling.

LADY BRITOMART. Andrew: don't be aggravating. And don't be wicked. At present you are both.

UNDERSHAFT. This conversation is part of the Undershaft tradition, Biddy. Every Undershaft's wife has treated him to it ever since the house[14] was founded. It is mere waste of breath. If the tradition be ever broken it will be for an abler man than Stephen.

LADY BRITOMART. [*pouting*] Then go away.

UNDERSHAFT. [*deprecatory*] Go away!

LADY BRITOMART. Yes: go away. If you will do nothing for Stephen, you are not wanted here. Go to your foundling, whoever he is; and look after him.

UNDERSHAFT. The fact is, Biddy—

LADY BRITOMART. Don't call me Biddy. I don't call you Andy.

UNDERSHAFT. I will not call my wife Britomart: it is not good sense. Seriously, my love, the Undershaft tradition has landed me in a difficulty. I am getting on in years; and my partner Lazarus has at last made a stand and insisted that the succession must be settled one way or the other. Of course he is quite right. But I haven't found a fit successor yet.

LADY BRITOMART. [*obstinately*] There is Stephen.

UNDERSHAFT. That's just it: all the foundlings I can find are exactly like Stephen.

LADY BRITOMART. Andrew!!

UNDERSHAFT. I want a man with no relations and no schooling: that is, a man who would be out of the running[15] altogether if he were not a strong man. And I can't find him. Every blessed foundling nowadays is snapped up[16] in his infancy by Barnardo homes, or School Board officers, or Boards of Guardians; and if he shews the least ability he is fastened[17] on by schoolmasters; trained to win scholarships like a racehorse; crammed with secondhand ideas; drilled and disciplined in docility and what they call good taste; and lamed for life. If you want to keep the foundry in the family, you had better find an eligible foundling and marry him to Barbara.

LADY BRITOMART. Ah! Barbara! Your pet! You would sacrifice Stephen to Barbara.

UNDERSHAFT. Cheerfully. And you, my dear, would boil Barbara to make soup for Stephen.

LADY BRITOMART. Andrew: this is not a question of our likings and dislikings: it is a question of duty. It is your duty to make Stephen your successor.

UNDERSHAFT. Just as much as it is your duty to submit to your husband. Come, Biddy! these tricks of the governing class don't go down with me. I am one of the governing class myself; and it is waste of time giving tracts[18] to a missionary. I have the power in this matter; and I am not to be humbugged[19] into using it for your purposes.

LADY BRITOMART. Andrew: you can talk my head off; but you can't change wrong into right. And your tie is all on one side. Put it straight.

UNDERSHAFT. [*disconcerted*]It won't stay unless it's pinned [*he fumbles at it with childish grimaces*]—

Stephen comes in.

STEPHEN. [*at the door*]I beg your pardon. [*about to retire*]

LADY BRITOMART. No: come in, Stephen. [*Stephen comes forward to his mother's writing table.*]

UNDERSHAFT. [*not very cordially*]Good morning.

STEPHEN. [*coldly*]Good morning.

UNDERSHAFT. [*to Lady Britomart*] He knows all about the tradition, I suppose?

LADY BRITOMART. Yes. [*to Stephen*] It is what I told you last night, Stephen.

UNDERSHAFT. [*sulkily*]I understand you want to come into the cannon business.

STEPHEN. I go into trade! Certainly not.

UNDERSHAFT. [*opening his eyes, greatly eased in mind and manner*]Oh! in that case—

LADY BRITOMART. Cannons are not trade, Stephen. They are enterprise[20].

STEPHEN. I have no intention of becoming a man of business in any sense. I have no capacity for business and no taste for it. I intend to devote myself to politics.

UNDERSHAFT. [*rising*]My dear boy: this is an immense relief to me. And I trust it may prove an equally good thing for the country. I was afraid you would consider yourself disparaged and slighted. [*he moves towards Stephen as if to shake hands with him.*]

LADY BRITOMART. [*rising and interposing*] Stephen: I cannot allow you to throw away an enormous property like this.

STEPHEN. [*stiffly*]Mother: there must be an end to treating me as a child, if you please. [*Lady Britomart recoils, deeply wounded by his tone.*] Until last night I did not take your attitude seriously, because I did not think you meant it seriously. But I find now that you left me in the dark as to matters which you should have explained to me years ago. I am extremely hurt and offended. Any further discussion of my intentions had better take place with my father, as between one man and another.

LADY BRITOMART. Stephen! [*she sits down again, her eyes filling with tears.*]

UNDERSHAFT. [*with grave compassion*]You see, my dear, it is only the big men who can be treated as children.

STEPHEN. I am sorry, mother, that you have forced me—

UNDERSHAFT. [*stopping him*]Yes, yes, yes, yes: that's all right, Stephen. She won't interfere with you any more: your independence is achieved: you have won your latchkey. Don't rub it in[21]; and above all, don't apologize. [*he resumes his seat*]. Now what about your future, as between one man and another—I beg your pardon, Biddy: as between two men and a woman.

LADY BRITOMART. [*who has pulled herself together strongly*]I quite understand, Stephen. *By all means go your own way if you feel strong enough*. [*Stephen sits down magisterially in the chair at the writing table with an air of affirming his majority*.]

UNDERSHAFT. It is settled that you do not ask for the succession to the cannon business.

STEPHEN. I hope it is settled that I repudiate the cannon business.

UNDERSHAFT. Come, come! don't be so devilishly sulky: it's boyish. Freedom should be generous. Besides, I owe you a fair start in life in exchange for disinheriting you. You can't become prime minister all at once. Haven't you a turn for something? What about literature, art, and so forth?

STEPHEN. I have nothing of the artist about me, either in faculty or character, thank Heaven!

UNDERSHAFT. A philosopher, perhaps? Eh?

STEPHEN. I make no such ridiculous pretension.

UNDERSHAFT. Just so. Well, there is the army, the navy, the Church, the Bar. The Bar requires some ability. What about the Bar?

STEPHEN. I have not studied law. And I am afraid I have not the necessary push—I believe that is the name barristers give to their vulgarity—for success in pleading.

UNDERSHAFT. Rather a difficult case, Stephen. Hardly anything left but the stage, is there? [*Stephen makes an impatient movement*.] Well, come! is there anything you know or care for?

STEPHEN. [*rising and looking at him steadily*]I know the difference between right and wrong.

UNDERSHAFT. [*hugely tickled*] You don't say so! What! no

capacity for business, no knowledge of law, no sympathy with art, no pretension to philosophy; only a simple knowledge of the secret that has puzzled all the philosophers, baffled all the lawyers, muddled all the men of business, and ruined most of the artists: the secret of right and wrong. Why, man, you're a genius, a master of masters, a god! At twenty four, too!

STEPHEN. [*keeping his temper with difficulty*] You are pleased to be facetious. I pretend to nothing more than any honorable English gentleman claims as his birthright [*he sits down angrily*].

UNDERSHAFT. Oh, that's everybody's birthright: Look at poor little Jenny Hill, the Salvation lassie! she would think you were laughing at her if you asked her to stand up in the street and teach grammar or geography or mathematics or even drawing room dancing; but it never occurs to her to doubt that she can teach morals and religion. You are all alike, you respectable people. You can't tell me the bursting strain of a ten-inch gun, which is a very simple matter; but you all think you can tell me the bursting strain of a man under temptation. You daren't handle high explosives; but you're all ready to handle honesty and truth and justice and the whole duty of man, and kill one another at that game. What a country! What a world!

LADY BRITOMART. [*uneasily*] What do you think he had better do, Andrew?

UNDERSHAFT. Oh, just what he wants to do. He knows nothing and he thinks he knows everything. That points clearly to a political career. Get him a private secretaryship to someone who can get him an Under Secretaryship; and then leave him alone. He will find his natural and proper place in the end on the Treasury Bench.

STEPHEN. [*springing up again*] I am sorry, sir, that you force me to forget the respect due to you as my father. I am an Englishman and I will not hear the Government of my country insulted. [*He thrusts his hands in his pockets, and walks angrily across to the window*].

UNDERSHAFT. [*with a touch of brutality*] The government of your country! I am the government of your country: I, and Lazarus. Do you suppose that you and half a dozen amateurs like you, sitting in a row in that foolish gabble shop[22], can govern Undershaft and

Lazarus? No, my friend: you will do what pays us. You will make war when it suits us, and keep peace when it doesn't. You will find out that trade requires certain measures when we have decided on those measures. When I want anything to keep my dividends up, you will discover that my want is a national need. When other people want something to keep my dividends down, you will call out the police and military. And in return you shall have the support and applause of my newspapers, and the delight of imagining that you are a great statesman. Government of your country! Be off with you, my boy, and play with your caucuses[23] and leading articles and historic parties and great leaders and burning questions and the rest of your toys. I am going back to my counting-house to pay the piper and call the tune.[24]

STEPHEN. [*actually smiling, and putting his hand on his father's shoulder with indulgent patronage*] Really, my dear father, it is impossible to be angry with you. You don't know how absurd all this sounds to me. You are very properly proud of having been industrious enough to make money; and it is greatly to your credit that you have made so much of it. But it has kept you in circles where you are valued for your money and deferred to for it, instead of in the doubtless very old-fashioned and behind-the-times public school and university where I formed my habits of mind. It is natural for you to think that money governs England; but you must allow me to think I know better.

UNDERSHAFT. And what does govern England, pray?

STEPHEN. Character[25], father, character.

UNDERSHAFT. Whose character? Yours or mine?

STEPHEN. Neither yours nor mine, father, but the best elements in the English national character.

UNDERSHAFT. Stephen: I've found your profession for you. You're a born journalist. I'll start you with a hightoned weekly review. There!

Before Stephen can reply Sarah, Barbara, Lomax, and Cusins come in ready for walking. Barbara crosses the room to the window and looks out. Cusins drifts amiably to the armchair. Lomax remains near the door, whilst Sarah comes to her mother.

Stephen goes to the smaller writing table and busies himself with his letters.

SARAH. Go and get ready, mamma: the car is waiting.

Lady Britomart leaves the room.

UNDERSHAFT. [*to Sarah*]Good day, my dear. Good morning, Mr Lomax.

LOMAX. [*vaguely*]Ahdedoo.

UNDERSHAFT. [*to Cusins*]Quite well after last night, Euripides[26], eh?

CUSINS. As well as can be expected.

UNDERSHAFT. That's right. [*to Barbara*]So you are coming to see my death and devastation factory, Barbara?

BARBARA. [*at the window*]You came yesterday to see my salvation factory. I promised you a return visit.

LOMAX. [*coming forward between Sarah and Undershaft*]You'll find it awfully interesting. I've been through the Woolwich Arsenal; and it gives you a ripping feeling of security, you know, to think of the lot of beggars we could kill if it came to fighting. [*to Undershaft, with sudden solemnity*]Still, it must be rather an awful reflection for you, from the religious point of view as it were. You're getting on, you know, and all that.

SARAH. You don't mind Cholly, papa, do you?

LOMAX. [*much taken aback*] Oh I say!

UNDERSHAFT. Mr Lomax looks at the matter in a very proper spirit, my dear.

LOMAX. Just so. That's all I meant, I assure you.

SARAH. Are you coming, Stephen?

STEPHEN. Well, I am rather busy—er—[*magnanimously*[27]]Oh well, yes: I'll come. That is, if there is room for me.

UNDERSHAFT. I can take two with me in a little motor I am experimenting with for field use. You won't mind its being rather unfashionable. It's not painted yet; but it's bullet proof.

LOMAX. [*appalled at the prospect of confronting Wilton Crescent in an unpainted motor*]Oh I say!

SARAH. Our own car for me, thank you. Barbara doesn't mind what she's seen in.

LOMAX. I say, Dolly, old chap: do you really mind the car being a guy[28]? Because of course if you do I'll go in it. Still—

CUSINS. I prefer it.

LOMAX. Thanks awfully, old man. Come, my ownest. [*he hurries out. Sarah follows him.*]

CUSINS. [*moodily walking across to Lady Britomart's writing table*] Why are we two coming to this Works Department of Hell? that is what I ask myself.

BARBARA. I have always thought of it as a sort of pit where lost creatures with blackened faces stirred up smoky fires and were driven and tormented by my father. Is it like that, dad?

UNDERSHAFT. [*scandalized*] My dear! It is a spotlessly clean and beautiful hillside town.

CUSINS. With a Methodist chapel? Oh do say there's a Methodist chapel.

UNDERSHAFT. There are several, all of different persuasions.[29] My men are all strongly religious. In the High Explosives Sheds they object to the presence of Agnostics[30] as unsafe.

BARBARA. And yet they obey all your orders?

UNDERSHAFT. I never give them any orders. When I speak to one of them it is "Well, Jones, is the baby doing well? and has Mrs Jones made a good recovery?" "Nicely, thank you, sir." And that's all.

CUSINS. But Jones has to be kept in order. How do you maintain discipline among your men?

UNDERSHAFT. I don't. They do. You see, the one thing Jones wont stand is any rebellion from the man under him, or any assertion of social equality between the wife of the man with 4 shillings a week less than himself, and Mrs Jones! Of course they all rebel against me, theoretically. Practically, every man of them keeps the man just below him in his place. I never meddle with them. I never bully them. I don't even bully Lazarus. I say that certain things are to be done; but I don't order anybody to do them. I don't say, mind you, that there is no ordering about and snubbing[31] and even bullying. The men snub the boys and order them about; the carmen snub the sweepers; the artisans snub the unskilled laborers; the foremen drive and bully both the laborers and artisans; the assistant engineers find fault with the foremen; the chief engineers drop on the assistants; the departmental managers worry the chiefs; and the clerks have tall hats and hymnbooks and keep up the social tone by refusing to associate on equal terms with anybody. The result is a considerable profit, some of which is spent in this house.

CUSINS. [*revolted*]You really are a—well, what I was saying yesterday.

BARBARA. What was he saying yesterday?

UNDERSHAFT. Never mind, my dear. He thinks I have made you unhappy. Have I ?

BARBARA. Do you think I can be happy in this vulgar silly dress? I! who have worn the uniform. Do you understand what you have done to me? Yesterday I had a man's soul in my hand. I set him in the way of life with his face to salvation. But when we took your money he turned back to drunkenness and derision. [*with intense conviction*] I will never forgive you that. If I had a child, and you destroyed its body with your explosives—if you murdered Dolly with your horrible guns—I could forgive you if my forgiveness would open the gates of heaven to you. But to take a human soul from me, and turn it into the soul of a wolf! that is worse than any murder.

UNDERSHAFT. Does my daughter despair so easily? Can you strike a man to the heart and leave no mark on him?

BARBARA. [*her face lighting up*]Oh, you are right: he can never be lost now: where was my faith?

CUSINS. Oh, clever clever devil!

BARBARA. You may be a devil; but God speaks through you sometimes. [*she takes her father's hands and kisses them.*] You have given me back my happiness: I feel it deep down now, though my spirit is troubled.

UNDERSHAFT. You have learnt something. That always feels at first as if you had lost something.

BARBARA. Well, take me to the factory of death; and let me learn something more. There must be some truth or other behind all this frightful irony. Come, Dolly. [*she goes out.*]

CUSINS. My guardian angel! [*to Undershaft*]Avaunt[32]! [*he follows Barbara.*]

STEPHEN. [*quietly, at the writing table*]You must not mind Cusins, father. He is a very amiable good fellow; but he is a Greek scholar and naturally a little eccentric.

UNDERSHAFT. Ah, quite so. Thank you, Stephen. Thank you. [*he goes out.*]

Stephen smiles patronizingly; buttons his coat responsibly; and crosses the room to the door. Lady Britomart, dressed for out-of-doors, opens it before he reaches it. She looks round for the others; looks at Stephen; and turns to go without a word.

STEPHEN. [*embarrassed*] Mother—

LADY BRITOMART. Don't be apologetic, Stephen. And don't forget that you have outgrown your mother. [*she goes out.*]

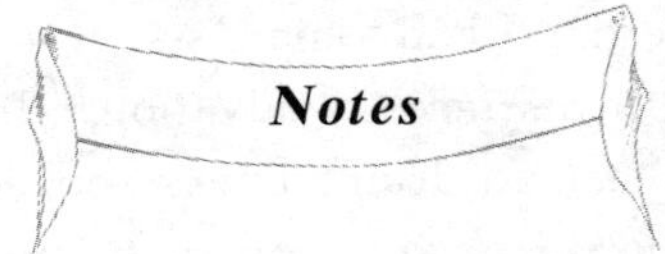

1. **Wilton Crescent**: the place where Lady Britomart lives with her son Stephen Undershaft and two daughters, Barbara Undershaft and Sarah Undershaft.
2. **Morrison**: the man servant of the house.
3. **Mr Cusins**: Adolphus Cusins, a professor of Greek, engaged to Barbara.
4. **Mr Lomax**: Charles Lomax, son of a millionaire, engaged to Sarah.
5. **premises**: building with its grounds, here referring to Undershaft's munition factory.
6. **hangover**: sick after-effects of drunkenness.
7. **Dolly**: pet name for Cusins.
8. **kippers**: salmons split open, seasoned and dried(腌晒的鲱鱼).
9. **Temperance**: moderation in the use of alcoholic liquors, and even entire abstinence from them. Here Cusins is using the word wittily.
10. **tosh**: nonsense.
11. **chucked**: abandoned or dismissed.
12. **Cholly**: pet name for Lomax.
13. **emetic** [ɪˈmetɪk]: medicine used to cause vomiting(催吐的).
14. **the house**: here referring to the munition factory.
15. **out of running**: having no chance to succeed.
16. **snapped up**: seized suddenly.
17. **fastened**: tied up.
18. **tracts**: short pamphlets, usu. on some moral or religious subject.
19. **humbugged**: deceived, swindled.
20. **enterprise**: an undertaking, especially a bold or difficult one.
21. **rub it in**: keep repeating or emphasizing something unimportant.
22. **that foolish gabble shop**: Shaw's contemptible term for Parliament (gabble = meaningless and foolish talk).
23. **caucuses** [ˈkɔːkəsɪs]: meetings of a small group of political party leaders to decide

policy, etc.

24. **I am going back to my counting-house to pay the piper and call the tune**: I am the boss behind the scene, and with my money I'll let the government do whatever suits me.
25. **Character**: a composite of good moral qualities typically of moral excellence and firmness blended with resolution, self-discipline, high ethics, and judgment.
26. **Euripides**: Greek tragedian(ca. 480 B. C. —406 B. C.).
27. **Magnanimously**: High-mindedly.
28. **guy**: an odd figure.
29. **persuasions**: particular sects of religion.
30. **Agnostics**: people who believe that nothing can be known about the existence of God or of anything except material things (不可知论者).
31. **snubbing**: treating with scorn.
32. **Avaunt**: Move on.

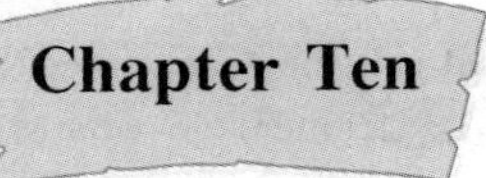

Chapter Ten

The Twentieth Century

The twentieth century was marked by the two World Wars which deprived hundred millions of lives. The two World Wars were the direct result of the conflicts between rival imperialist countries and their ambition to dominate the world.

Roughly speaking, the development of English literature in the twentieth century can be divided into two stages, that is, literature between the two World Wars, and literature after World War Ⅱ.

Three main trends of literature are worth our attention.

They are Modernism, The Angry Young Men, and The Theatre of the Absurd.

1. Modernism

Modernism is a rather vague term which is used to apply to the works of a group of poets, novelists, painters, and musicians between 1910 and the early years after the World War Ⅱ. The term includes various trends or schools, such as imagism, expressionism, dadaism, stream of consciousness, and existentialism. It means a departure from the conventional criteria or established values of the Victorian age. This departure from the conventions was prepared for by the aesthetic movement during the later decades of the 19th century, affected by the sickness of fin de siecle (世纪末), and sped up by the World War I. Though England had won the war, many intellectuals were disillusioned with the condition of their country. Besides economic and political causes, the English intellectuals were very much influenced by the psychology of Sigmund Freud (1856—1939), an Austrian psychoanalyst, who expounded that all human actions are determined by libido (sexual desire) which people subconsciously suppress.

Alienation and loneliness are the basic themes of modernism. In the eyes of modernist writers, the modern world is a chaotic one and is incomprehensible. Although modern society is materially rich, it is spiritually barren. It is a land of spiritual and emotional sterility. Human beings are helpless before an incomprehensible world and no longer able to do things that their forefathers once did.

The characteristics of modernist writings can be roughly summed up as below.

(1) Complexity and obscurity

The works of the modernist writers are complex and obscure because they express the subjective world of individual writers. As the consciousness and subconsciousness of a particular writer shifts from time to time, usually there is no time sequence in their writings. The past, present, and future are mixed together. The past is juxtaposed with the present and with the future. In addition, there is no limitation of space in their works. At one moment, the character might be in New York; at another moment he might be in Paris. The old tradition of Time and Space is done away with. It is difficult for a reader to follow the time and space shifts in their writings.

(2) The use of symbols

A symbol is something that represents or stands for something else. Like metaphors and similes, symbols are another kind of figurative language. But a symbol has a larger meaning than a metaphor or simile—a meaning which can often be multiple or ambiguous. It is more suggestive, more complex, and often hard to interpret. The modern poets and writers find in symbol a means to express their inexpressible selves. As a symbol is subject to different interpretations, the reader is often bewildered to find the real meaning.

(3) Allusion

Allusion is an indirect reference to another work of literature, art, history, or religion. By means of allusion, the modernist writer tries to unite the past, present, and future. He assumes the reader has the same knowledge as he has. Allusion enriches the meaning of the work, gives it depth, and makes the work understandable to the elite. The use of allusion also helps to achieve effects of irony, for allusions set the past against the present and thus exhibit a decay of past standards of morality and glory, showing the shallowness and degradation of the modern world.

(4) Irony

Irony is an expression of one's meaning by using words that mean the direct opposite of what one really intends to convey. In this way a writer is able to ridicule a person or a thing he dislikes or abhors, or to show contempt, or to express his humourous attitude. In short, it shows a contrast between what is and what is said. As modernist writers think themselves helpless in this chaotic world, they find their life ironical. Sometimes it is difficult for a reader to catch the irony.

Thomas Stearns Eliot (1888—1965)

Eliot was born in the United States. He received high education at Harvard University. It was there he wrote his earliest poem, "The Love Song of J. Alfred Prufrock" (1911). He was an assistant at Harvard in the academic year 1913—1914. Then he went to Germany. When the war broke out, he went to London, where he met another American poet Ezra Pound (1885—1972), who got Eliot's poem published in 1915. Then he became a clerk at a bank and worked there for eight years. In 1921 he wrote *The Waste Land*, and with the help of Pound, it was published in 1922. It established Eliot's status in modern literature. For no one had been able to embrace so much material with such skill as Eliot did in writing this poem. In the poem, London is presented as an arid, waste land. The central symbols are drought and flood, representing death and rebirth. Eliot saw the modern world falling apart and spiritually barren. He was engaged in a spiritual search, to which he finally found the solution in the Anglican Church. He said he was "classicist in literature, royalist in politics and Anglo-Catholic in religion" (*Lancelot Andrews* 1928). His other poems are *Ash Wednesday* (1930), *Murder in the Cathedral* (1935) and *The Family Reunion* (1939).

Besides poetry and dramatic poetry, Eliot also wrote many essays and much literary criticism. His essays are praised for their lucidity and precision.

"The Love Song of J. Alfred Prufrock" is a typical example of modernist poetry. The poem is noted for its irony, and the allusions to classical literary works add to the depth of irony. In the poem we can also see the technique of stream of consciousness, for the mind of Prufrock jumps from one subject to another without transitionary words. The images throughout the poem reflect the helplessness, torpor, submissiveness, and triviality of a modern man.

The Love Song of J. Alfred Prufrock[1,2]

S'io credessi che mia risposta fosse
A persona che mai tornasse al mondo,
Questa fiamma staria senza più scosse.
Ma percioche giammai di questo fondo
Non tornò vivo alcun, s'i'odo il vero,
Senza tema d'in famia ti rispondo.[3]

Let us go then, you and I,[4]
When the evening is spread out against the sky
Like a patient etherised upon a table;[5]
Let us go, through certain half-deserted streets,
The muttering retreats[6]
Of restless nights in one-night cheap hotels[7]

And sawdust restaurants with oyster-shells:[8]
Streets that follow like a tedious argument
Of insidious intent
To lead you to an overwhelming question...[9]
Oh, do not ask, "What is it?"
Let us go and make our visit.

In the room the women come and go
Talking of Michelangelo.[10]

The yellow fog that rubs its back upon the window-panes,
The yellow smoke that rubs its muzzle on the window-panes,
Licked its tongue into the corners of the evening,
Lingered upon the pools that stand in drains,
Let fall upon its back the soot that falls from chimneys,
Slipped by the terrace, made a sudden leap,

And seeing that it was a soft October night,
Curled once about the house, and fell asleep.[11]

And indeed there will be time
For the yellow smoke that slides along the street
Rubbing its back upon the window-panes;
There will be time, there will be time
To prepare a face to meet the faces that you meet;
There will be time to murder and create,
And time for all the works and days[12] of hands
That lift and drop a question on your plate;[13]
Time for you and time for me,
And time yet for a hundred indecisions,
And for a hundred visions[14] and revisions,[15]
Before the taking of a toast and tea.[16]

In the room the women come and go
Talking of Michelangelo.

And indeed there will be time
To wonder, "Do I dare?" and, "Do I dare?"
Time to turn back and descend the stair,
With a bald spot in the middle of my hair—[17]
(They will say: 'How his hair is growing thin!')
My morning coat, my collar mounting firmly to the chin, My necktie rich and modest, but asserted[18] by a simple pin—
(They will say: 'But how his arms and legs are thin!')
Do I dare
Disturb the universe?[19]
In a minute there is time
For decisions and revisions which a minute will reverse.[20]

For I have known them all already, known them all—
Have known the evenings, mornings, afternoons,
I have measured out my life with coffee spoons;[21]
I know the voices dying with a dying fall
Beneath the music from a farther room.
So how should I presume?[22]

And I have known the eyes already, known them all—

The eyes that fix you in a formulated phrase,[23]
And when I am formulated, sprawling on a pin,[24]
When I am pinned and wriggling on the wall,
Then how should I begin
To spit out all the butt-ends[25] of my days and ways?
　And how should I presume?

And I have known the arms already, known them all—
Arms that are braceleted and white and bare
(But in the lamplight, downed with light brown hair!)[26]
Is it perfume from a dress

That makes me so digress?
Arms that lie along a table, or wrap about a shawl.
　And should I then presume?
　And how should I begin?
　　. . . . .
Shall I say, I have gone at dusk through narrow streets
And watched the smoke that rises from the pipes
Of lonely men in shirt-sleeves, leaning out of windows?...

I should have been a pair of ragged claws
Scuttling across the floors of silent seas.[27]

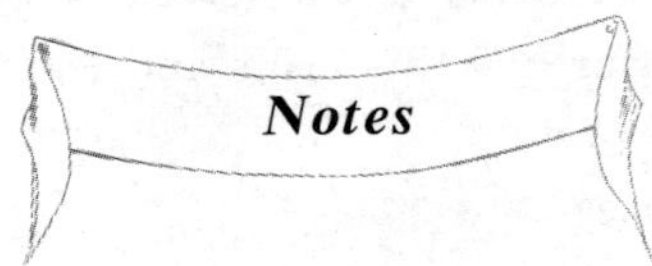

1. The poem is written in irregular metrical form.
2. The very title is ironical. A love song should be full of warm emotions, but what we find in the poem is just the contrary. The very name of the character is also ironical. It is a combination of two words, i. e., "prude" + "frock". "Prude" means "a person who is excessively or priggishly attentive to propriety or oversensitive to slight breaches of decorum"; "frock" means "an outer garment, chiefly worn by men when formally dressed". From the name we can have the first glimpse of the character and social status of Mr Prufrock.
3. The epigram in Latin is from Dante's *Inferno*, Canto XXVII, when Dante in Inferno meets Guido da Montefeltro, who, wrapped in flame, tells Dante about his shameful life because he believes that Dante will never return to earth to tell other people. He says, "If I thought that I was speaking / to someone who would

go back to the world, / this flame would shake no more, / But since nobody has ever / gone back alive from this place, if what I hear is true, / I answer you without fear of infamy."

4. **Let us go then, you and I** : This is a dramatic monologue, as there is an imaginary listener in the poem. But some scholars suggest that the other person is Mr Prufrock's alter ego.
5. **Like a patient etherised upon a table**: Here the evening is compared to a patient who is etherized (ether = a liquid produced from alcohol; it quickly changes into vapour and is used by doctors to make people unconscious of pain). "Table" = operation table. The image of the evening is in fact the projection of Prufrock's mind. It suggests Prufrock's benumbedness, submission, and his waiting for something grim to happen.
6. **retreats**: Retreat is a place of shelter which should give one peace and calm, but here there is no restfulness.
7. **one-night cheap hotels**: cheap hotels at which people would stay for one night.
8. **sawdust restaurants with oyster-shells**: an image of the combination of the ugly present and the glorious past. Sawdust spread on the ground suggests that this is a cheap restaurant. Oyster-shells suggests the refined and elegant life of the people of the upper class, who could afford to eat oysters, which were expensive in old times.
9. **Streets that follow... an overwhelming question**: Several images are juxtaposed in the sentence to express Prufrock's mind, which is obsessed with a question. The first image is the streets which are boringly long and full of twists and turns (as suggested by the second image of "a tedious argument / Of insidious intent") and which treacherously lead you to "an overwhelming question" (the third image). The reader is taken by surprise, as usually he expects the streets will lead someone to some place.
10. **In the room the women come and go / Talking of Michelangelo**: Without any transitionary words, Prufrock is in a room, evidently a room where there are women of the upper class, as they are talking of Michelangelo (1475—1564), a great Italian painter in the age of the Renaissance. But the irony lies in the fact that the women do not take Michelangelo seriously.
11. **The yellow fog that rubs its back upon the window-panes...... Curled once about the house, and fell asleep**: This stanza presents a very unpleasant nasty picture of an evening in London. The lifeless "fog" and "smoke" are animated. They appear like yellow cats. The image suggests torpor, inaction, stagnation, sluggishness, triviality, and the emptiness of Prufrock's state of mind.
12. **works and days**: the title of a poem by the Greek poet Hesiod (8th century B. C.), which celebrates farm work.
13. **That lift and drop a question on your plate**: The reader is expecting something important to happen after such sentences as "There will be time... to prepare a face to meet the faces that you meet" and "There will be time to murder and

create", but unexpectedly he finds something very insignificant.

14. **visions**: something seen in the mind, an idea, or desire.
15. **revisions**: change of mind.
16. **Before the taking of a toast and tea**: This line repeats the previous line: "That lift and drop a question on your plate". Naturally the reader is expecting something significant to happen after lines such as "time yet for a hundred indecisions" and "And for a hundred visions and revisions", but what he reads is "the taking of a toast and tea", which is a very trivial thing.
17. **With a bald spot in the middle of my hair**: Prufrock is gathering up his courage to ask the hand of the woman who is in the room among the women coming and going, but no sooner had he thought of doing so, than he turns his back, conscious of the bald spot in his hair. He is feeling insecure in the presence of the woman, as he is conscious of his middle age.
18. **asserted**: Here referring to "made fixed".
19. **Do I dare / Disturb the universe?** : Notice the irony of this question. What Prufrock intends to do is a very trivial thing.
20. **In a minute there is time / For decisions and revisions which a minute will reverse**: In a minute he will make up his mind, but he will change it again and again.
21. **I have measured out my life with coffee spoons**: The implied meaning of the line is that he has spent his life in trivial things.
22. **presume**: to claim something that one has no right to. The sudden shift from the question "Do I dare?" to "how should I presume?" shows that his resolution to make the proposal is growing weaker.
23. **The eyes that fix you in a formulated phrase**: "Formulated" means "to be reduced to a formula, or to be expressed in a short clear form". Here the meaning of the line is that the women in the room have a fixed impression of Prufrock.
24. **And when I am formulated, sprawling on a pin, /When I am pinned and wriggling on the wall**: Here Prufrock is comparing himself to a butterfly or an insect, pinned on the wall with wings or limbs spread and twisting. The two lines repeat the idea of the previous line.
25. **butt-ends**: the ends of cigarettes, meaning trivial things here. Prufrock is comparing the remaining years of his life to the ends of cigarettes.
26. **(But in the lamplight, downed with light brown hair!)** : The women who look beautiful are ugly when you look at them in close quarters. The light brown hair is an ironical reference to the "bald head".
27. **I should have been a pair of ragged claws/ Scuttling across the floors of silent seas**: The image of a sea crab with uneven claws, running hastily at the bottom of the sea is introduced here. A crab with its shell has a world of its own and is self-sufficient, with no need to be sociable. Prufrock is admiring the crab.

James Joyce (1882—1941)

Like Bernard Shaw, James Joyce was an Irishman born in Dublin and received education first at Catholic schools and later at the University College at Dublin. He was expected to be a Catholic priest, but instead of being a priest, he took to aesthetics and went to live in Paris and other European cities. His first major novel is *A Portrait of the Artist as a Young Man* (1916), a semi-autobiographical novel which tells the story of a young man, Stephen Dedalus, from his birth to young adulthood, describing how he rejected his education, his family, and his religion. In 1922, Joyce published his masterpiece *Ulysses*, in which he used the technique of stream of consciousness, a term coined by William James in *Principles of Psychology* (1890) to denote the flow of inner experiences. It refers to that technique which seeks to depict the multitudinous thoughts and feelings which pass through the mind. Another phrase for it is "interior monologue".

Ulysses has virtually no story, nor plot, almost no action. Broadly speaking the novel concerns the thoughts, experiences, and above all the encounter of two men during a single day, from 8 o'clock in the morning of June 16, 1904, to 2 o'clock in the morning of June 17—a day marked nothing outwardly notable, a day of no historical significance, nor even of any clear personal significance to the protagonists. The technique used in the book is what is called "stream of consciousness", though what Joyce writes is not of consciousness, but the activity of the part of the mind which lies somewhat between deliberate thought and the subconsciousness. It is this area which Joyce particularly explores.

The book centers round two protagonists. One is Leopold Bloom, born in 1866, married, a Dublin Jew and a canvasser for advertisements; his wife Molly, a distinguished singer, has some illicit love affair with a man called Boyan. The other protagonist is Stephen Dedalus, who appeared in *A Portrait of the Artist as a Young Man* as a would be artist. Both of them are possessed with a feeling of loneliness and isolation, for Stephen has been living as an exile, and Bloom is a Dublin Jew. They are both exiles in Dublin. Stephen, whose real father betrayed him by fecklessness and drunkenness, is yearning for a spiritual father; Bloom, whose actual son died in infancy, is preoccupied with a yearning for a spiritual son.

Finally, Bloom and Stephen, who have just been missing each other all day, get together. By this time it is too late, for Stephen is dead drunk. Bloom takes the unresponsive Stephen home and gives him a meal. After Stephen's departure, Bloom retires to bed with his wife Molly, representing the principle of sex, ends the book with a long monologue.

It is significant to note that the structure of the novel closely follows the story of the journey of Ulysses which he took after the war at Troy on his way to Greece. The book is divided into three parts, corresponding to the story in the epic: the opening section dealing with the son Telemanchus (Stephen), the central section dealing with the wandering of Ulysses (Bloom wandering in Dublin), the final section dealing with the get together of Ulysses and Telemanchus (Bloom and Stephen).

The following section is chosen from Part Ⅱ of the novel. It corresponds to Book Ⅹ of Homer's *Ulysses*, in which Ulysses comes to the land of Lestrygonians, who are cannibals. It is lunch time in Dublin, and the descriptions are about food and the slaughter of victims.

Ulysses

Pineapple rock, lemon platt, butter scotch.[1] A sugarsticky[2] girl shovelling scoopfuls of creams for a Christian brother[3]. Some school treat.[4] Bad for their tummies[5]. Lozenge and comfit manufacturer to His Majesty the King.[6] God. Save. Our?[7] Sitting on his throne sucking red juiubes white.[8]

A sombre Y. M. C. A. young man,[9] watchful among the warm sweet fumes of Graham Lemon's,[10] placed a throwaway[11] in a hand of Mr Bloom.

Heart to heart talks.

Bloo... Me? No.[12]

Blood of the Lamb.[13]

His slow feet walked him riverward, reading. Are you saved? All are washed in the blood of the lamb. God wants blood victim. Birth, hymen, martyr, war, foundation of a building, sacrifice, kidney burntoffering, druids'[14] altars. Elijah[15] is coming. Dr John Alexander Dowie, restorer of the church in Zion[16], is coming.

Is coming ! Is coming !! Is coming !!!
All heartily welcome.

Paying game. Torry and Alexander last year. Polygamy. His wife[17] will put the stopper on that. Where was that ad[18] some Birmingham firm the luminous crucifix.[19] Our Saviour. Wake up in the dead of night and see him on the wall, hanging. Pepper's[20] ghost idea. Iron Nails Ran In.

Phosphorus it must be done with. If you leave a bit of codfish for instance. I could see the bluey silver over it. Night I went down to the pantry in the kitchen. Don't like all the smells in it waiting to rush out. What was it she wanted? [21] The Malaga raisins. Thinking of Spain. Before Rudy[22] was born. The phosphorescence, that bluey greeny. Very good for the brain.

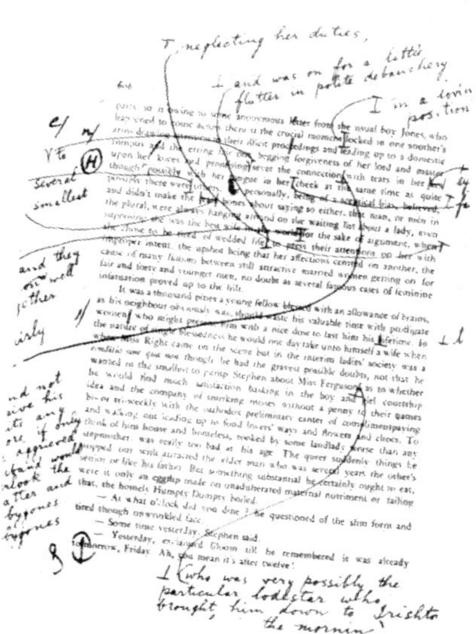

James Joyce's manuscript

From Butler's monument house corner he glanced along Bachelor's walk. Dedalus' daughter there still outside Dillon's auctionrooms. Must be selling off some old furniture. Knew her eyes at once from the father. Lobbing about waiting for him. Home always breaks up when the mother goes. Fifteen children he had. Birth every year almost. That's in their theology or the priest won't give the poor woman the confession, the absolution. Increase and multiply. Did you ever hear such an idea? Eat you out of house and home. No families themselves[23] to feed. Living on the fat of the land. Their butteries and larders.[24] I'd like to see them do the black fast[25] Yom Kippur.[26] Crossbuns[27]. One meal and a collation[28] for fear he'd collapse on the altar. A housekeeper of one of those fellows if you could pick it out of her. Never pick it out of her. Like getting £. s. d.[29] out of him. Does himself well. No guests. All for number one. Watching his water. Bring your own bread and butter. His reverence. Mum's the word.

Good Lord, that poor child's dress is in flitters. Underfed she looks too. Potatoes and marge, marge and potatoes. It's after they feel it. Proof of the pudding.[30] Undermines the constitution.

As he set foot on O Connell bridge a puffball of smoke plumed up from the parapet. Brewery barge with export stout. England. Sea air sours it, I heard. Be interesting some day get a pass through Hancock[31] to see the brewery. Regular world in itself. Vats of porter, wonderful. Rats get in too. Drink themselves bloated as big as a collie floating. Dead drunk on the porter. Drink till they puke again like Christians. Imagine drinking that! Rats: vats. Well of course if we knew all the things.

Looking down he saw flapping strongly, wheeling between the gaunt[32] quaywalls, gulls. Rough weather outside. If I threw myself down? Reuben J's son[33] must have swallowed a good bellyful of that sewage. One and eightpence too much. Hhhhm. It's the droll way he comes out with the things. Knows how to tell a story too.

They[34] wheeled lower. Looking for grub. Wait.

He threw down among them a crumpled paper ball. Elijah thirty-two feet per sec is com.[35] Not a bit. The ball bobbed unheeded on the wake of swells, floated under by the bridgepiers. Not such damn fools. Also the day I threw that stale cake out of the Erin's King[36] picked it up in the wake fifty yards astern. Live by their wits. They wheeled, flapping.

The hungry famished gull
Flaps o'er the waters dull.

That is how poets write, the similar sounds. But then Shakespeare has no rhymes: blank verse. The flow of the language it is. The thoughts. Solemn.

Hamlet, I am thy father's spirit
Doomed for a certain time to walk the earth.[37]

—Two apples a penny! Two for a penny!

His gaze passed over the glazed apples serried on her stand. Australians they must be this time of year. Shiny peels: polishes them up with a rag or a handkerchief.

Wait. Those poor birds.

He halted again and bought from the old applewoman two Banbury cakes for a penny and broke the brittle paste and threw its fragments down into the Liffey. See that? The gulls swooped silently two, then all from their heights, pouncing on prey. Gone. Every morsel!

Aware of their greed and cunning he shook the powdery crumb from his hands. They never expected that. Manna[38]. Live on fishy flesh they have to, all seabirds, gulls, seagoose. Swans from Anna Liffey swim down here sometimes to preen themselves. No accounting for tastes. Wonder what kind is swanmeat. Robinson Crusoe had to live on them.

They wheeled, flapping weakly. I'm not going to throw any more. Penny quite enough. Lot of thanks I get. Not even a caw[39]. They spread foot and mouth disease too. If you cram a turkey, say, on chestnutmeal it tastes like that. Eat pig like pig. But then why is it that saltwater fish are not salty? How is that?

1. **Pineapple rock, lemon platt, butter scotch**: As Bloom passes by a sweet shop, his eyes catch sight of the sweets.
2. **sugarsticky**: "Sugarstick" means "sticky sweets"; here Joyce invents the word "sugarsticky", which vividly describes both her appearance and what she is

doing.

3. **Christian brother**: a lay member of a men's religious order.
4. **Some school treat**: The Christian brother is obviously working for some school and he is buying creams for the school children.
5. **tummies**: stomaches.
6. **Lozenge and comfit manufacturer to His Majesty the King**: These are the words either on the window glass or on the outside wall of the shop to show that the shop manufactures sweets for the king.
7. **God. Save. Our**? : From the very words "His Majesty" Bloom's thought jumps to the national anthem of England, which is "God Save Our King."
8. **Sitting on his throne sucking red juiubes white**: This is Bloom's fanciful idea. He imagines the king as a child sucking gum on the throne.
9. **A sombre Y. M. C. A. young man**: a serious young man from the Young Men's Christian Association.
10. **Graham Lemon's** : the name of the sweet shop.
11. **throwaway**: a leaflet advertising the coming of Dr. John Alexander Dowie to preach in Dublin.
12. **Bloo... Me? No.** : Bloom's eyes catch the word "Bloo..." He mistakes "Blood" for "Bloom".
13. **Blood of the Lamb**: Lamb usually refers to Jesus Christ.
14. **druids**: priests of the ancient Celtic religion of Britain and Gaul.
15. **Elijah**: the name of an ancient prophet of Israel. Here Elijah refers to Dr. John Alexander Dowie, who was a Scottish-American evangelist and established the "Christian Catholic Apostolic Church in Zion" in 1901.
16. **Zion**: a height in the northeastern part of Jerusalem.
17. **His wife**: Here refers to his wife Molly who has an illicit love affair, so there is no need for polygamy.
18. **ad**: advertisement.
19. **the luminous crucifix**: A crucifix is a cross bearing the sculptured figure of Christ. Here the crucifix is made of phosphorus, so that it shines in darkness.
20. **Pepper**: the name of the inventor of the crucifix.
21. **What was it she wanted**? : As Bloom was in the kitchen, his wife also came downstairs.
22. **Rudy**: their son, who died in infancy eleven years before.
23. **themselves**: Here refers to the priest.
24. **butteries and larders**: Both words mean storeroom.
25. **black fast**: a fast of the most severe kind.
26. **Yom Kippur**: the Jewish day of Atonement, the most solemn day of the Jewish year, observed with fasting and prayers of repentance.
27. **Crossbuns**: sweet cakes indented with a cross.
28. **collation**: a light meal, especially at an unusual time.
29. **£. s. d.** : abbreviations, respectively, for pounds, shillings, and pence.

30. **Proof of the pudding**: an imcomplete English saying: Proof of the pudding is in the eating.
31. **Hancock**: the name of some person Bloom knows.
32. **gaunt**: grim and forbidding.
33. **Reuben J's son**: Reuben J. Dodd was a solicitor in Dublin. His son fell into the Liffey River and was rescued by a man to whom Reuben gave two shillings as a reward. "One and eightpence too much" was the remark of Simon Dedalus, the father of Stephen Dedlus when he discussed the matter with Bloom earlier that morning.
34. **They**: Here refers to the gulls.
35. **Elijah thirty-two feet per sec is com**: The pamphlet printed with "Elijah is coming" falls down at the rate of 32 feet per second.
36. **Erin's King**: the name of a ferry boat.
37. **Hamlet, I am thy father's spirit / Doomed for a certain time to walk the earth**: a slightly misquoted quotation from *Hamlet* I. v. 9—10.
38. **Manna**: the food miraculously supplied to the Israelites in the wilderness (see Exodus, 16 : 15).
39. **caw**: the cry of a gull or crow.

Stephen Spender (1909—1995)

Spender was the son of a distinguished journalist. He received education at University College, Oxford. He was one of the left-wing poets in the thirties. In his poetry we can see the influence of T. S. Eliot. The following poem shows his disillusionment with modern civilization.

The Landscape near an Aerodrome[1]

MORE beautiful and soft than any moth
With burring[2] furred antennae[3] feeling its huge path
Through dusk, the air liner[4] with shut-off engines
Glides over suburbs and the sleeves[5] set trailing tall
To point the wind. Gently, broadly, she falls,
Scarcely disturbing charted currents of air.[6]

Lulled by descent, the travellers across sea
And across feminine land indulging[7] its easy[8] limbs
In miles of softness, now let their eyes trained by watching[9]
Penetrate through dusk the outskirts of this town
Here where industry shows a fraying edge.[10]
Here they may see what is being done.

Beyond the winking masthead light
And the landing ground, they observe the outposts
Of work: chimneys like lank black fingers[11]
Or figures, frightening and mad:[12] and squat buildings
With their strange air behind trees, like women's faces

Shattered by grief.[13] Here where few houses

Moan with faint light behind their blinds,[14]
They[15] remark[16] the unhomely sense of complaint, like a dog
Shut out and shivering at the foreign moon.

In the last sweep of love,[17] they pass over fields
Behind the aerodrome, where boys play all day[18]
Hacking dead grass: whose cries, like wild birds,
Settle upon the nearest roofs
But soon are hid under the loud city.

Then, as they land, they hear the tolling bell
Reaching across the landscape of hysteria,
To where, louder than all those batteries
And charcoaled towers against that dying sky,[19]
Religion stands, the Church blocking the sun.

1. The poem is written in irregular meter.
2. **burring**: making a whirling sound.
3. **furred antennae**: The antennae is covered with frost as if coated with fur.
4. **the air liner**: In the poem the poet is contrasting the beauty of the landing airplane with the ugliness of the industrial city.
5. **the sleeves**: the wings of the airplane.
6. **charted currents of air**: the currents of air drawn on a chart.
7. **indulging**: taking unrestrained pleasure in.
8. **easy**: comfortable. The antecedent of "its" is "feminine land".
9. **their eyes trained by watching**: The travellers have been looking out of the windows, watching the scene outside; their eyes seem to have received training all the way to be watchful.
10. **where industry shows a fraying edge**: The plane is sliding over the outskirts of a city where there are spots of factories (fraying edge=the threads are loose at the edge of a piece of clothing by over-wearing; the word "fraying" carries a derogatory sense).
11. **chimneys like lank black fingers**: Notice the ghostlike sight of chimneys.
12. **figures, frightening and mad**: may refer to any kind of figures, which are

threatening and mad, another horrible sight of an industrial city, which is a land of hysteria.

13. **squat buildings /With their strange air behind trees, like women's faces / Shattered by grief**: From the airplane, the high buildings of a city look like crouching behind trees in a strange manner. As the buildings are behind trees, they also look like women's faces stricken by grief.
14. **few houses /Moan with faint light behind their blinds**: Notice the similarity between this image and images in Eliot's "The Love Song of J. Alfred Prufrock".
15. **They**: the travellers in the airplane.
16. **remark**: notice.
17. **love**: the love between the earth and the airplane.
18. **where boys play all day**: a glimpse of life and vivacity in the deadened city.
19. **louder than all those batteries/And charcoaled towers against that dying sky**: Images of war and devastation further point to the horror of the deathlike city.

Wystan Hugh Auden (1907—1973)

Auden was born in York, the son of a doctor. He received education at Christ Church, Oxford University. Like Spenser, he was one of the left-wing poets in the thirties and the influence of T. S. Eliot is visible in his poetry. He went to Spain and was an ambulance driver for the Republicans during the Spanish Civil War. After his visit to Iceland and China, he went to the United States in 1939 and became an American citizen in 1946. The poem below is written during the Spanish Civil War.

Spain 1937 [1]

YESTERDAY all the past. The language of size[2]
Spreading to China along the trade-routes; the diffusion[3]
    Of the counting-frame[4] and the cromlech[5];
Yesterday the shadow-reckoning[6] in the sunny climates.

Yesterday the assessment of insurance by cards[7],
The divination of water[8]; yesterday the invention
    Of cart-wheels and clocks, the taming of
Horses; yesterday the bustling world of navigators.

Yesterday the abolition of fairies and giants[9];
The fortress like a motionless eagle eyeing the valley,[10]
    The chapel built in the forest;
Yesterday the carving of angels and of frightening gargoyles.[11]

The trial of heretics among the columns of stone;[12]
Yesterday the theological feuds in the taverns[13]
    And the miraculous cure at the fountain;
Yesterday the Sabbath of Witches[14]. But to-day the struggle[15].

Yesterday the installation of dynamos and turbines;
The construction of railways in the colonial desert;
Yesterday the classic lecture
On the origin of Mankind[16]. But to-day the struggle.

Yesterday the belief in the absolute value of Greek[17];
The fall of the curtain upon the death of a hero[18];
Yesterday the prayer to the sunset[19],
And the adoration of madmen[20]. But to-day the struggle.

As the poet whispers, startled among the pines
Or, where the loose waterfall sings, compact, or upright
On the crag by the leaning tower:[21]
"O my vision. O send me the luck of the sailor.[22]"

And the investigator[23] peers through his instruments
At the inhuman provinces[24], the virile bacillus
Or enormous Jupiter finished:
"But the lives of my friends. I inquire, I inquire."[25]

And the poor in their fireless lodgings dropping the sheets
Of the evening paper: "Our day is our loss. O show us
History the operator; the
Organizer, Time the refreshing river."[26]

And the nations combine each cry[27], invoking the life[28]
That shapes the individual belly and orders
The private nocturnal terror:[29]
"Did you not found once the city state of the sponge,"[30]

"Raise the vast military empires of the shark
And the tiger[31], establish the robin's plucky canton?[32]
Intervene, O descend as a dove[33] or
A furious papa[34] or a mild engineer[35]: but descend."

And the life, if it answers at all, replies from the heart

And the eyes and the lungs, from the shops and squares of the city
    "O no, I am not the Mover, [36]
Not to-day, not to you. To you I'm the"

"Yes-man, the bar-companion, the easily-duped;
I am whatever you do; I am your vow to be
    Good, your humorous story;
I am your business voice; I am your marriage."

"What's your proposal? To build the Just City? I will.
I agree. Or is it the suicide pact[37], the romantic
    Death? Very well, I accept, for
I am your choice, your decision: yes, I am Spain."

Many have heard it on remote peninsulas,
On sleepy plains, in the aberrant fisherman's islands,
    In the corrupt heart of the city;
Have heard and migrated like gulls or the seeds of a flower.

They clung like burrs[38] to the long expresses that lurch
Through the unjust lands, through the night,
through the alpine[39] tunnel;
    They floated over the oceans;
They walked the passes: they came to present their lives.

On that arid square, that fragment nipped off from hot
Africa, soldered so crudely to inventive Europe[40],
    On that tableland scored by rivers,
Our fever's menacing shapes are precise and alive.[41]

    To-morrow, perhaps, the future: the research on fatigue[42]
And the movements of packers[43]; the gradual exploring of all the
    Octaves of radiation[44];
To-morrow the enlarging of consciousness by diet and breathing[45].

To-morrow the rediscovery of romantic love:
The photographing of ravens; all the fun under

Liberty's masterful shadow;
To-morrow the hour of the pageant-master[46] and
the musician.

To-morrow, for the young, the poets exploding like bombs,
The walks by the lake, the winter of perfect communion;
To-morrow the bicycle races
Through the suburbs on summer evenings: but today the struggle.

To-day the inevitable increase in the chances of death[47],
The conscious acceptance of guilt in the fact of murder[48];
To-day the expending of powers
On the flat ephemeral pamphlet and the boring meeting.[49]

To-day the makeshift consolations[50]; the shared cigarette;
The cards in the candle-lit barn and the scraping concert[51],
The masculine jokes; to-day the
Fumbled and unsatisfactory embrace before hurting.

The stars are dead; the animals will not look:
We are left alone with our day, and the time is short and
History to the defeated
May say Alas but cannot help or pardon.[52]

1. The poem consists of 23 quatrains, with the first, second, and the fourth lines of each quatrain generally having 5 stressed syllables, and the third line having 3 stressed syllables and a varying number of unstressed syllables in each line.

   The poem is composed of four sections. The first six quatrains form the first section, which describes the development of human civilization with a phrase "today the struggle" echoing through the section. The second section contains the next eleven quatrains, in which people invoke life (Life Force) to descend to them, but life wants them to "build the Just City" by their own efforts. The third section is comprised of the next three quatrains, which describes the bright future. The last section includes the last three quatrains of the poem, in which the poet describes people's struggle today and points out that they must rely on their own efforts, for if they fail, History can only say, "Alas but cannot help or pardon."

2. **the language of size**: Arabic figures.
3. **diffusion**: spreading.
4. **counting-frame**: abacus.
5. **cromlech**: a structure of prehistoric age consisting of a large flat unhewn stone resting horizontally on three or more stones set upright, found especially in Wales, Devonshire, Cornwell, and Ireland.
6. **shadow-reckoning**: Here refers to the sun-dial.
7. **cards**: fortune telling cards.
8. **divination of water**: the discovery of underground water by magical means. Auden regards superstition and magic as part of human civilization.
9. **the abolition of fairies and giants**: With the development of science man no longer believed in the existence of fairies and giants.
10. **The fortress like a motionless eagle eyeing the valley**: In feudal times a castle was built on a mountain, overlooking the valley like an eagle.
11. **the carving of angels and of frightening gargoyles**: Here refers to the architecture in medieval times (gargoyles = grotesquely carved figures of animals or human beings).
12. **The trial of heretics among the columns of stone**: In medieval times, heretics were tried on the footsteps of a cathedral. Auden regards the trial of heretics as a stage in the development of human civilization.
13. **theological feuds in the taverns**: the quarrels between the Catholics and the Protestants in the wineshops.
14. **the Sabbath of Witches**: the day the witches set for their worship.
15. **to-day the struggle**: the struggle of the Spanish people and progressive people against Fascism.
16. **the classic lecture / On the origin of Mankind**: Here refers to the theory of Charles Darwin.
17. **the absolute value of Greek**: Greek literature and philosophy was regarded for several centuries in European countries as the acme of human knowledge.
18. **The fall of the curtain upon the death of a hero**: The line may refer to Shakespeare's tragedies.
19. **the prayer to the sunset**: Here refers to the romantic poetry in the 19th century.
20. **the adoration of madmen**: Here refers to the theory of Sigmund Freud.
21. **As the poet whispers, startled among the pines... by the leaning tower**: Auden, the poet is among the pines, or sings by waterfalls or by the leaning tower in the mountain.
22. **O send me the luck of the sailor**: Auden wishes to be a sailor who gets inspiration from the sea.
23. **investigator**: scientist who makes study of the world around him. Here Auden appears as an investigator.
24. **provinces**: fields of knowledge.

25. **But the lives of my friends, I inquire, I inquire**: Auden means that though he knows inhuman things, he does not know what is happening to his friends who are persecuted by the Fascists.
26. **O show us / History the operator; the /Organizer, Time the refreshing river**: The poor people wish some change will happen to put an end to Fascism. History is compared to someone who operates or organizes things in the human world. Time will change things. Here the poor people invoke History and Time.
27. **the nations combine each cry**: The nations combine the cry of the poet, the investigator, and the poor people.
28. **life**: Here refers to the Life Force.
29. **That shapes the individual belly and orders /The private nocturnal terror**: The Life Force feeds on our bellies and creates our nightmares. According to Auden, the Life Force dominates human life.
30. **Did you not found once the city state of the sponge**: Wasn't it you, the Life Force, who once established the "city state" of the sponge, which is the most primitive living animal?
31. **Raise the vast military empires of the shark / And the tiger**: Wasn't it you, the Life Force, who created the "military empires" of the shark and the tiger?
32. **establish the robin's plucky canton?**: Wasn't it you, the Life Force, who founded the robin's brave democratic state (canton= one of the sovereign states of the Swiss confederation)? Auden, in using the allegorical images (the city state of the sponge, the military empires of the shark and the tiger, and the robin's plucky canton) is denoting the development of the political structure of human society, from the lowest form to the highest form, which is dictated by the Life Force.
33. **as a dove**: as God.
34. **papa**: God.
35. **a mild engineer**: also God; in the 18th century people regarded God as one (engineer) who makes the universe working.
36. **I am not the Mover**: The life Force answers that he is not God (the Mover) and that people must rely on themselves.
37. **the suicide pact**: Death wish was very popular among the romantic poets.
38. **burrs**: a plant's seedcase of flowers that clings to hair or clothes.
39. **alpine**: of high mountains.
40. **soldered so crudely to inventive Europe**: Spain is cut off from Africa by the Strait of Gibraltar.
41. **Our fever's menacing shapes are precise and alive**: Here refers to the threatening power of Fascism.
42. **the research on fatigue**: Auden is thinking of inventions in the future that will make people less tired in work.
43. **packers**: machines taking place of hand pickers, who pick fruits or cotton in harvesting time.
44. **all the / Octaves of radiation**: the whole range of the wave length of radiation.

45. **the enlarging of consciousness by diet and breathing**: Auden believes that in the future by improving diet and way of breathing people can be wiser and more knowledgeable.
46. **pageant-master**: the man who organizes a procession or parade with elaborate spectacular display.
47. **the chances of death**: Here refers to the fighting in Spain.
48. **The conscious acceptance of guilt in the fact of murder**: Killing is an act of murder, but in war people consciously accept killing.
49. **the expending of powers / On the flat ephemeral pamphlet and the boring meeting**: In wartime Auden wastes his energy in writing monotonous short-lived leaflets and in attending boring meetings.
50. **the makeshift consolations**: temporary substitute for comforts. The makeshift comforts are listed in the following lines.
51. **scraping concert**: As the soldiers don't play musical instruments well, they make a harsh, unpleasant sound when they are holding a concert.
52. **History to the defeated / May say Alas but cannot help or pardon**: If we should be defeated, in the future when History looks back towards us, it cannot help us and will not pardon us for not doing enough to guard ourselves against defeat.

2. Angry Young Men

In 1945 the Labour Party won in the general election, for it had promised the people that it would establish a welfare state which would provide welfare to the people and jobs for adults. But after it took office, though some reforms were taken and some welfare projects were implemented, such as the establishment of free medical care, there were still growing disappointments and complaints among the people, especially because the government failed to give jobs to all adults. When the Conservatives succeeded the Labour, things were not getting any better, especially among the young people who refused to cooperate with the government and strongly criticized state, church, and society.

During the fifties there appeared a group of young writers who were fiercely critical of the established order. They were called "Angry Young Men", a term taken from John Osborne's play *Look Back in Anger*, which first appeared on stage in 1956. The writers belonging to this group are Kingsley Amis, author of *Lucky Jim* (1954), John Wain, author of *Hurry on Down* (1953), John Braine, author of *Room at the Top* (1957); and Alan Sillitoe, author of *Saturday Night and Sunday Morning* (1958). Most of them came from working class families and lower middle families. They wrote about the ugliness and sordidness of life and exposed the hypocrisy of the genteel class. Their works were written in ordinary, sometimes dirty language. The scenes were usually set in the dark rooms or kitchens of industrial cities instead of the drawing rooms. The "heroes" were not men with high ideals. They were bitter defeated men in society.

Look Back in Anger is about the story of a young man named Jimmy Porter who is of working class parentage, has received high education, and has served in war. But after the war, he cannot find a job, although he has tried many things—journalism, advertising, etc. Now he is running a sweet stall with his friend Cliff and has married Alison, daughter of a middle class family. He loves her but takes her as a hostage against those sections of society he has declared war on. Alison's father is a retired colonel from India. Jimmy and his friend Cliff would burst into the middle class families and do all kinds of mischiefs at parties. They wolf down food and drink, smoke cigars as a way to take revenge on the society that has deprived them of the opportunity of a nice living. Alison, after living with her husband for four years and finding that she is going to have a baby, can no longer endure this kind of life. And her girl friend Helena who has advised her to leave her husband takes her place and comes to live with Jimmy. Finally Alison comes back to Jimmy.

Jimmy is a typical angry young man, who is angry with all people around him. He flings abuse at Alison. He thinks that English society is hopeless and there is no way out. But he does not take action besides doing vandalism in rich men's houses and flinging curses at the society.

The selection below is taken from the first act of the play.

John James Osborne (1929—1994)

John James Osborne was an English playwright, screenwriter, actor, known for his excoriating prose and intense critical stance towards established social and political norms. The success of his 1956 play *Look Back in Anger* transformed English theatre. In a productive life of more than 40 years, Osborne explored many themes and genres, writing for stage, film and TV. He was one of the first writers to address Britain's purpose in the post-imperial age, and was the first to question the point of the monarchy on a prominent public stage. His personal life was extravagant and iconoclastic. He was notorious for the ornate violence of his language, not only on behalf of the political causes he supported but also against his own family, including his wives and children.

Look Back in Anger

Act I

The Porters' one-room flat in a large Midland town. Early evening. April.

The scene is a fairly large attic room, at the top of a large Victorian house. The ceiling slopes down quite sharply from L. to R. Down R. are two small low windows. In front of these is a dark oak dressing table. Most of the furniture is simple, and rather old. Up R. is a double bed, running the length of most of the back wall, the rest of which is taken up with a shelf of books. Down R. below the bed is a heavy chest of drawers, covered with books, neckties and odds and ends, including a large, tattered toy teddy bear and soft, woolly squirrel. Up L. is a door. Below this a small wardrobe. Most of the wall L. is taken up with a high, oblong window. This looks out on to the landing, but light comes through it from a skylight beyond. Below the wardrobe is a gas stove, and, beside this, a wooden food cupboard, on which is a small, portable radio. Down C. is a sturdy dining table and three chairs, and, below this, L. and R., two deep, shabby leather armchairs.

AT RISE OF CURTAIN, JIMMY and CLIFF are seated in the two armchairs R. and L., respectively. All that we can see of either of them is two pairs of legs, sprawled way out beyond the newspapers which hide the rest of them from sight. They are both reading. Beside them, and between them, is a jungle of newspapers and weeklies. When we do eventually see them, we find that JIMMY is a tall, thin young man about twenty-five, wearing a very worn tweed jacket and flannels. Clouds of smoke fill the room from the pipe he is smoking. He is a disconcerting mixture of sincerity and cheerful malice[1], of tenderness and freebooting cruelty[2]; restless, importunate[3], full of pride, a combination which alienates the sensitive and insensitive alike. Blistering honesty[4], or apparent honesty, like his, makes few friends. To many he may seem sensitive to the point of vulgarity. To others, he is simply a loudmouth. To be as vehement as he is is to be almost non-committal. CLIFF is the same age, short, dark, big boned, wearing a pullover and grey, new, but very creased trousers. He is easy and relaxed, almost to lethargy, with the rather sad, natural intelligence of the self-taught. If JIMMY alienates love, CLIFF seems to exact it—demonstrations of it, at least, even from the cautious. He is a soothing, natural counterpoint to JIMMY.

Standing L., below the food cupboard, is ALISON. She is leaning over an ironing board. Beside her is a pile of clothes. Hers is the most elusive personality[5] to catch in the uneasy polyphony[6] of these three people. She is turned in a different key, a key of well-bred malaise[7] that is often drowned in the robust orchestration of the other two. Hanging over the grubby, but expensive, skirt she is wearing is a cherry red shirt of JIMMY's, but she manages somehow to look quite elegant in it. She is roughly the same age as the men. Somehow, their combined physical oddity makes her beauty more striking than it really is. She is tall, slim, dark. The bones of her face are long and delicate. There is a surprising reservation about her eyes, which are so large and deep they should make equivocation impossible.[8] The room is still, smoke filled. The only sound is the occasional thud of ALISON's iron on the board. It is one of those chilly Spring evenings, all cloud and shadows. Presently, JIMMY throws his paper down.

JIMMY: Why do I do this every Sunday? Even the book reviews seem to be the same as last week's. Different books—same reviews. Have you finished that one yet?

CLIFF: Not yet.

JIMMY: I've just read three whole columns on the English Novel. Half of it's in French. Do the Sunday papers make *you* feel ignorant?

CLIFF: Not' arf.

JIMMY: Well, you *are* ignorant. You're just a peasant. (*to Alison*) What about you? You're not a peasant are you?

ALISON: (*absently*) What's that?

JIMMY: I said do the papers make you feel you're not so brilliant after all?

ALISON: Oh—I haven't read them yet.

JIMMY: I didn't ask you that. I said——

CLIFF: Leave the poor girlie alone. She's busy.

JIMMY: Well, she can talk, can't she? You can talk, can't you? You can express an opinion. Or does the White Woman's Burden make it impossible to think?

ALISON: I'm sorry. I wasn't listening properly.

JIMMY: You bet you weren't listening. Old Porter[9] talks, and everyone turns over and goes to sleep. And Mrs. Porter gets'em all going with the first yawn.

CLIFF: Leave her alone, I said.

JIMMY: (*shouting*) All right, dear. Go back to sleep. It was only me talking. You know? Talking? Remember? I'm sorry.

CLIFF: Stop yelling. I'm trying to read.

JIMMY: Why do you bother? You can't understand a word of it.

CLIFF: Uh huh.

JIMMY: You're too ignorant.

CLIFF: Yes, and uneducated. Now shut up, will you?

JIMMY: Why don't you get my wife to explain it to you? She's educated. (*to her*) That's right, isn't it?

CLIFF: (*kicking out at him from behind his paper*) Leave her alone, I said.

JIMMY: Do that again, you Welsh ruffian, and I'll pull your ears off.

He bangs Cliff's paper out of his hands.

CLIFF: (*leaning forward*) Listen— I'm trying to better myself. Let me get on with it, you big, horrible man. Give it me. (*puts his hand out for paper*)

ALISON: Oh, give it to him, Jimmy, for heaven's sake! I can't think!

CLIFF: Yes, come on, give me the paper. She can't think.

JIMMY: Can't think! (*throws the paper back at him.*) She hasn't had a thought for years! Have you?

ALISON: No.

JIMMY: (*picks up a weekly*) I'm getting hungry.

ALISON: Oh no, not already!

CLIFF: He's a bloody pig.

JIMMY: I'm not a pig. I just like food—that's all.

CLIFF: Like it! You're like a sexual maniac—only with you it's food. You'll end up in the *News of the World*, boyo, you wait. James Porter, aged twenty-five, was bound over last week after pleading guilty to interfering with a small cabbage and two tins of beans of his way home from the Builder's Arms. The accused said he hadn't been feeling well for some time, and had been having black-outs[10]. He asked for his good record as an air-raid warden, second class, to be taken into account.

JIMMY: (*grins*) Oh, yes, yes, yes. I like to eat. I'd like to live too. Do you mind?

CLIFF: Don't see any use in your eating at all. You never get any fatter.

JIMMY: People like me don't get fat. I've tried to tell you before. We just burn everything up[11]. Now shut up while I read. You can make me some more tea.

CLIFF: Good God, you've just had a great potful! I only had one cup.

JIMMY: Like hell! Make some more.

CLIFF: (*to Alison*) Isn't that right? Didn't I only have one cup?

ALISON: (*without looking up*) That's right.

CLIFF: There you are. And she only had one cup too. I saw her. You guzzled the lot.

JIMMY: (*reading his weekly*) Put the kettle on.

CLIFF: Put it on yourself. You've creased up my paper.

JIMMY: I'm the only one who knows how to treat a paper, or

anything else, in this house. (*picks up another paper*) Girl here wants to know whether her boy friend will lose all respect for her if she gives him what he asks for. Stupid bitch.

CLIFF: Just let me get at her, that's all.

JIMMY: Who buys this damned thing? (*throws it down*) Haven't you read the other posh paper yet?

CLIFF: Which?

JIMMY: Well, there are only two posh papers on a Sunday—the one you're reading, and this one. Come on, let me have that one, and you take this.

CLIFF: Oh, all right.

They exchange.

I was only reading the Bishop of Bromley. (*puts out his hand to Alison*) How are you, dullin'?

ALISON: All right thank you, dear.

CLIFF: (*grasping her hand*) Why don't you leave all that, and sit down for a bit? You look tired.

ALISON: (*smiling*) I haven't much more to do.

CLIFF: (*kisses her hand, and puts her fingers in his mouth.*) She's a beautiful girl, isn't she?

JIMMY: That's what they all tell me.

His eyes meet hers.

CLIFF: It's a lovely, delicious paw you've got. Ummmmm. I'm going to bite it off.

ALISON: Don't! I'll burn his shirt.

JIMMY: Give her her finger back, and don't be so sickening. What's the Bishop of Bromley say?

CLIFF: (*letting go of Alison*) Oh, it says here that he makes a very moving appeal to all Christians to do all they can to assist in the manufacture of the H-Bomb.

JIMMY: Yes, well, that's quite moving, I suppose. (*to Alison*) Are you moved, my darling?

ALISON: Well, naturally.

JIMMY: There you are: even my wife is moved. I ought to send the Bishop a subscription. Let's see. What else does he say. Dumdidumdidumdidum. Ah yes. He's upset because someone has suggested that he supports the rich against the poor. He says he denies the difference of class distinctions. "This idea has been persistently and wickedly fostered by—the working classes!" Well! *He looks up at both of them for reaction, but Cliff is reading, and Alison is intent on her ironing.*

JIMMY: (*to Cliff*) Did you read that bit?

CLIFF: Um?

He has lost them, and he knows it, but he won't leave it.

JIMMY: (*to Alison*) You don't suppose your father could have written it, do you?

ALISON: Written what?

JIMMY: What I just read out, of course.

ALISON: Why should my father have written it?

JIMMY: Sounds rather like Daddy, don't you think?

ALISON: Does it?

JIMMY: Is the Bishop of Bromley his nom de plume[12], do you think?

CLIFF: Don't take any notice of him. He's being offensive. And it's so easy for him.

JIMMY: (*quickly*) Did you read about the woman who went to the mass meeting of a certain American evangelist at Earls Court? She went forward, to declare herself for love or whatever it is, and, in the rush of converts to get to the front, she broke four ribs and got kicked in the head. She was yelling her head off in agony, but with 50,000 people putting all they'd got into "Onward Christian Soldiers", nobody even knew she was there. *He looks up sharply for a response, but there isn't any.* Sometimes, I wonder if there isn't something wrong with me. What about that tea?

CLIFF: (*still behind paper*) What tea?

JIMMY: Put the kettle on.

Alison looks up at him.

ALISON: Do you want some more tea?

JIMMY: I don't know. No, I don't think so.

ALISON: Do you want some, Cliff?

JIMMY: No, he doesn't. How much longer will you be doing that?

ALISON: Won't be long.

JIMMY: God, how I hate Sundays! It's always so depressing, always the same. We never seem to get any further, do we? Always the same ritual. Reading the papers, drinking tea, ironing. A few more hours, and another week gone. Our youth is slipping away. Do you know that?

CLIFF: (*throws down paper*) What's that?

JIMMY: (*casually*) Oh, nothing, nothing. Damn you, damn both of you, damn them all.

CLIFF: Let's go to the pictures. (*to Alison*) What do you say, lovely?

ALISON: I don't think I'll be able to. Perhaps Jimmy would like to go. (*to Jimmy*) Would you like to?

JIMMY: And have my enjoyment ruined by the Sunday night yobs[13] in the front row? No, thank you. (*pause*) Did you read Priestley's piece this week? Why on earth I ask I don't know. I know damned well you haven't. why do I spend ninepence on that damned paper every week? Nobody reads it except me. Nobody can be bothered. No one can raise themselves out of their delicious sloth. You two will drive me round the bend[14] soon—I know it, as sure as I'm sitting here. I know you're going to drive me mad. Oh heavens, how I long for a little ordinary human enthusiasm. Just enthusiasm—that's all. I want to hear a warm, thrilling voice cry out Hallelujah! (*he bangs his breast theatrically.*) Hallelujah! I'm alive! I've an idea. Why don't we have a little game? Let's pretend that we're human beings, and that we're actually alive. Just for a while. What do you say? Let's pretend we're human. (*he looks from one to the other.*) Oh, brother, it's such a long time since I was with anyone who got enthusiastic about anything.

CLIFF: What did he say?

JIMMY: (*resentful of being dragged away from his pursuit of Alison*) What did who say?

CLIFF: Mr. Priestley.

JIMMY: What he always says, I suppose. He's like Daddy—still casting well-fed glances back to the Edwardian twilight[15] from his comfortable, disenfranchised[16] wilderness. What the devil have you done to those trousers?

CLIFF: Done?

JIMMY: Are they the ones you bought last week-end? Look at them. Do you see what he's done to those new trousers?

ALISON: You are naughty, Cliff. They look dreadful.

JIMMY: You spend good money on a new pair of trousers, and then sprawl about in them like a savage. What do you think you're going to do when I'm not around to look after you? Well, what are you going to do? Tell me?

CLIFF: (*grinning*) I don't know. (*to Alison*) What am I going to do, lovely?

ALISON: You'd better take them off.

JIMMY: Yes, go on. Take'em off. And I'll kick your behind for you.

ALISON: I'll give them a press while I've got the iron on.

CLIFF: O. K. (*starts taking them off.*) I'll just empty the pockets. (*takes out keys, matches, handkerchief.*)

JIMMY: Give me those matches, will you?

CLIFF: Oh, you're not going to start up that old pipe again, are you? It stinks the place out. (*to Alison*) Doesn't it smell awful?

Jimmy grabs the matches, and lights up.

ALISON: I don't mind it. I've got used to it.

JIMMY: She's a great one for getting used to things. If she were to die, and wake up in paradise—after the first five minutes, she'd have got used to it.

CLIFF: (*hands her the trousers.*) Thank you, lovely. Give me a cigarette, will you?

JIMMY: Don't give him one.

CLIFF: I can't stand the stink of that old pipe any longer. I must have a cigarette.

JIMMY: I thought the doctor said no cigarettes?

CLIFF: Oh, why doesn't he shut up?

JIMMY: All right. They're your ulcers[17]. Go ahead, and have a bellyache, if that's what you want. I give up. I give up. I'm sick of doing things for people. And all for what?

Alison gives Cliff a cigarette. They both light up, and she goes on with her ironing.

Nobody thinks, nobody cares. No beliefs, no convictions and no enthusiasm. Just another Sunday evening.

Cliff sits down again, in his pullover and shorts.

Perhaps there's a concert on. (*picks up* Radio Times.) Ah. (*nudges Cliff with his foot.*) Make some more tea. *Cliff grunts. He is reading again.* Oh, yes. There's a Vaughan Williams. Well, that's something, anyway. Something strong, something simple, something English. I suppose people like me aren't supposed to be very patriotic. Somebody said—what was it—we get our cooking from Paris (that's a laugh), our politics from Moscow, and our morals from Port Said. Something like that, anyway. Who was it? (*pause*) Well, you wouldn't know anyway. I hate to admit it, but I think I can understand how her Daddy must have felt when he came back from India, after all those years away. The old Edwardian brigade do make their brief little world look pretty tempting. All homemade cakes and croquet, bright ideas, bright uniforms. Always the same picture: high summer, the long days in the sun, slim volumes of verse, crisp linen, the smell of starch. What a romantic picture. Phoney too, of course. It must have rained sometimes. Still, even I regret it somehow, phoney or not. If you've no world of your own, it's rather pleasant to regret the passing of someone else's. I must be getting sentimental. But I must say it's pretty dreary living in the American Age—unless you're an American of course. Perhaps all our children will be Americans. That's a thought isn't it?

He gives Cliff a kick, and shouts at him.

I said that's a thought!

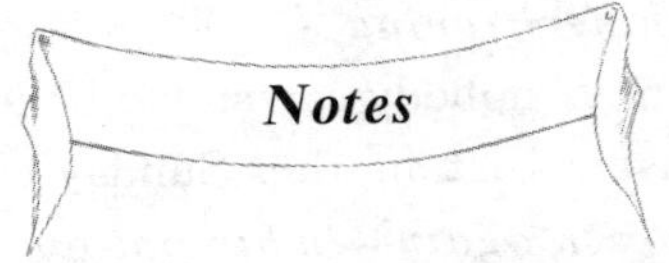

1. **cheerful malice**: the desire to hurt or tease people in good spirits.
2. **freebooting cruelty**: being cruel in plundering people's things.
3. **importunate**: being persistent in demand.
4. **Blistering honesty**: Honesty that hurts (blister = a bubble-like swelling on the skin, filled with watery liquid).
5. **elusive personality**: Her personality is hard to comprehend.
6. **polyphony**: a musical composition in which two or more melodies are harmoniously intertwined(复调音乐).
7. **malaise**: a vague feeling of uneasiness and discomfort.
8. **make equivocation impossible**: The implied meaning is that it is impossible for her to hide her real emotions. (equivocate = to use ambiguous words in order to conceal truth).
9. **Old Porter**: Jim is referring to himself.
10. **black-outs**: temporary loss of consciousness.
11. **We just burn everything up**: We just exhaust every thing we eat.
12. **nom de plume**: pen name.
13. **yobs**: (*slang*) fellows.
14. **round the bend**: crazy.
15. **Edwardian twilight**: Here refers to the reign of King Edward Ⅶ (1901—1910), in which England enjoyed the last glow of prosperity.
16. **disenfranchised**: deprived of the privileges.
17. **ulcers**: open sores on the skin.

3. The Theatre of the Absurd

The Theatre of the Absurd is a term applied to a group of dramatists who were active in the 50's. The name was probably coined by Martin Esslin in his book *The Theatre of the Absurd*, published in 1961.

"Absurd" originally means "out of harmony" or "inharmonious" in a musical context. Here it means "out of harmony with reason or propriety". It is a step further from what Joyce wrote in his works. Joyce was interested in depicting the psychology of the irrational, but at least the reader can understand the subconscious or even preconscious mind of the character described in his works. The generation after the first World War regarded the world as a waste land, but the generation after the second World War regarded the world as an irrational one.

The word "absurd" was first suggested by Camus in 1942 in *The Myth of Sisphyus*, in which Camus tries to diagnose the human situation in the world of shattered belief, as he said: "A world that can be explained by reasoning, however faulty, is a familiar world. But in a universe that is suddenly deprived of illusions and of light, man feels a stranger. He is an irremediable exile, because he is deprived of memories of a lost homeland as much as he lacks the hope of a promised land to come. This divorce between man and life, the actor and his setting, truly constitutes the feeling of Absurdity." According to Ionesco, who was born in Rumania but lived in Paris, "absurd" means "devoid of purpose... Cut off from his religious, meataphysical, and transcendental roots, man is lost, all his actions become senseless, absurd, useless." The absurdity of human conditions is the main theme of the plays of the school of the theatre of the absurd. In the plays the dramatists express that life has no pattern of meaning or ultimate significance and that no activity is more or less valuable than another.

Samuel Beckett (1906—1989)

Samuel Beckett is an Irishman, who lives in Paris. His philosophy is one of complete pessimism. Man's reason is unreliable. Truth does not exist, or if it does, man can never know it, because no human acts have meaning or purpose and life as a whole is tedious. There is no hope of communication with other human beings, for we are all unreal or false to one another. Knowledge of others and of self is impossible. Man is essentially an intellectual cripple, struggling to survive in an universe for no apparent purpose.

Waiting for Godot was published in book form in 1952 and was put on stage in 1953. In the play Beckett is discussing the absurdity of human life. He is exploring an answer to such questions as "Who am I?", or "What am I living for?" but in this world of absurdity he cannot find the answer.

What actually happens in the play?

Near a bare roadside tree, two tramps meet as they daily meet. They are waiting for Godot. Estragon (Gogo) fusses with his boots. Vladimir (Didi) fusses with his hat. Gogo naps but cannot recount his dreams because Didi won't listen. They discuss separation but make up, suicide but defer it, vegetables, religion, Didi's urinary troubles and Godot. Passing through are Pozzo, with a whip in hand, and his serf Lucky, on a leash, carrying Pozzo's coat, etc. Pozzo, who owns the surrounding land, introduces himself, discussing selling the serf. Lucky weeps but kicks Gogo when Gogo offers him a handkerchief. Pozzo commands Lucky to "dance" and "think". Master and slave resume their travelling. A goatboy comes and brings a message: Godot will come tomorrow. Gogo and Didi decide to leave, but they stand still. The next day the tree has five leaves. The tramps resume waiting with games, light gymnastic exercises, philosophical talks. Pozzo, now blind, and Lucky, now mute, return and collapse. The tramps deliberate over whether to help. They go to help, but they fall too. Finally, they help Pozzo up. Pozzo goads Lucky into travelling. Didi soliloquizes on his predicament. The boy brings the message: Godot will come tomorrow. Night falls. Agreeing to leave, they stand still.

What is the meaning of the play? Who is Godot? Why are they waiting? What do all their talks mean? What are the boots, hats, leash, and tree intended to symbolize?

Why do the tramps talk of separation and leaving, but always stand still? What do Pozzo and Lucky stand for? All these questions puzzle the reader/audience.

The message of the play may be like this. At the bottom, life is cyclical. It is spiraling downward. In either case life seems repetitious, empty, boring, with no meaning in the sense of "purpose" or "progress". The passive ones (Gogo and Didi) know this and show it more clearly. The active ones succeed for a time, but finally they are even worse than the passive ones. What should men do in this world? Wait for Godot. One does not know whether he will come or not, but wait.

The selected part is chosen from Act I, in which we can have a glimpse of the relations between the two tramps.

Waiting for Godot

Act I

Estragon, sitting on a low mound, is trying to take off his boot. He pulls at it with both hands, panting. He gives up, exhausted, rests, tries again.

As before.

Enter Vladimir.

ESTRAGON: (*giving up again*) Nothing to be done.

VLADIMIR: (*advancing with short, stiff strides, legs wide apart*). I'm beginning to come round to that opinion. All my life I've tried to put it from me, saying, Vladimir, be reasonable, you haven't yet tried everything. And I resumed the struggle. (*he broods, musing on the struggle. turning to Estragon.*) So there you are again.

ESTRAGON: Am I ?

VLADIMIR: I'm glad to see you back. I thought you were gone for ever.

ESTRAGON: Me too.

VLADIMIR: Together again at last! We'll have to celebrate this. But how? (*he reflects.*) Get up till I embrace you.

ESTRAGON: (*irritably*) Not now, not now.

VLADIMIR: (*hurt, coldly*) May one inquire where His Highness spent the night?

ESTRAGON: In a ditch.

VLADIMIR: (*admiringly*) A ditch! Where?

ESTRAGON: (*without gesture*) Over there.

VLADIMIR: And they didn't beat you?

ESTRAGON: Beat me? Certainly they beat me.

VLADIMIR: The same lot as usual?

ESTRAGON: The same? I don't know.

VLADIMIR: When I think of it... all these years... but for me... where would you be...

(*decisively*) You'd be nothing more than a little heap of bones at the present minute, no doubt about it.

ESTRAGON: And what of it?

VLADIMIR: (*gloomily*) It's too much for one man. (*pause. cheerfully*) On the other hand what's the good of losing heart now, that's what I say. We should have thought of it a million years ago, in the nineties. [1]

ESTRAGON: Ah stop blathering and help me off with this bloody thing.

VLADIMIR: Hand in hand from the top of the Eiffel Tower, among the first. We were respectable in those days. Now it's too late. They wouldn't even let us up. (*Estragon tears at his boot.*) What are you doing?

ESTRAGON: Taking off my boot. Did that never happen to you?

VLADIMIR: Boots must be taken off every day, I'm tired telling you that. why don't you listen to me?

ESTRAGON: (*feebly*) Help me!

VLADIMIR: It hurts?

ESTRAGON: (*angrily*) Hurts! He wants to know if it hurts!

VLADIMIR: (*angrily*) No one ever suffers but you. I don't count. I'd like to hear what you'd say if you had what I have.

ESTRAGON: It hurts?

VLADIMIR: (*angrily*) Hurts! He wants to know if it hurts!

ESTRAGON: (*pointing*) You might button it all the same.

VLADIMIR: (*stooping*) True. (*he buttons his fly.*) Never neglect the little things of life.

ESTRAGON: What do you expect, you always wait till the last moment.

VLADIMIR: (*musingly*) The last moment... (*he meditates.*) Hope deferred[2] maketh the something sick, who said that?

ESTRAGON: Why don't you help me?

VLADIMIR: Sometimes I feel it coming all the same. Then I go all queer. (*he takes off his hat, peers inside it, feels about inside it, shakes it, puts it on again.*) How shall I say? Relieved and at the same time... (*he searches for the word.*) ... appalled. (*with emphasis*) AP-PALLED. (*he takes off his hat again, peers inside it.*) Funny. (*He knocks on the crown as though to dislodge a foreign body, peers into it again, puts it on again.*) Nothing to be done. (*Estragon with a supreme effort succeeds in pulling off his boot. He peers inside it, feels about inside it, turns it upside down, shakes it, looks on the ground to see if anything has fallen out, finds nothing, feels inside it again, staring sightlessly before him.*) Well?

ESTRAGON: Nothing.

VLADIMIR: Show.

ESTRAGON: There's nothing to show.

VLADIMIR: Try and put it on again.

ESTRAGON: (*examining his foot*) I'll air it for a bit.

VLADIMIR: There's man all over for you, blaming on his boots the faults of his feet. (*he takes off his hat again, peers inside it, feels about inside it, knocks on the crown, blows into it, puts it on again.*) This is getting alarming. (*silence. Vladimir deep in thought, Estragon pulling at his toes.*) One of the thieves was saved. (*pause*) It's a reasonable percentage. (*pause*) Gogo.

ESTRAGON: What?

VLADIMIR: Suppose we repented.

ESTRAGON: Repented what?

VLADIMIR: Oh... (*he reflects.*) We wouldn't have to go into the details.

ESTRAGON: Our being born?

Vladimir breaks into a hearty laugh which he immediately stifles, his hand pressed to his pubis, his face contorted.

VLADIMIR: One daren't even laugh any more.

ESTRAGON: Dreadful privation.

VLADIMIR: Merely smile. (*he smiles suddenly from ear to ear, keeps smiling, ceases as suddenly.*) It's not the same thing. Nothing to be done. (*pause*) Gogo.

ESTRAGON: (*irritably*) What is it?

VLADIMIR: Did you ever read the Bible?

ESTRAGON: The Bible... (*he reflects.*) I must have taken a look at it.

VLADIMIR: Do you remember the Gospels?

ESTRAGON: I remember the maps of the Holy Land. Coloured they were. Very pretty. The Dead Sea was pale blue. The very look of it made me thirsty. That's where we'll go, I used to say, that's where we'll go for our honeymoon. We'll swim. We'll be happy.

VLADIMIR: You should have been a poet.

ESTRAGON: I was. (*gesture towards his rags.*) Isn't that obvious?

Silence.

VLADIMIR: Where was I... How's your foot?

ESTRAGON: Swelling visibly.

VLADIMIR: Ah yes, the two thieves. Do you remember the story?

ESTRAGON: No.

VLADIMIR: Shall I tell it to you?

ESTRAGON: No.

VLADIMIR: It'll pass the time. (*pause*) Two thieves, crucified at the same time as our Saviour. One—

ESTRAGON: Our what?

VLADIMIR: Our Saviour. Two thieves. One is supposed to have been saved and the other... (*he searches for the contrary of saved*)... damned.

ESTRAGON: Saved from what?

VLADIMIR: Hell.

ESTRAGON: I'm going.

He does not move.

VLADIMIR: And yet... (*pause*)... how is it—this is not boring you I hope—how is it that of the four Evangelists[3] only one speaks of a thief being saved. The four of them were there—or there-abouts—and only one speaks of a thief being saved. (*pause*) Come on, Gogo, return the ball,[4] can't you, once in a way?

ESTRAGON: (*with exaggerated enthusiasm*) I find this really most extraordinarily interesting.

VLADIMIR: One out of four. Of the other three two don't mention any thieves at all and the third says that both of them abused him.

ESTRAGON: Who?

VLADIMIR: What?

ESTRAGON: What's all this about? Abused who?

VLADIMIR: The Saviour.

ESTRAGON: Why?

VLADIMIR: Because he wouldn't save them.

ESTRAGON: From hell?

VLADIMIR: Imbecile! From death.

ESTRAGON: I thought you said hell.

VLADIMIR: From death from death.

ESTRAGON: Well what of it?

VLADIMIR: Then the two of them must have been damned.

ESTRAGON: And why not?

VLADIMIR: But one of the four says that one of the two was saved.

ESTRAGON: Well? They don't agree and that's all there is to it.

VLADIMIR: But all four were there. And only one speaks of a thief being saved. Why believe him rather than the others?

ESTRAGON: Who believes him?

VLADIMIR: Everybody. It's the only version they know.

ESTRAGON: People are bloody ignorant apes.

He rises painfully, goes limping to extreme left, halts, gazes into distance off with his hand screening his eyes, turns, goes to extreme right, gazes into distance. Vladimir watches him, then goes and picks up the boot, peers into it, drops it hastily.

VLADIMIR: Pah!

He spits. Extragon moves to center, halts with his back to auditorium.

ESTRAGON: Charming spot. (*he turns, advances to front, halts facing auditorium.*) Inspiring prospects. (*he turns to Vladimir.*) Let's go.

VLADIMIR: We can't.

ESTRAGON: Why not?

VLADIMIR: We're waiting for Godot.

ESTRAGON: (*despairingly*) Ah! (*pause*) You're sure it was here?

VLADIMIR: What?

ESTRAGON: That we were to wait.

VLADIMIR: He said by the tree. (*they look at the tree.*) Do you see any others?

ESTRAGON: What is it?

VLADIMIR: I don't know. A willow.

ESTRAGON: Where are the leaves?

VLADIMIR: It must be dead.

ESTRAGON: No more weeping.

VLADIMIR: Or perhaps it's not the season.

ESTRAGON: Looks to me more like a bush.

VLADIMIR: A shrub.

ESTRAGON: A bush.

VLADIMIR: A—. What are you insinuating? That we've come to the wrong place?

ESTRAGON: He should be here.

VLADIMIR: He didn't say for sure he'd come.

ESTRAGON: And if he doesn't come?

VLADIMIR: We'll come back to-morrow.

ESTRAGON: And then the day after to-morrow.

VLADIMIR: Possibly.

ESTRAGON: And so on.

VLADIMIR: The point is—

ESTRAGON: Until he comes.

VLADIMIR: You're merciless.

ESTRAGON: We came here yesterday.

VLADIMIR: Ah no, there you're mistaken.

ESTRAGON: What did we do yesterday?

VLADIMIR: What did we do yesterday?
ESTRAGON: Yes.
VLADIMIR: Why... (*angrily*) Nothing is certain when you're about.
ESTRAGON: In my opinion we were here.
VLADIMIR: (*looking round*) You recognize the place?
ESTRAGON: I didn't say that.
VLADIMIR: Well?
ESTRAGON: That makes no difference.
VLADIMIR: All the same... that tree... (*turning towards auditorium*) that bog...
ESTRAGON: You're sure it was this evening?
VLADIMIR: What?
ESTRAGON: That we were to wait.
VLADIMIR: He said Saturday. (*pause*) I think.
ESTRAGON: You think.
VLADIMIR: I must have made a note of it. (*he fumbles in his pockets, bursting with miscellaneous rubbish.*)
ESTRAGON: (*very insidious*) But what Saturday? And is it Saturday? Is it not rather Sunday? (*pause*) Or Monday? (*pause*) Or Friday?
VLADIMIR: (*looking wildly about him, as though the date was inscribed in the landscape*) It's not possible!
ESTRAGON: Or Thursday?
VLADIMIR: What'll we do?
ESTRAGON: If he came yesterday and we weren't here you may be sure he won't come again to-day.
VLADIMIR: But you say we were here yesterday.
ESTRAGON: I may be mistaken. (*pause*) Let's stop talking for a minute, do you mind?
VLADIMIR: (*feebly*) All right. (*Estragon sits down on the mound. Vladimir paces agitatedly to and fro, halting from time to time to gaze into distance off. Estragon falls asleep. Vladimir halts finally before Estragon.*) Gogo!... Gogo!... GOGO! Estragon wakes with a start.
ESTRAGON: (*restored to the horror of his situation.*) I was asleep! (*despairingly*) Why will you never let me sleep?

VLADIMIR: I felt lonely.
ESTRAGON: I had a dream.
VLADIMIR: Don't tell me!
ESTRAGON: I dreamt that—
VLADIMIR: DON'T TELL ME!
ESTRAGON: (*gesture towards the universe*) This one is enough for you? (*silence*) it's not nice of you, Didi. Who am I to tell my private nightmares to if I can't tell them to you?
VLADIMIR: Let them remain private. You know I can't bear that.
ESTRAGON: (*coldly*) There are times when I wonder if it wouldn't be better for us to part.
VLADIMIR: You wouldn't go far.
ESTRAGON: That would be too bad, really too bad. (*pause*) Wouldn't it, Didi, be really too bad? (*pause*) When you think of the beauty of the way. (*pause*) And the goodness of the wayfarers. (*pause, wheedling.*) Wouldn't it, Didi?

1. **We should have thought of it a million years ago, in the nineties**: According to the context, Vladimir is saying that they should have committed suicide long ago.
2. **Hope deferred**: Hope delayed.
3. **the four Evangelists**: Here refers to the four of Jesus Christ's disciples who wrote the four Gospels. They were St. Matthew, St. Mark, St. Luke, and St. John.
4. **return the ball**: answer me.

4. Iris Murdoch (1919—1999)

Iris Murdoch, in full Dame Jean Iris Murdoch, married name Mrs. J. O. Bailey, is a British writer, university lecturer and prolific and highly professional novelist. She was born in Dublin of Anglo-Irish parents. She went to Badminton School, Bristol, and read classics at Somerville College, Oxford. In 1956, she married John Bailey, don and critic. In her mainly philosophical novels, Iris Murdoch dealt with everyday ethical or moral issues, sometimes in the light of myths. Beginning from 1954, she published more than forty novels, including *Under the Net* (1954), *The Flight from the Enchanter* (1956), *The Bell* (1958), *A Severed Head* (1961), *The Unicorn* (1963), *The Red and Green* (1965), *A Fairly Honourable Defeat* (1970), *The Black Prince* (1973), *The Sea, The Sea* (1978), *The Philosopher's Pupil* (1983), *The Green Knight* (1993).

A Severed Head

In the story, Antonia, the wife of Martin Lynch-Gibbon, an upper class wine merchant, tells her husband that she is in love with their best friend, Palmer Anderson. Palmer and Antonia want to deal with the situation in a civilized way, by remaining friends with Martin. Meanwhile Martin tries to keep his mistress, Georgie Hands, a secret, but Palmer's sister, Honor Klein, who taught Georgie at Oxford, tells Palmer and Antonia about her. Furthermore, Honor introduces Georgie to Martin's womanizing brother, Alexander. This is just the beginning of a series of intricate relationships and liaisons.

Thirteen

I[1] SIMPLY had to see Antonia[2] again. It was with her as we left Pelham Crescent, that the weight of my love and concern remained. I could no more separate my being from her than if she had been my mother; and the confrontation of the two women had made me feel, perhaps momentarily but with desperate sadness, the concreteness of my bond with her, the abstractness of my bond with Georgie.[3] Yet how much Antonia exasperated me. I felt, every twist and turn of it, Georgie's exasperation, her so fastidious curling up.[4] At the same time I resented this wincing in Georgie, resented even her cautious, scrupulous, after her own fashion dignified, approach to a judgement. I had to depart with Georgie; but I had to return to Antonia.

I took Georgie home in the car. We were both silent, exhausted really. Once inside she offered me supper, and I stayed to eat bread and cheese. Georgie was no cook and I had no heart for cooking anything myself. We ate the bread and cheese, wolfishly and with surly looks, washing it down with whisky and water. I felt I could not bear any display of emotion just then from Georgie; I wanted to get away. She taxed[5] me, as we were finishing our meal, with just this, and I could not find the protestations which would console her. She spared me her tears. But it was in both our minds that she had said "it is unlikely that he will marry me". For her, I think, these words were a barrier between us which she wished me now lovingly and tempestuously to remove. For me they constituted rather a kind of moratorium, a momentary neutral zone where I could, and how very much in my weariness I needed it, absolutely rest. I had not got it in me to produce for Georgie the passionate reassuring speeches which she wanted. Her words had been intended as a provocation. I accepted them gratefully and in silence as a resting place.

Just before I left we achieved a sort of peace together, lying down for a moment beside the gas fire, forehead to forehead and foot to foot. Georgie's so familiar face, close to mine, in repose at last, her big eyes gentle now, her mouth relaxed, resting from my kisses, was a beloved landscape. Without words we gazed and murmured each other into quietness, until it was as if we had talked in detail for a long time, so spiritual a thing is the human face.

I left Georgie taking aspirins and promising to go to bed at once. I did not suggest and she did not demand that I should remain with her. The prospect of a night together, so eagerly grasped in the old days, was now a problem and not a prize. We were both in a state of emotional exhaustion, and what we really needed for the moment was a rest from each other. In addition I required, with anxiety and with eagerness, to see Antonia once more, however, briefly, before I went to bed. I drove the car back to Palmer's[6] house.

It was beginning to be foggy again. A yellow sulphurous haze hung about the street lamps of Pelham Crescent imposing its own infernal curfew, and my steps as I crossed the pavement left moist sticky traces. There were no traffic noises here. The place was sunk in the stricken silence of the gathering fog. The great London night contracted about me into a cold brown kernel, where the damp curled and crept, diminishing, and already too opaque to return an echo. I hurried up to the door and stepped quietly into the warm fresh-smelling hall. I had stayed long with Georgie. The time was a little after ten o'clock.

The lights were on in the hall and the upstairs landing. I listened. There was no sound of voices. I crossed to the drawing-room door and opened it. The fire was burning brightly but there was no one there. I turned the lamps on from the door. The room came into being[7] before me, still, yet tense with its own sinister life. I closed the door behind me and stood there a while. Something of Palmer and Antonia was present, some tall shadow of them, which illicitly and with an almost guilty relish I enjoyed, simply standing in the empty room. I moved towards the fire and realized then that I was a bit drunk. I had had no lunch and precious little supper and I had consumed, with Georgie, a formidable amount of whisky. I sat heavily into an armchair and reflected on how pleasant it was to be alone and not to have to think of ways of justifying myself.

I became aware that I was filled with undirected sexual desire. I wanted somebody. I suppose, after a little while, that it was Antonia that I wanted. I had certainly not wanted Georgie. I had envisaged with a trapped gloom the possibility that she might suggest our going to bed together; I had accepted gratefully her obvious desire to be, for the moment, rid of me. I had not had, for her, the right words, the proper consolations. Later, I knew, I would be able to soothe and delight her with these. Now, however, with a resentment which I knew to be unjust, I was prepared to keep her in suspense and to greet her weary disappointed dismissal with a sigh of relief. No. it was about Antonia, in a sad and confused way, that my imagination now played; and it was evident to me that I had not yet accepted that I had lost her. It was as if recent events represented a mock barrier between us, an element as it were in a flirtation, over and past which I would later sweep to a reunion. I imagined myself, ultimately and safely, at home in her arms.

I shook myself out of these dreams. There were places where my thoughts must not go; and as I then reflected how few places were left where they *could* now go without incurring pain or guilt I decided that I needed some more whisky and recalled that Palmer kept some in the sideboard in the dining-room. Leaving the lights on I crossed the hall. The dining-room door was closed. I opened it and went in.

The room was not dark and my hand hesitated on the electric-light switch. Candles were burning still in the silver candlesticks on the long table, making the room a cave of warm dim luminosity to which my eyes became in a moment accustomed. I stood still, a little surprised, and closed the door behind me. Then I saw that there was someone sitting alone at the far end of the table.

It was Honor Klein[8]. As I saw her the consciousness returned to me, but without being distressing, that I was somewhat tipsy; and I stood there for a moment longer leaning against the door. I could not see her clearly. But I apprehended at once, and it struck me as a trifle strange, that she was not particularly concerned about my arrival. It was like an arrival at the shrine of some remote and self absorbed deity. She was plunged in thoughts of her own.

I came slowly down the length of the table. I saw as I came that Palmer and Antonia had dined. Again there were the two places set, and the bottle, this time of Lynch-Gibbon Château Malmaison[9] 1953, almost emptied. Two table napkins lay in disarray beside the places and there was a wide scattering of crumbs upon the polished surface beneath which the light of the candles seemed to burn again. As I approached Honor Klein I saw that without moving her head she was following me with her eyes. It was like the animation of a corpse. I looked down at her with a sort of fastidious surprise and then found that I had sat down beside her.

I said, "Excuse me, I was looking for Palmer's whisky. Where are they anyway?"

"At the opera,"[10] said Honor. She spoke in an abstracted[11] tone, as if I had only a small corner of her attention. She stared ahead of her now toward the candles. I wondered for a moment if she was drunk, but decided probably it was only I who was drunk.

"At the opera," I said. It occurred to me as scandalous that Palmer and Antonia, after the scene in which I had taken part in the drawing-room, should have gone out to the opera. Antonia ought to have been waiting for me to come back. I resented this indifference to the tempo of my own drama.

"What's on?"I said.

"*Götterdämmerung*."[12]

I laughed.

Presently I got up and went to the cupboard to look for whisky. As I passed behind her I saw something lying upon the table. It was the Japanese sword, encased in its scabbard of lacquered wood, which usually hung in the hall. Honor Klein had evidently been continuing her dismantling activities.[13] There was no whisky but I found a bottle of excellent brandy. I returned to the table with the bottle and two glasses. "You'll join me?"

With a sort of effort she gave me her glance. Her face, in which I now apprehended a fugitive resemblance to Palmer,[14] had a slumbrous look which I could not decipher. It might have been sheer weariness, it might have been resignation. She said after a moment, "Thank you, yes, why not." I realized, but without understanding and without curiosity, that somehow, in some way, she was *in extremis*.[15] I poured out the brandy.

We sat in silence for a while. The room was beginning to seem abnormally dark. Perhaps some of the fog had drifted in from outside. One of the candles began to flicker, and its flame foundered sizzling in a sea of melted wax. As I saw it go I felt frightened and then wondered if I had rightly identified the thing which clutched at my heart.

I said to Honor Klein, "You didn't waste much time in having me brought to justice."

She kept her eyes on the candles and smiled very slightly. "Was it unpleasant?"

"I don't know," I said. "I suppose so. Everything is so unpleasant nowadays it's hard to tell." I found I could talk to her with remarkable directness. Our conversations were refreshingly lacking in formality. As I spoke I reached out automatically toward the sword, which lay with the blunt-ended scabbard towards me; but Honor Klein drew it away a little and I left my hand upon the table to fiddle with the bread crumbs.

I wondered if I should ask her why she had made Georgie confess,[16] but found that I could not bring myself to do so. A nervous shrinking which was not exactly dislike made me hesitate to probe the motives of such a being. Therewith some vague yet powerful train of thought led me to say, "I'm a broken reed[17] after all."

I was not sure why I said this, but some subterranean affinity with the thoughts of my companion must have prompted it, for she replied at once, "Yes. It doesn't matter."

We both sighed. My hand moved restlessly upon the table. I began to stare at the sword and to want very much to get hold of it. Honor was holding it in a possessive predatory way, her two hands on the scabbard, like a large animal holding down a small one. She faced the candles looking pale and rather haggard, her eyes screwed up as against a great light, and I tried in vain to detect what it was, other than a certain elusive air of authority, which made her resemble her brother;

for the fact was that Palmer was beautiful while she was very nearly ugly. I contemplated her sallow cheek which shone dully like wax, and the black gleaming bair, oily straight, and brutally short. She was a subject for Goya.[18] Only the curve of her nostril and the curve of her mouth hinted, with a Jewish strength, a possible Jewish refinement. I said, "Is the sword yours?" and as I spoke I put my hand on the end of the scabbard.

She stared a little and said, "Yes. It's a Japanese Samurai sword,[19] a very fine one. I used to have a great interest in Japan. I worked there for a time." She drew the sword away again.

"You were with Palmer in Japan?"

"Yes."She spoke as out of a deep dream.

I wanted her to know that I was present. I said, "May I see the sword?"

I thought for a moment that she was going to ignore me. But she turned towards me as if taking thought. Then she twisted the thing about on the polished surface of the table. I expected her to offer me the hilt, but instead, as I reached for it, she took the hilt in her own hand and with a swift movement drew the sword from the scabbard. At the same time she rose to her feet.

The sword came out with a swishing clattering sound and the disturbed candles flashed for a moment in the blade. She laid the scabbard on the table and let the blade descend more slowly until it lay along her thigh. Its bright surface showed against the dark material of her dress as with head bowed she gazed down along its slightly curving length.

When she spoke her voice was dry. She might have been in the lecture room. "In Japan these swords are practically religious objects. They are forged not only with great care but with great reverence. And the use of them is not merely an art but a spiritual exercise."

"So I have heard," I said. I moved her chair out of the way so as to see her better and made myself comfortable, crossing one leg over the other. "I am not attracted by the idea of decapitating people as a spiritual exercise."

Somewhere, seeming at first to be inside my head, I heard a small sound. Then I realized it was a very distant peal of church bells; and I brought to mind that it was New Year's Eve. Some nearer bells took up the peal. We both listened for a moment in silence. Soon it would be the turn of the year.

Honor let the sword droop towards the floor. She said, "Being a Christian, you connect spirit with love. These people connect it with control, with power."

"What do you connect it with?"

She shrugged her shoulders. "I am a Jew."

"But you believe in the dark gods," I said.

"I believe in people," said Honor Klein. It was a rather unexpected reply.

I said, "You sound rather like a fox saying it believes in geese."

She laughed suddenly, and with that she laid her other hand upon the hilt and drew the sword upward with surprising swiftness to describe a great arc at the level of her head. It made a sound like a whip moving. The point came down within an inch of the arm of my chair and then descended again to the floor. I resisted an impulse to move back. I said, "You can use it?"

"I studied it for several years in Japan, but I never got beyond the beginning."

"Show me something," I said. I wanted to see her moving again.

She said, "I am not a performer," and turned away again towards the table. In the distance the church bells continued their mathematical jargoning.

The remnants of Palmer and Antonia's dinner lay derelict under the falling candles. She drew towards her their two crumpled table napkins and looked at them thoughtfully. Then with one hand she tossed one of the napkins high in the air into the darkness of the high-ceilinged room. As it descended the sword was already moving with immense speed. The two halves of the napkin fluttered to the floor. She threw up the other napkin and decapitated it.[20] I picked up one of the pieces. It was cleanly cut.

As I held it, looking up at her, I suddenly recalled the scene in the drawing-room when I had first seen Honor Klein confronting the other two like a young and ruthless captain. I laid the piece of linen on the table and said, "That was a good trick."

"It was not a *trick*," said Honor. She had been standing before me, still holding the hilt in a two-handed grip, and looking down at one of the severed napkins. I saw that she was breathing deeply. Now she moved her chair back to the table and sat down. For a moment or two she lifted the sword, moving it as if it had become very heavy, and cooled her forehead on the blade, turning her head slowly against it with a caressing motion. Then she laid it down again on the table, still keeping one hand on the hilt. I looked at the corded hilt, long and dark, continuing the gentle sinister backward curve of the blade, the inner casing, which seemed like snake-skin, decorated with silver flowers, appearing through the diamond-shaped slits of the black cordage. Her large pale hand was firmly closed about it. I felt an intense desire to take the sword from her, but something prevented me. I put my hand on the blade, moving it up towards the hilt and feeling the cutting edge. It was hideously sharp. My hand stopped. The blade felt as if it were charged with electricity and I had to let go. No longer now attending to me she moved the sword back and laid it across her knees in the attitude of a patient executioner. I realized that the church bells had become silent and it was the New Year.

1. "I" here is Martin Lynch-Gibbon.
2. Antonia is the much-pampered wife of Martin.
3. Because of her lower middle-class background, Georgie Hands is in a disadvantageous position in a mainly upper-class circle.
4. **curl up**: to lie comfortably with the limbs drawn close to the body.
5. **tax**: to make heavy demands (on sb.); to tire (sb.)
6. Palmer Anderson is a psychiatrist.
7. **come into being**: to begin to exist; here, to become visible.
8. **Honor Klein**: Palmer's sister, intellectual, and university lecturer.
9. **Lynch-Gibbon Château Malmaison**: As Martin is a wealthy upper-class merchant, it is natural that Martin's residence has an impressive name.
10. **the opera**: the theatre where operas are performed.
11. **abstracted**: inattentive to what is happening.
12. ***Götterdämmerung***: *German for Twilight of the Gods*, Richard Wagener's famous opera. Its accepted Chinese translation is "众神的黄昏".
13. **dismantling activities**: In the story, Honor Klein has important thematic and narrative functions, that is, to destroy or dismantle the outward character of people and compel them to face the truths.

14. **a fugitive resemblance to Palmer**: Remember Honor Klein is Palmer's sister.
15. ***in extremis***: Latin, roughly meaning in crises.
16. Honor Klein has made Georgie confess that she is Martin's mistress.
17. **a broken reed**: a helper who cannot be trusted.
18. The subjects of Goya, a famous painter, are often the grotesque.
19. **a Japanese Samurai sword**: 日本武士战刀。
20. **She threw up the other napkin and decapitated it**: Toward the end of *A Severed Head* (Chapter 27), Honor Klein says, "I am a severed head such as primitive tribes and old alchemists used to use, anointing it with oil and putting a morsel of gold upon its tongue to make it utter prophecies. And who knows but that long acquaintance with a severed head might not lead to strange knowledge." For a fruitful understanding of this novel, it is necessary to connect this passage to her "decapitating" and "dismantling" activities.

5. William Golding (1911—1993)

William Golding was born in Cornwall in 1911 and was educated at Marlborough Grammar School and at Brasenose College, Oxford. Apart from writing, his occupations include being a schoolmaster, a lecturer, an actor, a sailor, and a musician. His father was a schoolmaster and his mother was a suffragette. He was brought up to be a scientist, but revolted. After two years at Oxford he read English literature instead. He spent five years at Oxford. published a volume of poems in 1935. Taught at Bishop Wordsworth's School, Salisbury. Joined the Royal Navy in 1940 and spent six years afloat. After the war he returned to teaching, and began to write again. In 1980 he won the "Booker Prize". In 1983, he won the Nobel Prize for Literature. He retired from teaching in 1962. After that, he lived in Wiltshire, listing as his hobbies music, sailing, archaeology and classical Greek. Apart from *Lord of the Flies* (1954), his other novels are *The Inheritors* (1955), *Pincher Martin* (1965) *Free Fall* (1959), *The Spire* (1964), *The Pyramid* (1967), *The Scorpion God* (three short novels) (1971), *Darkness Visible* (1979), *Rites of Passage* (1980), *The Paper Men* (1984), *Close Quarters* (1987), *Fire Down Below* (1989).

Lord of the Flies

The main idea of the story could be summarized as follows. Because of a large-scale War, a group of children are stranded on an island and thus a children's society begins to operate. However, in such activities as hunting for food, building shelters and keeping a fire for rescue signal, the children soon abandon all the civilized conducts that have been taught them and start killing each other. William Golding himself describes the theme of the novel as "an attempt to trace the defects of society back to the defects of human nature". Obviously *Lord of the Flies* is more than a children's tale and its moral applies to adult society with equal weight, as is indicated again by Golding: "The whole book is symbolic in nature except the rescue in the end where adult life appears, dignified and capable, but in reality enmeshed in the same evil as the symbolic life of the children on the island."

Chapter Nine

A View to a Death

Over the island the build-up of clouds continued. A steady current of heated air rose all day from the mountain and was thrust to ten thousand feet; revolving masses of gas piled up the static until the air was ready to explode. By early evening the sun had gone and a brassy glare had taken the place of clear daylight. Even the air that pushed in from the sea was hot and held no refreshment. Colours drained[1] from water and trees and pink surfaces of rock, and the white and brown clouds brooded. Nothing prospered but the flies who blackened their lord[2] and made the spilt guts look like a heap of glistening coal. Even when the vessel broke in Simon's[3] nose and the blood gushed out they left him alone, preferring the pig's high flavour.

With the running of the blood Simon's fit[4] passed into the weariness of sleep. He lay in the mat of creepers while the evening advanced and the cannon continued to play. At last he woke and saw dimly the dark earth close by his cheek. Still he did not move but lay there, his face sideways on the earth, his eyes looking dully before him. Then he turned over, drew his feet under him and laid hold of the creepers to pull himself up. When the creepers shook the flies exploded from the guts with a vicious note and clamped back on again. Simon got to his feet. The light was unearthly. The Lord of the Flies[5] hung on his stick like a black ball.

Simon spoke aloud to the clearing.

"What else is there to do?"

Nothing replied. Simon turned away from the open space and crawled through the creepers till he was in the dusk of the forest. He walked drearily between the trunks, his face empty of expression, and the blood was dry round his mouth and chin. Only sometimes as he lifted the ropes of creeper aside and chose his direction from the trend of the land, he mouthed words that did not reach the air.

Presently the creepers festooned the trees less frequently and there was a scatter of pearly light from the sky down through the trees. This was the backbone of the island, the slightly higher land that lay beneath the mountain where the forest was no longer deep jungle. Here there were wide spaces interspersed with thickets and huge trees and the trend of the ground led him up as the forest opened. He pushed on, staggering sometimes with his weariness but never stopping. The usual brightness was gone from his eyes and he walked with a sort of glum determination like an old man.

A buffet of wind made him stagger and he saw that he was out in the open, on rock, under a brassy sky. He found his legs were weak and his tongue gave him pain all the time. When the wind reached the mountain-top he could see something happen, a flicker of blue stuff against brown clouds. He pushed himself forward and the wind came again, stronger now, cuffing the forest heads till they ducked and roared. Simon saw a humped thing suddenly sit up on the top[6] and look down at him. He hid his face, and toiled on.

The flies had found the figure too. The life-like movement would scare them off for a moment so that they made a dark cloud round the head. Then as the blue material of the parachute collapsed the corpulent figure would bow forward, sighing, and the flies settle once more.

Simon felt his knees smack the rock. He crawled forward and soon he understood. The tangle of lines showed him the mechanics of this parody; he examined the white nasal bones, the teeth, the colours of corruption. He saw how pitilessly the layers of rubber and canvas held together the poor body that should be rotting away. Then the wind blew again and the figure lifted, bowed, and breathed foully at him. Simon knelt on all fours and was sick till his stomach was empty. Then he took the lines in his hands; he freed them from the rocks and the figure from the wind's indignity.

At last he turned away and looked down at the beaches. The fire by the platform appeared to be out, or at least making no smoke. Further along the beach, beyond the little river and near a great slab of rock, a thin trickle of smoke was climbing into the sky. Simon, forgetful of the flies, shaded his eyes with both hands and peered at the smoke. Even at that distance it was possible to see that most of the boys—perhaps all the boys—were there. So they had shifted camp then, away from the beast. As Simon thought this, he turned to the poor broken thing that sat stinking by his side. The beast was harmless and horrible; and the news must reach the others as soon as possible. He started down the mountain and his legs gave beneath him. Even with great care the best he could do was a stagger.

"Bathing," said Ralph,[7] "that's the only thing to do."

Piggy[8] was inspecting the looming sky through his glass.

"I don't like them clouds.[9] Remember how it rained just after we landed?"

"Going to rain again."

Ralph dived into the pool. A couple of littluns[10] were playing at the edge, trying to extract comfort from a wetness warmer than blood. Piggy took off his glasses, stepped primly into the water and then put them on again. Ralph came to the surface and squirted a jet of water at him.

"Mind my specs," said Piggy. "If I get water on the glass I got to get out and clean'em."

Ralph squirted again and missed. He laughed at Piggy, expecting him to retire meekly as usual and in pained silence. Instead, Piggy beat the water with his hands.

"Stop it!" He shouted, "D'you hear?"

Furiously he drove the water into Ralph's face.

"All right, all right," said Ralph. "Keep your hair on.[11]" Piggy stopped beating the water.

"I got a pain in my head. I wish the air was cooler."

"I wish the rain would come."

"I wish we could go home"

Piggy lay back against the sloping sand-side of the pool. His stomach protruded and the water dried on it. Ralph squirted up at the sky. One could guess at the movement of the sun by the progress of a light patch among the clouds. He knelt in the water and looked round.

"Where's everybody?"

Piggy sat up.

"P'raps they're lying in the shelter."

"Where's Samneric?"

"And Bill?"

Piggy pointed beyond the platform.

"That's where they've gone. Jack's party.[12]"

"Let them go," said Ralph, uneasily, "I don't care."

"Just for some meat—"

"And for hunting," said Ralph, wisely, "and for pretending to be a tribe, and putting on war-paint."

Piggy stirred the sand under water and did not look at Ralph.

"P'raps we ought to go too."

Ralph looked at him quickly and Piggy blushed.

"I mean—to make sure nothing happens."

Ralph squirted water again.

Long before Ralph and Piggy came up with Jack's lot, they could hear the party. There was a stretch of grass in a place where the palms left a wide band of turf between the forest and the shore. Just one step down from the edge of the turf was the white, blown sand of above high water, warm, dry, trodden. Below that again was a rock that stretched away towards the lagoon. Beyond was a short stretch of sand and then the edge of the water. A fire burned on the rock and fat dripped from the roasting pigmeat into the invisible flames. All the boys of the island, except Piggy, Ralph, Simon, and the two tending the pig, were grouped on the turf. They were laughing, singing, lying, squatting, or standing on the grass, holding food in their hands. But to judge by the greasy faces, the meat-eating was almost done; and some held coconut shells in their hands and were drinking from them. Before the party had started a great log had been dragged into the centre of the lawn and Jack, painted and garlanded, sat there like an idol.[13] There were piles of meat on green leaves near him, and fruit, and coconut shells full of drink.

Piggy and Ralph came to the edge of the grassy platform; and the boys, as they noticed them, fell silent one by one till only the boy next to Jack was talking. Then the silence intruded even there and Jack turned where he sat. For a time he looked at them and the crackle of the fire was the loudest noise over the bourdon of the reef. Ralph looked away; and Sam, thinking that Ralph had turned to him accusingly, put down his gnawed bone with a nervous giggle. Ralph took an uncertain step, pointed to a palm tree, and whispered something inaudible to Piggy; and they both giggled like Sam. Lifting his feet high out of the sand, Ralph started to stroll past. Piggy tried to whistle.

At this moment the boys who were cooking at the fire suddenly hauled off a great chunk of meat and ran with it towards the grass. They bumped Piggy who was burnt, and yelled and danced. Immediately, Ralph and the crowd of boys were united and relieved by a storm of laughter. Piggy once more was the centre of social derision so that everyone felt cheerful and normal.[14]

Jack stood up and waved his spear.

"Take them some meat."

The boys with the spit gave Ralph and Piggy each a succulent chunk. They took the gift, dribbling. So they stood and ate beneath a sky of thunderous brass that rang with the storm-coming.

Jack waved his spear again.

"Has everybody eaten as much as they want?"

There was still food left, sizzling on the wooden spits, heaped on the green platters. Betrayed by his stomach, Piggy threw a picked bone down on the beach and stooped for more.

Jack spoke again, impatiently.

"Has everybody eaten as much as they want?"

His tone conveyed a warning, given out of the pride of ownership, and the boys ate faster while there was still time. Seeing there was no immediate likelihood of a pause, Jack rose from the log that was his throne and sauntered to the edge of the grass. He looked down from behind his paint at Ralph and Piggy. They moved a little further off over the sand and Ralph watched the fire as he ate. He noticed, without understanding, how the flames were visible now against the dull light. Evening was come, not with calm beauty but with the threat of violence.

Jack spoke.

"Give me a drink."

Henry brought him a shell and he drank, watching Piggy and Ralph over the jagged rim. Power lay in the brown swell of his forearms: authority sat on his shoulder and chattered in his ear like an ape.[15]

"All sit down."

The boys ranged themselves in rows on the grass before him but Ralph and Piggy stayed a foot lower, standing on the soft sand. Jack ignored them for the moment, turned his mask down to the seated boys and pointed at them with the spear.

"Who is going to join my tribe?"

Ralph made a sudden movement that became a stumble. Some of the boys turned towards him.

"I gave you food," said Jack, "and my hunters will protect you from the beast. Who will join my tribe?"

"I'm chief," said Ralph, "because you chose me. And we were going to keep the fire going. Now you run after food—"

"You ran yourself!" shouted Jack. "Look at that bone in your hands!"

Ralph went crimson.

"I said you were hunters. That was your job."

Jack ignored him again.

"Who'll join my tribe and have fun?"

"I'm chief," said Ralph tremulously. "And what about the fire? and I've got the conch—"[16]

"You haven't got it with you," said Jack, sneering. "You left it behind. See, clever? And the conch doesn't count at this end of the island—"

All at once the thunder struck. Instead of the dull boom there was a point of impact in the explosion.

"The conch counts here too," said Ralph, "and all over the island."

"What are you going to do about it then?"

Ralph examined the ranks of boys. There was no help in them and he looked away, confused and sweating. Piggy whispered.

"The fire—rescue."[17]

"Who'll join my tribe?"

"I will."

"Me."

"I will."

"I'll blow the conch," said Ralph breathlessly, "and call an assembly."

"We shan't hear it."

Piggy touched Ralph's wrist.

"Come away. There's going to be trouble. And we've had our meat."

There was a blink of bright light beyond the forest and the thunder exploded again so that a littlun started to whine. Big drops of rain fell among them making individual sounds when they struck.

"Going to be a storm," said Ralph, "and you'll have rain like when we dropped here. Who's clever now? Where are your shelters? What are you going to do about that?"

The hunters were looking uneasily at the sky, flinching from the stroke of the drops. A wave of restlessness set the boys swaying and moving aimlessly. The flickering light became brighter and the blows of the thunder were only just bearable. The littluns began to run about, screaming.

Jack leapt on to the sand.

"Do our dance! Come on! Dance!"

He ran stumbling through the thick sand to the open space of rock beyond the fire. Between the flashes of lightning the air was dark and terrible; and the boys followed him, clamorously. Roger became the pig, grunting and charging at Jack, who side-stepped. The hunters took their spears, the cooks took spits, and the rest clubs of fire-wood. A circling movement developed and a chant. While Roger mimed the terror of the pig, the littluns ran and jumped on the outside of the circle. Piggy and Ralph, under the threat of the sky, found themselves eager to take a place in this demented but partly secure society. They were glad to touch the brown backs of the fence that hemmed in the terror and made it governable.

"*Kill the beast! Gut his throat! Spill his blood!*"

The movement became regular while the chant lost its first superficial excitement and began to beat like a steady pulse. Roger ceased to be a pig and became a hunter, so that the centre of the ring yawned emptily. Some of the littluns started a ring on their own; and the complementary circles went round and round as though repetition would achieve safety of itself. There was the throb and stamp of a single organism.

The dark sky was shattered by a blue-white scar. [18] An instant later the noise was on them like the blow of a gigantic whip. The chant rose a tone in agony.

"*Kill the beast! Gut his throat! Spill his blood!*"

Now out of the terror rose another desire, thick, urgent, blind.

"*Kill the beast! Gut his throat! Spill his blood!*"

Again the blue-white scar jagged above them and the sulphurous explosion beat down. The littluns screamed and blundered about, fleeing from the edge of the forest, and one of them broke the ring of biguns in his terror.

"Him! Him!"

The circle became a horseshoe. A thing was crawling out of the forest. It came darkly, uncertainly. The shrill screaming that rose before the beast was like a pain. The beast stumbled into the horseshoe. [19]

"*Kill the beast! Gut his throat! Spill his blood!*"

The blue-white scar was constant, the noise unendurable. Simon was crying out something about a dead man on a hill.

"*Kill the beast! Gut his throat! Spill his blood! Do him in!*"

The sticks fell and the mouth of the new circle crunched and screamed. The beast was on its knees in the centre, its arms folded over its face. It was crying out against the abominable noise something about a body on the hill. The beast struggled forward, broke the ring and fell over the steep edge of the rock to the sand by the water. At once the crowd surged after it, poured down the rock, leapt on to the beast, screamed, struck, bit, tore. There were no words, and no movements but the tearing of teeth and claws. [20]

Then the clouds opened and let down the rain like a waterfall. The water bounded from the mountain-top, tore leaves and branches from the trees, poured like a cold shower over the struggling heap on the sand. Presently the heap broke up and figures staggered away. Only the beast lay still, a few yards from the sea. Even in the rain they could see how small a beast it was; and already its blood was staining the sand.

Now a great wind blew the rain sideways, cascading the water from the forest trees. On the mountain-top the parachute filled and moved; the figure slid, rose to its feet, spun, swayed down through a vastness of wet air and trod with ungainly feet the tops of the high trees; falling, still falling, it sank towards the beach and the boys rushed screaming into the darkness. The parachute took the figure forward, furrowing the lagoon, and bumped it over the reef and out to sea.

Towards midnight the rain ceased and the clouds drifted away, so that the sky was scattered once more with the incredible lamps of stars. Then the breeze died too and there was no noise save the drip and trickle of water that ran out of clefts and spilled down, leaf by leaf, to the brown earth of the island. The air was cool, moist, and clear; and presently even the sound of the water was still. The beast lay huddled on the pale beach and the stains spread, inch by inch.

The edge of the lagoon became a streak of Phosphorescence which advanced minutely, as the great wave of the tide flowed. The clear water mirrored the clear sky and the angular bright constellations. The line of phosphorescence bulged about the sand grains and little pebbles; it held them each in a dimple of tension, then suddenly accepted them with an inaudible syllable and moved on.

Along the shoreward edge of the shallows the advancing clearness was full of strange, moonbeam-bodied creatures with fiery eyes. Here and there a larger pebble clung to its own air and was covered with a coat of pearls. The tide swelled in over the rain-pitted sand and smoothed everything with a layer of silver. Now it touched the first of the stains that seeped from the broken body and the creatures made a moving patch of light as they gathered at the edge. The water rose further and dressed Simon's coarse hair with brightness. The line of his cheek silvered and the turn of his shoulder became sculptured marble. The strange, attendant creatures, with their fiery eyes and trailing vapours, busied themselves round his head. The body lifted a fraction of an inch from the sand and a bubble of air escaped from the mouth with a wet plop. Then it turned gently in the water.

Somewhere over the darkened curve of the world the sun and moon were pulling; and the film of water on the earth planet was held, bulging slightly on one side while the solid core turned. The great wave of the tide moved further along the island and the water lifted. Softly, surrounded by a fringe of inquisitive bright creatures, itself a silver shape beneath the steadfast constellations, Simon's dead body moved out towards the open sea.

1. **Colours drained**: became less and less visible.
2. **lord**: the head of a decapitated pig.
3. Different from all the other children, Simon enjoys solitude or an isolation largely inflicted by himself.
4. **Simon's fit**: fits of fainting attack Simon from time to time.
5. **The Lord of the Flies**: It is not only a pig's head that attracts flies but also a symbol of evil. To the Jews, Baalzebub or "Lord of the Flies" is the chief representative of the false gods. In *Matthew* xii 24 of the *Bible*, he is referred to as "the prince of the devils" and similarly in *Mark* i i i, 22 and *Luke* xi, 15.
6. **Simon saw a humped thing suddenly sit up on the top**: Although the "humped thing" is the corpse of a pilot, the children do not know the truth and are not willing to find out. It therefore engenders irrational fears among them, as something representing evil. A question could therefore be asked: is evil essentially outside or within human beings?
7. Ralph, a bigger child, somehow represents reason in the story.
8. Piggy, also a bigger child, is Ralph's friend. Because of his fatness and shortsightedness, he often falls prey to derision of the other children.
9. **them clouds**: non-standard English.
10. **littluns**: little ones, non-standard English.
11. **Keep your hair on**: Stay calm. Do not get into a temper.
12. **Jack's party**: Jack is the head of a pack of children who function as hunters of the children's society on the island. The "hunters" constitute a natural "party" as opposed to such non-allied children as Ralph and Piggy, who do not hunt.
13. Pay attention to what kind of personage Jack has become in the eyes of the other children.
14. Golding here is giving a picture of mass psychology via a herd of children.
15. Here it is clear that Jack has no respect for the democratic power that Ralph believes he is to exercise.
16. At the beginning of the story it is agreed among the children that as Ralph has the conch with him, he is the "chief".
17. A fire needs to be kept as rescue signal.
18. Pay attention to Golding's peculiar language in rendering a natural phenomenon.
19. Pay attention to Golding's peculiar language in using the children's point of view

and adopting their voice in referring to Simon as a "thing" and a "beast".

20. As before, the children's dance here escalates into real attacking, but this time the consequence is very different.

6. V. S. Naipaul (1932—)

V. S. Naipaul was born into an Indian family in Trinidad in 1932. He went to England on a scholarship in 1950. After four years at Oxford he began to write, and since then he has followed no other profession. He is the author of more than twenty books of fiction and nonfiction. For his literary achievement, hs received numerous honours, including the Booker Prize (Britain's most prestigious literary prize) in 1971. a knighthood for services to literature in 1990, and the Nobel Prize in 2001. He published the following fictional works:

The Mystic Masseur (1957),
Miguel Street (1958),
A House for Mr. Biswas (1961),
The Mimic Man (1967),
In a Free State (1971),
Guerrillas (1975),
A Bend in the River (1979),
The Enigma of Arrival (1987),
A Way in the World (1997),
Half a Life (1999).

His best-known nonfictional works include:

Between Father and Son: Family Letters,
Beyond beliefs: Islamic Excursions Among the Converted,
Peoples, Among the Believers: an Islamic Journey,
India: a Million Mutinies Now,
India: a Wounded Civilization.

In a Free State

In a Free State consists of five apparently independent stories or novellas: (1) "Prologue, From a Journal: The Tramp at Piraeus", (2) "One out of Many", (3)

"Tell Me Who to Kill", (4) "In a Free State" and (5) "Epilogue, from a Journal: The Circus at Luxor". The following excerpt is taken from "Epilogue". In the story, the Egyptians are presented as lacking in dignity or self-respect, indifferent to their fellow countrymen's sufferings and humiliations, as in the case of the first-person narrator's driver, and even trying to please the western sightseers or earn their money by insulting their compatriots, as in the case of the man with the camel-whip. Close attention should be paid, however, to Naipaul's treatment of the Chinese Circus, which is actually at the center of the entire story. Although this episode is presented in a subtle and highly detached manner, it is by no means friendly toward China.

Epilogue, from a Journal:

The Circus at Luxor

To me these boys[1], springing up expectantly out of rock and sand when men approached, were like a type of sand animal. But my driver knew some of them by name; when he shooed them away it was with a languid gesture which also contained a wave. He was a young man, the driver, of the desert himself, and once no doubt he had been a boy in a jibbah[2]. but he had grown up differently. He wore trousers and shirt and was vain of his good looks. He was reliable and correct, without the frenzy of the desert guide. Somehow in the desert he had learned boredom. His thoughts were of Cairo and a real job. He was bored with the antiquities[3], the tourists and the tourist routine.

I was spending the whole of that day in the desert, and now it was time for lunch. I had a Winter Palace lunch-box, and I had seen somewhere in the desert the new government rest-house where tourists could sit at tables and eat their sandwiches and buy coffee. I thought the driver was taking me there. But we went by unfamiliar ways to a little oasis with palm trees and a large, dried-up timber hut. There were no cars, no minibuses, no tourists, only anxious Egyptian serving-people in rough clothes. I didn't want to stay. The driver seemed about to argue, but then he was only bored. He drove to the new rest-house, set me down and said he would come back for me later.

The rest-house was crowded. Sunglassed tourists, exploring their cardboard lunch-boxes, chattered in various European languages. I sat on the terrace at a table with two young Germans. A brisk middle-aged

Egyptian in Arab dress moved among the tables and served coffee. He had a camel-whip at his waist, and I saw, but only slowly, that for some way around the rest-house the hummocked[4] sand was alive with little desert children. The desert was clean, the air was clean; these children were very dirty.

The rest-house was out of bounds to[5] them. When they came close, tempted by the offer of a sandwich or an apple, the man with the camel-whip gave a camel-frightening shout. Sometimes he ran out among them, beating the sand with his whip, and they skittered[6] away, thin little sand-smoothed legs frantic below swinging jibbahs. There was no rebuke for the tourists who had offered the food; this was an Egyptian game with Egyptian rules.

It was hardly a disturbance. The young Germans at my table paid no attention. The English students inside the rest-house, behind glass, were talking competitively about Carter[7] and Lord Carnarvon[8]. But the middle-aged Italian group on the terrace, as they understood the rules of the game, became playful. They threw apples and made the children run far. Experimentally they broke up sandwiches and threw the pieces out onto the sand; and they got the children to come up quite close. Soon it was all action around the Italians; and the man with the camel-whip, like a man understanding what was required of him, energetically patrolled the end of the terrace, shouting, beating the sand, earning his paper piastres[9].

A tall Italian in a cerise[10] jersey stood up and took out his camera. He laid out food just below the terrace and the children came running. But this time, as though it had to be real for the camera, the camel-whip fell not on sand but on their backs, with louder, quicker camel-shouts. And still, among the tourists in the rest-house and among the Egyptian drivers standing about their cars and minibuses, there was no disturbance. Only the man with the whip and the children scrabbling in the sand were frantic. The Italians were cool. The man in the cerise jersey was opening another packet of sandwiches. A shorter, older man in a white suit had stood up and was adjusting his camera. More food was thrown out; the camel-whip continued to fall; the shouts of the man with the whip turned to resonant grunts.

Still the Germans at my table didn't notice; the students inside were still talking. I saw that my hand was trembling. I put down the sandwich I was eating on the metal table; it was my last decision. Lucidity, and anxiety, came to me only when I was almost on the man with the camel-whip. I was shouting. I took the whip away, threw it on the sand. He was astonished, relieved. I said, "I will report this to Cairo." He was frightened; he began to plead in Arabic. The children were puzzled; they ran off a little way and stood up to watch. The two Italians, fingering cameras, looked quite calm behind their sunglasses. The women in the party leaned back in their chairs to consider me.

I felt exposed, futile, and wanted only to be back at my table. When I got back I took up my sandwich. It had happened quickly; there had been no disturbance. The Germans started at me. But I was indifferent to them now as I was indifferent to the Italian in the cerise jersey. The Italian women had stood up, the group was leaving; and he was ostentatiously shaking out lunchboxes and sandwich wrappers onto the sand.

The children remained where they were. The man from whom I had taken the whip came to give me coffee and to plead again in Arabic and English. The coffee was free; it was his gift to me. But even while he was talking the children had begun to come closer. Soon they would be back, raking the sand for what they had seen the Italian throw out.

I didn't want to see that. the driver was waiting, leaning against the car door, his bare arms crossed. He had seen all that had happened. From him, an emancipated young man of the desert in belted trousers and sports shirt, with his thoughts of Cairo, I was expecting some gesture, some sign of approval. He smiled at me with the corners of his wide mouth, with his narrow eyes. He crushed his cigarette in the sand and slowly breathed out smoke through his lips; he sighed. But that was his way of smoking. I couldn't tell what he thought. He was as correct as before, he looked as bored.

Everywhere I went that afternoon I saw the pea-green Volks-wagen minibus of the Italian group. Everywhere I saw the cerise jersey. I learned to recognize the plump, squiffy[11], short-stepped walk that went with it, the dark glasses, the receding hairline, the little stiff swing of the arms. At the ferry I thought I had managed to escape; but the minibus arrived, the Italians got out. I thought we would separate on the Luxor bank. But they too were staying at the Winter Palace. The cerise jersey bobbed[12] confidently through bowing Egyptian servants in the lobby, the bar, the grand dining-room with fresh flowers and intricately folded napkins. In Egypt that year there was only paper money.

I stayed for a day or two on the Luxor bank. Dutifully, I saw Karnak[13] by moonlight. When I went back to the desert I was anxious to avoid the rest-house. The driver understood. Without any show of triumph he took me when the time came to the timber hut among the palm trees. They were doing more business that day. There were about four or five parked minibuses. Inside, the hut was dark, cool and uncluttered[14]. A number of tables had been joined together; and at this central dining-board there were about forty or fifty Chinese, men and women, chattering softly. They were part of the circus I had seen in Milan.

The two elderly Chinese sat together at the end of the long table, next to a small, finely made lady who looked just a little too old to be an acrobat. I had missed her in the crowd in Milan. Again, when the time came to pay, the man with the fat wallet used his hands awkwardly. The lady spoke to the Egyptian waiter. He called the other waiters and they all formed a line. For each waiter the lady had a handshake and gifts, money, something in an envelope, a medal. The ragged waiters stood stiffly, with serious averted faces, like soldiers being decorated. Then all the Chinese rose and, chattering, laughing softly, shuffled out of the echoing hut with their relaxed, slightly splayed gait. They didn't look at me; they appeared scarcely to notice the hut. They were as cool and well-dressed in the desert, the men in suits, the girls in slacks[15], as they had been in the rain of Milan. So self-contained, so handsome and healthy, so silently content with one another: it was hard to think of them as sightseers.

The waiter, his face still tense with pleasure, showed the medal on his dirty striped jibbah. It had been turned out from a mould that had lost its sharpness; but the ill-defined face was no doubt Chinese and no doubt that of the leader[16]. In the envelope were pretty coloured postcards of Chinese peonies.

Peonies, China! So many empires had come here. Not far from where we were was the colossus on whose shin the Emperor Hadrian[17] had caused to be carved verses in praise of himself, to commemorate his visit. On the other bank, not far from the Winter Palace, was a stone with a rougher Roman inscription marking the southern limit of the Empire, defining an area of retreat. Now another, more remote empire was announcing itself. A medal, a postcard; and all that was asked in return was anger and a sense of injustice.

Notes

1. **these boys**: some Egyptian beggar boys hiding behind a hillock.
2. **jibbah**: a kind of outer garment worn by Arabs.
3. **antiquities**: (*usually plural*) a building, work of art, etc., remaining from an ancient time.
4. **hummock**: a small hillock.
5. **out of bounds to**: forbidden to be visited (by).
6. **skitter**: (of a small creature) to run quickly and lightly.
7. **Carter**: Howard Carter (1873—1939), British archeologist and Egyptologist, who made the richest and most celebrated contributions to Egyptology: the discovery (1922) of the largely intact tomb of King Tutankhamen.
8. **Lord Carnarvon**: George Edward Stanhope Molyneux Herbert, 5th earl of Carnarvon, Baron Porchester of Highclere (1866—1923), British Egyptologist who was the patron and associate of archaeologist Howard Carter in the discovery of the tomb of King Tutankhamen.
9. **piastre**: a small coin or banknote in Turkey, Egypt, Syria, the Lebanon, and the Sudan.
10. **cerise**: having a clear red colour.
11. **squiffy**: (*British English*, *informal*) slightly drunk.
12. **bobbed**: moved back and forth quickly.
13. **Karnak**: also called Al-Karnak, village in *Qina muhafazah* (governorate), Upper Egypt, which has given its name to the northern half of the ruins of Thebes on the east bank of the Nile, with the ruins of the Great Temple of Amon.
14. **uncluttered**: not yet made untidy or confused.
15. **slacks**: trousers, especially of a loosefitting informal kind.
16. **the leader**: Chairman Mao Zedong.
17. **Hadrian**: born in AD 76 and died in 138, Roman emperor (117 — 138), the emperor Trajan's nephew and successor, who was a cultivated admirer of Greek civilization and who unified and consolidated Rome's vast empire.

7. Martin Amis (1949—)

Martin Amis is probably the most widely acclaimed writer in contemporary Britain. He was born in Oxford on 25th August, 1949 and was educated in Britain, Spain and the USA, attending a lot of schools and then a series of crammers (a special school that prepares people quickly for an examination) in London and Brighton. He received his formal university education at Exeter College, Oxford, graduating with distinctions. For some time, he was an editorial assistant on the *Times Literary Supplement* and was Literary Editor of the *New Statesman* from 1977 to 1979. He then worked as a Special Writer on the *Observer*. Ever since the early 1970s, he has published nine novels: *The Rachel Papers* (1973), which won the 1974 Somerset Maugham Award, *Dead Babies* (1975), *Success* (1978), *Other People: a Mystery Story* 1981), *Money: a Suicide Note* (1984), *London Fields* (1989), *Time's Arrow* (1991), *The Information* (1995), *Night Train* (1997), and a story collection called *Einstein's Monsters* (1986). His non-fictional writings include *Visiting Nabokov* (1993).

Money: A Suicide Note

Money: a Suicide Note is the novel that brought immense fame to Martin Amis. It tells a story of John Self, a film adman and screenplay-agent, who is spiritually rootless and morally corrupted, "suffering from a contemporary waste and fatigue, and living in collapsing urban jungles on both sides of the Atlantic in an age of globalism" (Malcolm Bradbury, *The Modern British Fiction*, 1994, p. 427) and who commits suicide toward the close of the story. In the following excerpt, John Self uses money to lure "Martin Amis" (an important figure in the novel who has the same name as Martin Amis the writer and like his creator, is himself a sort of writer) to rewrite a story written by a certain Doris Arthur, that is, to add nore sex and violence to it, so as to make it more acceptable to the film makers or ultimately to the film market. Here is the dialogue between John Self and "Martin Amis" the character.

"Answer me something. Do you sort of set yourself a time to write every day? Or do you just write when you feel like it. Or what." (This is asked by John Self—editor)

He ("Martin Amis" the character—editor) sighed and said, "You really want to know?... I get up at seven and write straight through till twelve. Twelve to one I read Russian poetry—in translation, alas. A quick lunch, then art history until three. After that it's philosophy for an hour—nothing technical, nothing hard. Four to five: European history, 1848[1] and all that. Five to six: I improve my German. And from then until dinner, well, I just relax and read whatever the hell I like. Usually Shakespeare."

"Yeah, I was re-reading a book the other day. *Animal Farm*[2]. What you reckon?"

"I've never read it, funnily enough."

"What about—what about *1984* [3]?"

"Oh, I'll get round to[4] it when the time comes. I'm not all that interested in the novel of ideas. I don't like coming up for air[5] either."

"Uh? —How much money do you earn?"

"It varies."

"But how much?"

He told me

"Then what the hell do you spend it on?"

(This paragraph is intended to be a sort of aside on the part of John Self; and there are other paragraphs like this in this excerpt—editor) I tell you, this Martin Amis ("Martin Amis" the character in the story, not Martin Amis the writer who was born in 1949, and is still writing— editor), lives like a student. I had inspected his flat with an adman's eye, mindful of outlay and lifestyle, of vocational expenditure. And there was nothing, no tape recorder or filing cabinets or electric typewriters or word processors. Just his pastel portable[6], like an ancient till[7]. Just biros, pads, pencils. Just two dust-furred rooms off a sooty square, with no hall or passage. And he earns enough. Why isn't he living right up to the hilt of his dough.[8] He must have a bad book-habit, this character. How much are books? It seems he has the reading thing real bad.[9]

"This feels like a good bit of work to me. It's certainly unusual," he said. Doris Arthur's screenplay lay cracked out on his lap. He had been flicking through it confidently. "Are these your jottings[10]? What's your problem?"

"We have a hero problem. We have a motivation problem. We have a fight problem. We have a realism problem."

"What's your realism problem?"

I told him. It took a long time.

"...and so, and so, yeah, that's where you come in," I (John Self—editor) said, winding it all up.

"That wouldn't be writing," he said. "That would be psychotherapy."

"Here's the deal."

"Talk to me."

I named the sum. That took quite a long time too. Jesus, it sounded an awful lot, for a writer.

Martin laughed. I think he gulped. "... Pounds or dollars?" He asked.

Selina[11] says I'm not capable of true love. It isn't true. I truly love money. Truly I do. Oh, money, I love you. You're so democratic: you've got no favourites. You even things out for me and my kind.

"Pounds," I said, offhand. "though of course the money's American. How busy are you?" I let him shrug and put for a while. "It may eat into your philosophy for a couple of weeks," I said, "but that's life. Shakespeare can hang fire[12]. History can wait." I coolly mentioned the cheque I had right here in my pocket, and tossed in a detail or two about the payment schedule. By now I was thinking—we're just pissing money away[13] on this kid ("Martin Amis" the character—editor). He did it for half the dough, easy. Think of all the books he can buy.

"I'm going to say no."

Dah! Son of a *bitch*! "What? Why?" I said with a rush of bitter heat—inordinate, stunning pain, as if a child of mine had been crudely slighted, or me, myself, running home from school in tears. Ooh, the world can still hurt. It's as sharp as ever it was.

"Nothing personal," he said. "I just don't know enough about you. I just don't know enough about *Good Money*[14]."

"I just told you all about it for Christ's sake."

"That's the trouble." He paused, and his head dipped.

"This film. Who's directing it? Are you... ? You give me the plot. You sound like a ten-year-old trying to remember a dirty joke. Now that doesn't really worry me. The film industry is full of thriving duffers[15] and speechless millionaires. What worries me is... To make a film you need energy, all this energy. That's what film directors are — people with all this energy. Now you, you look as though you're about to check into a sense-deprivation unit. I keep thinking, if he (Martin Amis the character—editor) blinks, he'll have a heart attack. I've seen you around and you're really a prodigy. You are something else."

Happening to have turned out as the human being I am, the first thing I wonder about a woman is: will I fuck it? Similarly, the first thing I wonder about a man is : will I fight it? Three yeas ago, three months ago, three weeks ago, I would have answered Martin's objections by hoisting him to his feet and nutting[16] him between the eyes. For some ambiguous reason (and I think it's to do with his name, so close to that of my pale minder[17]), I feel strangely protective of little Martin here: in a way, I would hate to damage him, or to see him damaged. But on another level, on another night, I can hear myself—I can smell myself—giving Martin the pasting[18] of his life, a real bad one, roused, blind, with nothing mattering. I sense he senses this sometimes, this stickiness between us. I scare him, for all his talk. Yes, he's clever, and I wish I had his articulation, but I sussed[19] him for a wimp, right from the start.

Sitting back, I let my heartbeat go ahead and take its time[20]. I glanced down at the ashtray before me, a mass grave, with its stools[21] and the crushed corpses of a dozen butts. I said,

"I'm going to double it." I named the revised figure, and felt a nauseous twinge in my balls[22]. "And that's just for a starting." I produced my chequebook. Now come on. Where do you get off, turning down that kind of money? Do it. Buy a present for your girlfriend. Or your mother. Do it. Come on, save my life."

"... I'll do it."

"Thank you, Martin."

"On one condition."

"What?"

"The cheque doesn't bounce[23]."

"The cheque's good," I said, handing it over. "I'll need the first draft in two weeks. Christ, all you're doing is a re-write."

He looked up at the tumbling zeros. He said, "This is—this isn't realistic."

I stood up sharply: energetically. Martin flinched. His eyes watched me. He knows what's going on between us. Or maybe he thinks he's just being paranoid[24].

He isn't. He isn't just being paranoid. I can assure him of that.

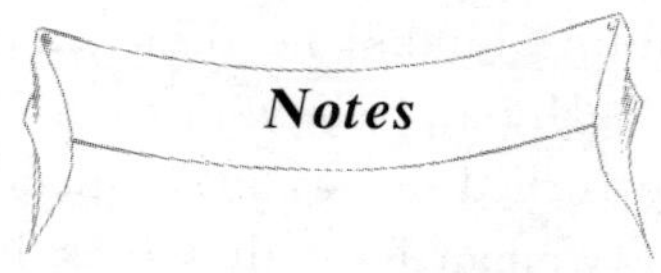

Notes

1. **1848**: the social tumults that occurred in many parts of Europe in 1848.
2. ***Animal Farm***: a novel by George Orwell (1903—1950) published in 1945.
3. ***1984***: a novel by George Orwell, published in 1949.
4. **get round to**: find time or have the time for (something or doing something).
5. **coming up for air**: here Martin Amis is apparently playing with the words of the name of *Coming Up for Air* (1939), another novel by George Orwell.
6. **portable**: a small and light typewriter.
7. **till**: a drawer where money is kept in a shop.
8. **Why isn't he living right up to the hilt of his dough**: Why doesn't he use up all his money and enjoy life thoroughly?
9. **It seems he has the reading thing real bad**: To John Self, reading is bad. Here he is disparaging Martin Amis the character's reading habit.
10. **jottings**: (*usually plural in form yet singular in meaning*) a rough note.
11. **Selina**: In the story, Selina (her complete name is Selina Street) is an expensive prostitute and John Self's girlfriend.
12. **hang fire**: to hesitate or to be slow in response.
13. **piss away**: waste (money, etc). Notice, "piss" means urinate. Like lots of other expressions used by John Self, "piss away" here is vulgar.
14. ***Good Money***: the name of the screenplay written by Doris Arthur and to be re-written by "Martin Amis". Notice, "good" here means real, or not fake. This indicates how obsessed with money everybody is in the story.
15. **duffer**: (*informal*) a foolish person or slow learner.
16. **nutting**: (*British slang*) striking hard with one's head.
17. **minder**: a child taken care of by a special institute or nursery school.
18. **pasting**: (*informal*) a hard beating.
19. **sussed**: (*British slang*) "sus somebody for..." means suspect somebody to be...
20. **I let my heartbeat go ahead and take its time**: I relaxed.
21. **stools**: (*formal and technical*) pieces of solid waste matter passed from the body.
22. **balls**: (*interjection, taboo, slang*) testicles.
23. **bounce**: (*slang*, of a cheque) to be returned by a bank as worthless.
24. **paranoid**: believing that others are purposely mistreating and hating oneself, or that one is a person of high rank or importance.

8. Seamus Heaney (1939—2013)

Seamus Heaney[1] was born in 1939 on a 50-acre family farm called Mossbawn in Co. Derry, Northern Ireland. He received higher education in the Queen's University of Belfast from 1957 to 1961. In 1962, after acquiring a postgraduate diploma for teachers' training at St Joseph's College of Education, Belfast, he started teaching in a secondary school and in November of that year he published his first poem, "Tractors", in the *Belfast Telegraph*. During the period he came into contact with Philip Hobsbaum, a poet who organized the renowned "Group" in London since the mid-50s, who was teaching in the Queen's University. With Hobsbaum as session-organizer, the "Belfast Group" soon came into being and played an important role in changing the previously discouraging literary atmosphere of the city. Besides Hobsbaum and Heaney, the Group (1963—1966) included, off and on, Michael Longley, Derek Mahon, Stewart Parker and James Simmons. From 1966 when Hobsbaum moved to Glasgow till 1970 the Group's sessions continued in Heaney's own house and attracted such younger poets as Paul Muldoon, Frank Ormsby and Michael Foley. In 1966 Heaney returned to the Queen's University to succeed Hobsbaum's lectureship which he maintained until 1972 when he moved to the Republic of Ireland. His first book of poetry, *Death of a Naturalist*, was published in 1966 and the second, *The Door into the Dark*, in 1969. Heaney has to date published more than 10 books of poetry, latest of which being *Electric Light* (2001), together with several books of literary criticism including *Preoccupations*, *The Government of Tongue*, *The Place of Writing* and *Redress of Poetry*. His translation of the old-English epic, *Beowulf*, was off the press in 1999. He was awarded the Nobel Prize for Literature in 1995, on the occasion of which he made the famous Nobel lecture, *Crediting Poetry*.

His poetry consists of mainly two genres: firstly, the observed and recollected facts of his early rural experience, i. e. the private or autobiographical theme as reflected in *Death of a Naturalist* and *Door into the Dark*; and secondly, the psychological meditation on the violence in Northern Ireland arising from religious and political conflicts, i. e. the public or political theme as reflected in *North* and in particular the so-called "bog poems". His poetic language is recommended for the vivid description of details and profound philosophical meditation.

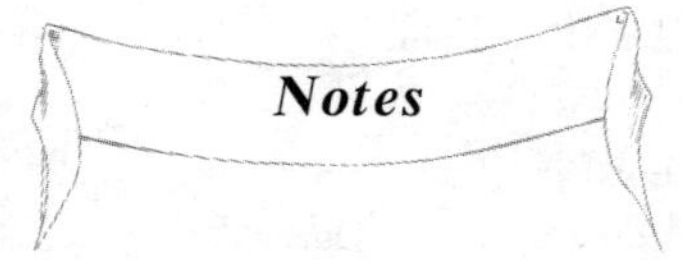

Notes

1. **Seamus Heaney**: "Seamus" is the Irish counterpart of "James", and its pronunciation is roughly /ʃeɪməs/, while "Heaney" sounds approximately /heɪnɪ:/.

Death of a Naturalist[1]

All year the flax-dam[2] festered in the heart
Of the townland; green and heavy-headed
Flax had rotted there, weighted down by huge sods[3].

Daily it sweltered in the punishing sun.
Bubbles gargled delicately, bluebottles[4]
Wove a strong gauze of sound around the smell.[5]

There were dragonflies, spotted butterflies.
But best of all was the warm thick slobber
Of frogspawn[6] that grew like clotted water
In the shade of the banks. Here, every spring
I would fill jampotfuls of the jellied
Specks to range on window-sills at home,
On shelves at school, and wait and watch until
The fattening dots burst into nimble—
Swimming tadpoles. Miss Walls[7] would tell us how
The daddy frog was called a bullfrog[8]
And how he croaked and how the mammy frog
Laid hundreds of little eggs and this was
Frogspawn. You could tell the weather by frogs too
For they were yellow in the sun and brown
In rain.

Then one hot day when fields were rank[9]
With cowdung in the grass the angry frogs
Invaded the flax-dam; I ducked through hedges[10]

To a coarse croaking that I had not heard
Before. The air was thick with a bass chorus[11].

Right down the dam gross-bellied frogs were cocked[12]
On sods; their loose necks pulsed like sails. Some hopped:
The slap and plop were obscene threats. Some sat[13]
Poised like mud grenades, their blunt heads farting.[14]

I sickened, turned, and ran. The great slime kings[15]
Were gathered there for vengeance[16] and I knew
That if I dipped my hand the spawn would clutch[17] it.

Notes

1. **"Death of a Naturalist"**: the name of Heaney's first book of poetry published in 1966, as well as the title-poem of the said book. The poem is generally considered one of Heaney's best autobiographical works. In the first of its two stanzas "I" was a "naturalist", while in the second the "naturalist" was scared to "death" out of the vengeance from the nature. The word "naturalist" here has been variously interpreted.
2. **flax-dam**: Here refers to a lake made by a dam in which newly harvested flax is put to get the fiber softened.
3. **huge sods**: huge pieces of earth used to keep the flax in place.
4. **bluebottle**: a kind of large blue fly.
5. **Wove a strong gauze of sound around the smell**: Here the poet conjures up a synaesthetic image as if sound and smell were something tangible.
6. **frogspawn**: an uncountable collective noun referring to the eggs laid by female frogs.
7. **Miss Walls**: name of a school teacher.
8. **bullfrog**: obviously here "bullfrog" is a grown-up male frog; but usually "bullfrog" refers to a species of large-size frog (牛蛙).
9. **rank**: having very strong and unpleasant smell.
10. **ducked through hedges**: lowering the head so that not to be hurt while going through the hedges (树篱).
11. **bass chorus**: low-pitch chorus by men (男低音大合唱).
12. **gross-bellied frogs were cocked**: the frogs with big bellies set themselves erect as if ready for fighting.
13. **The slap and plop...** : the use of these onomatopoeic words very vividly conveys the sound produced by the frogs' hopping. **obscene**: indecent.

14. **Poised**: calm and confident, ready for action; **grenade**: a small bomb that can be thrown by hand or fired by a rifle; **their blunt heads farting**: the big heads of the frogs sending out stinking smell.
15. **The great slime kings**: Here refers to the frogs.
16. **vengeance**: punishment as retaliation(报仇).
17. **clutch**: to hold something tightly.

Punishment[1]

I can feel the tug[2]
of the halter at the nape[3]
of her neck, the wind
on her naked front.

It blows her nipples
to amber beads,[4]
it shakes the frail rigging
of her ribs.[5]

I can see her drowned
body in the bog,
the weighing stone,
the floating rods and boughs.[6]

Under which at first
she was a barked sapling[7]
that is dug up
oak-bone, brain-firkin[8]

her shaved head
like a stubble of black corn,
her blindfold[9] a soiled bandage,
her noose a ring

to store
the memories of love.
Little adulteress,[10]

before they punished you

you were flaxen-haired,
undernourished, and your
tar-black face was beautiful.
My poor scapegoat[11],

I almost love you
but would have cast, I know,
the stones of silence.[12]
I am the artful voyeur[13]

of your brain's exposed
and darkened combs,
your muscles' webbing
And all your numbered bones:

I who have stood dumb
when your betraying sisters,
cauled in tar,[14]
wept by the railings,

who would connive[15]
in civilized courage[16]
yet understand the exact
and tribal, intimate revenge.[17]

Notes

1. **Punishment**: a poem from *North* (1975). It is generally agreed that the latter part of *Wintering Out* and *North* represent a turning point in Heaney's literary creation, i. e. beginning to be involved in public or political themes. "Punishment" is also one of Heaney's "bog poem" series which imply some psychological similarities between the contemporary violence in Northern Ireland and the killing for religious sacrifice in ancient Danish tribes. After writing "Tollund Man", the first "bog poem", Heaney visited Denmark in October 1973 and saw in the museum there the preserved bodies described in *The Bog People*, a

book by P. V. Glob, a Danish archaeologist.

2. **tug**: a sudden strong pull.
3. **halter**: Here refers to the noose used for hanging the girl; **nape**: the back of the neck.
4. **It blows her nipples / to amber beads**: the wind has blown for centuries and the dead body has turned fossil and, therefore, the nipples look like beads made of amber.
5. **rigging / of her ribs**: "rigging" here refers to the network of human ribs.
6. **weighing stone**: the stone fastened onto the body to keep it in place when drowned and to prevent it from floating up to the water surface; **floating rods and boughs**: rods and boughs fastened onto the body to indicate its position.
7. **barked sapling**: a sapling (young tree) whose exterior covering has been stripped.
8. **that is dug up / oak-bone, brain-firkin**: when it is dug up now it looks like a bone made of oak, and her head looks like a firkin (small wooden cask) housing the brain.
9. **blindfold**: the girl's eyes were covered with a blindfold before being killed.
10. **Little adulteress**: the girl was found to have committed adultery and, therefore, was given the "punishment".
11. **scapegoat**: the girl was drowned and offered as a religious sacrifice to bear the blames for the whole tribe, hence a scapegoat.
12. **... would have cast... the stones of silence**: if I were present I would not dare to say anything against the tribal punishment and would very possibly join the others in punishing the girl (by casting the stones at her).
13. **artful voyeur**: a "voyeur" is someone who enjoys watching other people's private affairs. The poet feels a guilty conscience and calls himself a "voyeur", though an artful one (capable of deceiving people).
14. **I who have stood dumb...** : It is an allusion to an event in Northern Ireland during 1960s when some Irish girls were found going with British soldiers and, as a result, were punished by being covered all over with feathers and tar. **caul**: to cover or wrap all over.
15. **connive**: pretend ignorant of or fail to take action against something one ought to oppose.
16. **civilized courage**: an irony referring to the allusion in note 14, "courage" here is actually "violence".
17. **yet understand the exact / and tribal, intimate revenge**: Here "intimate" means "from the deepest nature". The poet's message is that the violence occurring in present Northern Ireland is similar to the "revenge" committed in the ancient Danish tribe, as both are attributable to man's deepest nature.